HARD TIME

Liu Zongren

Also by Liu Zongren

TWO YEARS IN THE MELTING POT
6 TANYIN ALLEY

HARD TIME

THIRTY MONTHS IN A CHINESE LABOR CAMP

LIU ZONGREN

China Books & Periodicals, Inc.

SAN FRANCISCO

Edited by Erik Noyes & James J. Wang

Cover Design by Linda Revel
Book Design by Wendy K. Lee

First Edition 1995

2   4   6   8   10   9   7   5   3   1

Library of Congress Catalog Card Number: 95-069930
ISBN 0-8351-2542-4

Printed in Canada.

 China Books and Periodicals, Inc.
2929 24th St.
San Francisco, CA 94110

I dedicate this book to my wife Fengyun who suffered even more during the most difficult years of our lives.

Prologue

During my six years of service in the army air force, I had studied high school and college English-language textbooks on my own. After I was discharged, I took a year's course of intensive English and then found a job at the Beijing Foreign Trade Bureau as a practicing proofreader. I continued my self-study, hoping one day to become a full-fledged translator. As my bad luck would have it, the Cultural Revolution began and some of my friends and I were labeled "counter-revolutionary." Most of them went in prison while I was sent to a labor reform farm.

I was sent to Chadian in 1973 as a "labor reform element," to be disciplined and instructed for a period of three years. The sentence was later reduced by six months, and I was released in 1975. I returned in August 1979, after the incendiary label of "counter-revolutionary" was removed from my dossier. At that time, I returned to make sure that the labor reform farm had totally expunged my records so that in the future I wouldn't be suddenly summoned to a police station and told that I had to be put under surveillance because the country was being threatened by foreign invasion or by internal unrest, or just for my own "safety's sake."

I remember the February afternoon in 1973 when nearly 200 of us, dubiously labeled "labor reform elements," were transported from Beijing to Chadian by train. I remember the feeling of leaving my home to spend three years of my life in a labor reform farm. I tilted my head against the window and watched it all recede into the winter fog...

Upon arriving at Chadian, the police guards ordered us to throw our luggage and toiletries out the windows. Then, they pushed us out of the car doors which were exclusively designated for our entry and exit. The train stopped at Chadian for a mere two minutes – not nearly enough time for all of us to file out carefully. In addition to being rushed, the car we were in was the last passenger car on the train. Since the platform didn't reach that far, we had to jump down onto the gravel rail bed. Some fell and went rolling down the steep embankment. But since we were not human beings, our welfare mattered very little.

Heads popped out of windows of the other cars. All eyes were upon us and some of the other passengers yelled at us. "Traitors of the people!" they shouted, to show how knowledgeable they were. I remember that my ears tingled at the base and my eyes blurred with tears of shame and humiliation. No one should ever have to endure such ostracizing.

The name of Chadian was hardly known to Beijing residents before 1967. In that year, the Red Guard launched a citywide campaign to round up all of the street thugs, shop lifters, burglars, and all of the troublesome and overtly promiscuous high school students. They sent thousands of these youths to the juvenile delinquent centers at Tiantanhe and Tuanhe, on the outskirts of Beijing. After those two farms filled to capacity, the remainder of the delinquents were sent to Chadian. It seemed as if every family in Beijing had been affected by this massive sweep. Predictably, the name "Chadian," and its dismal reputation spread far and wide.

The Beijing police department managed five labor-reform farms in various parts of the country, Chadian being the oldest and largest. It took in both court-sentenced criminals and petty law breakers. It also had another name – Qinghe – which was the name of the county in Hebei province where the farm was, and still is, located. This name was used only by the security guards, their families and ex-inmates who were not allowed to return to Beijing, most of whom had been permanently assigned to jobs in the nine sub-farms and seven factories.

The area in which this labor reform farm was situated used to be an immense flat wilderness, bleached snow white by alkali. Because it was situated next to the Bohai Sea, many people over the years had tried to make use of the land, but failed. In 1911, revolutionaries staged an uprising in Wuchang that overthrew China's last imperial dynasty, the Qing. The new government set up the North China Reclamation Company to reclaim some of this wasteland. They dug small ditches to guide fresh water into a few small paddy fields for growing rice. The harvest was poor, but these shrewd fortune-seekers stumbled onto a more profitable crop: fresh water crabs from the many water holes that riddled the marshland.

After the Japanese occupied north China in 1931, they interred the Koreans in the Chadian area to produce rice. Japanese engineers and their Chinese and Korean conscripts dug a drainage canal and built a pumping station that was powered by steam boilers. If the war had lasted longer, or if the Japanese had won, Chadian might have been turned into a granary. But by the time the Japanese left, the area had not changed significantly for the better. Where the ground was not drenched by sluggish marsh water or covered by layers of alkaline frost, sage brush grew sparsely. Fish and the freshwater crabs, however, still flourished.

At the end of World War II, the nationalist government (Kuomintang) took over the area and opened a few more acres of rice fields. A wider and longer irrigation canal was dug. Then, in April 1948, the Kuomintang General Fu Zuoyi surrendered Beijing to the Communists.

Seventeen hundred prisoners of war – called trainees because most of them had surrendered on the orders from their commander – were transported into the swampland at Chadian. Two hundred officers and five hundred soldiers of the People's Liberation Army came with them. Together they pitched tents and propped up huge outdoor cast iron cauldrons to cook their meals. They dug a canal to lead fresh water from the Chaobai River into the drainage ditches which were already there. This was an attempt to guide the alkaline water into the sea. They also built row houses, with more packed earth than bricks, and opened the fields for rice production.

Chinese like to describe a rich place as a "land of fish and rice." Chadian teemed with fish and crabs wherever there was water, and now there was rice. The soil was saturated with the organic material it accumulated over many centuries. This fertile earth eagerly released its nourishment after the fresh water had flushed out the alkali in the soil.

In 1951, the Korean War broke out. Chiang Kai-shek, who had moved his defeated Kuomintang government to Taiwan, threatened to recapture the mainland. People in many nations were talking about a Third World War. Some of the trainees at Chadian became restless and hopeful that the Kuomintang could return and so they could once again "lord it over the common people." They began to organize secret groups to assist the Kuomintang army from within Communist borders.

During this period, and really ever since the founding of the People's Republic of China, campaigns had been launched, one after another, to purify this new society. As a result, Chadian began to receive an influx of gangsters who terrifed Beijings neighborhoods and markets, private merchants who speculated in grain and daily necessities, and merchants who made big money selling fake medicines, mildewed grain, and absorbent cotton made of old quilts or mattresses dug out of graves. Eventually the Communists even began to send their own people there to be reformed, members who had been corrupted by the "sugarcoated bullets" of merchants and private industrialists.

More campaigns rounded up more people. Trainloads of uprooted citizens arrived at Chadian. When the 1957 campaign against Rightists began, Chadian filled up with several thousand intellectuals: college students and graduates, doctors, engineers, professors, and teachers. These were the ones who had openly expressed their dissatisfaction with various ideas and practices of the Communist Party. New row houses of solid red brick were built to accommodate them. Then, Chadian farm added another section for the young malcontents, street thugs, hustlers, burglars, and school troublemakers.

By 1970, the farm had cleared and planted 11,000 hectares of rice in paddy fields. The Chadian directors had divided the whole compound into nine sub-farms. They used inmate labor to build a farm machinery repair plant, a paper mill, a feed factory, a chicken farm, a hat making workshop, a brick kiln, and a transportation corps. I became one of those inmates who labored.

During my two and half years at Chadian, I was confined at Farm 583, one of the nine sub-farms, and had to remain within its residential compound and the surrounding fields. I was allowed to go to the general headquarters for a bath every month during winter and occasionally on errands. I never saw the other sub-farms or workshops. Looking back at my time in Chadian, and comparing it to my current life, I wonder how many like me lost every shred of their dignity, and how many like me were able to regain it.

1

Three Years of Hard Labor for Ten Years of Loyalty

The bosses at the Beijing Foreign Trade Bureau named me as a core member of a counter-revolutionary clique which included some hundred young activists of the Cultural Revolution. Several of them were indeed my friends. All army veterans and most Party members, we would occasionally go for beers and talk politics. At those times we were boisterous in showing our political superiority to those pen pushers in the Bureau who lived in constant fear. They were sure that the Cultural Revolution would come knocking on their door, bringing disaster down on them at any moment. We believed confidently, and we had every right to, that our military service would keep us immune from any attacks by the Red Guards.

Furthermore, I had violated neither the National Constitution nor the Constitution of the Chinese Communist Party, to which I had belonged for ten years. Still, those bastards accused me of having committed crimes against Socialism, the Communist Party, and the Dictatorship of the Proletariat. And, as such, I was placed in solitary confinement for investigation.

After a month in solitary I was subjected to public meetings at which I was criticized and called names. Work at the Bureau became unbearable. First, they moved my desk out to the corridor, and eventually, they just stopped giving me work to proofread.

I felt deeply wronged. I had never beaten up anyone or shouted expletives, as many young people did during the Cultural Revolution. My major complaint was that the forced military drills in early morning were ruining family life. I criticized the endless study sessions of political doctrine. And said that shouting high sounding slogans of revolution could not produce food. And that forbidding people to air their views could not make people agree with the leaders. They seemed like trivial remarks to me, but because of these inconsequential rumblings, I was labeled "counter-revolutionary."

The ignominy became too much to bear. I began to pay regular visits to the Bureau chiefs' offices. I made a habit of making their lives as uncomfortable as I could, never believing that they could do any more harm to me than they already had.

Several members of the supposed "counter-revolutionary clique" had landed in prison. I heard a rumor that the police were asked to take me in too, but had refused, requesting more hard evidence. This boosted my determination to harass the Bureau big shots. "They can't put me in prison," I assured my wife, Shalin, when she urged me to stop provoking the officials.

How utterly foolish it was to believe that I was exempt from further punishment. At the time, I didn't know that besides the legal system's prisons, there were labor reform farms. But as I found out very quickly, certain government organizations were authorized to send their members directly there. Unfortunately, the Beijing Foreign Trade Bureau was one of them.

On a January morning in 1973, I was alone on the fourth floor of my office building. No longer allowed to sit in on political meetings except when I was the target of criticism, I was *ordered* (as a parent would instruct a child with a plate full of vegetables) to sit at my desk and study the writings of Chairman Mao. Through them, I would hopefully see what was wrong with my ideology. As always, the English language books I had were far more enticing.

That morning I was reading *David Copperfield*, buried in a copy of "China Pictorial", but could not settle into the novel. My mind refused to open to the stepfather beating the young protagonist. I put the book down and waited for what might befall me that day.

"Huang Longsen," Tang Wen came up the staircase and called to me. "Your presence is requested at this morning's meeting."

Tang Wen, a colleague of mine in his early thirties, had never shouted at me nor used ugly words in his criticisms at the office meetings. In fact, he had shared my political views before I came under investigation. Unlike him, my mouth had been too quick and too big. Now, Tang Wen was assigned to my case team. His task was to reconfirm the accusations against me, and to dig out more evidence. Ironically, I found myself pitying him. His position was no more comfortable than mine.

I followed him downstairs to the Bureau dining hall. We passed no one on the stairway, which was an eerie tense sensation. The dining hall door was left open – peculiar – despite the strong drafts coming down from the lobby. All of the benches and tables had been pushed aside and the entire eight hundred staff members were packed in, standing room only. It was like some sporting event was about to take place. Two square tables of raw wood just inside the door served as a presidium. The Bureau chief, three deputies and Director Hou of the political department stood around it, wrapped in quilted overcoats. Everyone looked toward me, my closer acquaintances were overtly self-conscious, their eyes shifting to avoid my gaze. The chiefs did not bother to raise their eyes from the documents they were reading, or pretending to read. I waited inside the door to be instructed where to stand. Tang Wen looked inquisitively at Director Hou who said, "It will take only a minute," indicating that I was to stay where I was. This was a modern-day Inquisition and I was the heretic *du jour*.

After an uncomfortable silence which seemed to last forever, the director announced with hatred and a trace of triumph, "Because Huang Longsen has stubbornly refused to repent of his counter-revolutionary ideological mistakes we have decided to send him to a labor re-form farm for three years." He glanced my way, tensed for my roaring protest. I looked at him coolly. "Take him out!" the director shouted. He must have been shocked that this time I did not call him a hypocrite or a lying son-of-a-bitch.

As they ushered me out the door, I began to feel a shortness of breath. I hissed at a deputy who sat by the aisle, "Go to hell, you damned hypocrites! All of you!" In my mind, I was cursing their ancestors, mothers, sisters – all of their families. I wanted to use all the curses I had learned as a kid in the slums of Beijing, but my tongue was as alienated from the words as I was from the boys of my childhood. And had I used those raw phrases, all of the allegations against me would simply be confirmed in the eyes of my colleagues. They would rest self-assured that I had deserved my sentence, and they would have no remorse or misgivings about banishing me for three years of my life to a little piece of hell in China.

Shalin, who worked in the Bureau library, was not allowed to attend meetings aimed at me. I did not ask to say good-bye to her. I would not deign to plead for mercy, rather I would show that separation from my family could not intimidate me.

An olive green police jeep stood in the compound behind the office building, its engine running. A Bureau car would have been too nice for a political criminal like me. Could it be that the police department had refused to lend a driver and escorts for such a criminal? Whatever the circumstance, Tang Wen and Wei Shao were assigned. And the Bureau's Driver Chang sat rigidly at the wheel.

A friend of mine had been taken away a couple of days earlier. He was thrown onto the floor of a similar jeep. The two policemen had practically stood on his back. I did not know how I would have reacted if they had done that to me. Fortunately, they had been polite to me, not even rushing me to get into the jeep.

We drove out of the Bureau's compound from the back gate. The side street was deserted. A dirty gray mist covered the long row of brick buildings while the jeep stole through the sleeping neighborhoods.

Forty minutes later we had wound out of the Beijing traffic and were speeding south on the highway, bumping in a dull rhythm over the seams of the concrete. The sky was dirty gray, and gloomy, typical of Beijing winter before a snow or sleet storm. The fields were just as desolate. In scattered spots where sun and wind did not reach, snow from previous falls remained, dirt encrusted.

I looked straight ahead over Driver Chang's shoulder in total indifference. "So be it," I thought, invoking the strength and indifference of the street thugs I had known in my youth. I knew the other men were nervous. They said nothing after we left the compound.

Since my family had moved to Beijing in 1951, I had not been south of the city. The Summer Palace, the Zoo, Fragrant Hill, the Ming Tombs, the Great Wall, the Fishing Terrace – all the places we visited during holidays – were to the west and north. The winter scene along the highway here was more primitive than the urbane neighborhoods to which I was accustomed. This was apparently Driver Chang's first time, too. He concentrated on the road, defensively swerving to avoid every pothole.

My mind was still, so still that I found tranquillity in the gray winter sky, the desolate fields, the whirling roadside litter, and the speeding trucks, lumbering horsedrawn carts, and struggling cyclists. Resting in that moment I had no feeling of being wronged, no hatred for those who had bestowed this disgrace on me, nor grievances against those colleagues who had exposed the "counterrevolutionary remarks" I had made in casual conversations. I became numb. I sublimated any and all concern for how Shalin would feel when she learned the news.

Several of my friends were in prison. It felt right that I was now about to share their sufferings. All of us had been fools. Urged by those in high places to carry out Chairman Mao's call to fight for the cause of the proletariat, we had criticized Party officials for their "revisionist and bourgeois ways," as well as those who had served the regime the Communists replaced. Now that the power structure was secure, the young zealots of the Cultural Revolution had become a nuisance and had to be taken out of society. Whom could I blame? If I had been smarter, I would not have become involved in that political havoc. My better educated colleagues kept quiet and stayed safe. We, who had helped the major bureaucrats wipe out their opponents, were being sacrificed. I wept bitter tears when I was denounced as a counterrevolutionary a year earlier. Now I had conquered that unmanly weakness.

I thought of Mr. Duan, my neighbor who worked in the Bureau. He had consoled me, "I have been a Party member for more than twenty years and have gone through many 'campaigns to expose impurities.' Many people have been wronged. Many have been executed or forced to take their own lives. I told you in the beginning of the Cultural Revolution to stand back. You did, but not far enough. Don't worry; you'll pull out of this all right. You only said a few unseemly things in a voice too loud. They won't send you to prison."

They did not put me in prison, but they had not let me slip away.

An hour out of Beijing, a lone farmer by the highway directed us down a gravel side road. It ended at a gate of steel plates interrupting a high wall of gray brick. A sign announced, "Newborn Machinery Plant."

This was the infamous police holding tank where labor reform elements were gathered and sent to the farms around Beijing. Some were sent as far away as the farm at Chadian on the Bohai Sea.

Driver Chang tapped the horn timidly, waited a couple of minutes, hit it a little harder, and waited again. A small door in the gate groaned, and soon a moon-shaped head popped out of the crack. "Papers," the gatekeeper grunted, as if we had woken him from his midmorning nap. Tang Wen got down, drew an envelope out of a black attaché case, and presented it with great respect.

The guard stretched one arm out of the gate, snatched

the official letter, propped a pair of glasses on his stubby nose and looked closely at the paper, his bald head shimmering in the weak sun. He withdrew what he had extended, and closed the door. Ten minutes later the heavy steel gate creaked open, the left half first and then the right. A sturdy man in police blue stood at the entrance with the official document in hand and waved the jeep in.

"You, come with me and sign the registration book!" Tang Wen followed him into the only multi-story building in this immense compound. The others got out to stretch their legs, while I tried to attach some profundity to the fact that I was going to be here for a long time. I couldn't muster any emotions at all, and I decided it would be just as well not to feel any. And so I stood there, straightening up my usually hunched back and blankly surveyed the place where I was to stay for some time.

I saw a sprawling grayness: the three-story building and long low inner walls were of gray brick, as were the two clusters of one-story houses that the inner walls sequestered. Two-thirds of the open area was committed to vegetable plots of gray earth. The people in the compound were also wearing gray, except for a dozen police guards identified by blue uniforms.

The sign outside had said it was a factory, but I could see no workshop. The only structure that might have resembled one was an auditorium, most of its windows patched with sheets of plywood. High, dead grass thrust up around its base and reminded me of the pubic hair of old men I had seen at the Beijing public baths.

The men came out. The policeman solemnly nodded his acceptance of me, and Tang Wen nodded his goodbye. My escorts and Driver Chang climbed back in the jeep. The motor coughed hoarsely and stalled, whined again and caught. The jeep made a tight turn in front of the building and sped out the gate, as if fleeing an impending bomb explosion. The guard laboriously pushed the steel gate closed, the right half, then the left. I was cut off from the civilized world.

"Come with me," the policeman said, his tone surprisingly mild, and walked back into the building. I followed, head high, chest out. I had not yielded to the bastards in the Bureau and was not going to yield to the guards.

The foyer had three offices to the left. Opposite them, an iron grille served as a check point to a long corridor. I followed the policeman into one of the offices.

"I'm Officer Sun." He introduced himself as if to a guest. His tone told me that the police who worked at the labor reform farms were not entirely unreasonable. "Now I have to bother you with a few standard procedures." I expected to have to sign some forms. "Take all the things out of your pockets and put them on the table."

I obeyed the mild instructions awkwardly. In films I had seen thieves booked at the police station. I hunched my shoulders and looked down, feeling enormously humiliated.

Officer Sun examined the contents of my wallet and made a list of the items with a ball point pen. "Your colleagues will be bringing your bedding and toiletries this afternoon. They can take these things back to your wife. Meanwhile, there's a form we'll need you to fill out." He took a sheet of paper from the drawer of the only desk in the room and handed it to me. I sat down on a stool to write.

NAME: Huang Longsen
EMPLOYER: Beijing Foreign Trade Bureau
AGE: 32
NATIONALITY: Han
EDUCATION: Middle School
FAMILY BACKGROUND: Middle class peasant
OCCUPATION: Proofreader
FATHER'S OCCUPATION: Electrical engineer
POLITICAL AFFILIATIONS: Young Pioneers, age 9; Communist Youth League, age 14; Communist Party, age 20
WHAT CRIME DID YOU COMMIT?

I looked up at Officer Sun. "I didn't commit any crime."

"You didn't?" he asked in his gentle tone. "Then why are you here?"

"They charged me with counter-revolutionary agitation," I explained, "but I never did anything harmful. I said some improper things all right. But I didn't violate the Constitution."

Officer Sun looked at me, his expression thoughtful. I detected a fleeting smile. "Everyone has to fill out this form. You were sent here by your work unit, not the police, so we don't have your dossier. There's no way for us to know the details of your...uh...verdict. Whether you fill in that line or not makes no difference as far as we're concerned here. We have to keep you on a farm for three years, no matter what. But if I were you, I'd fill it in. If you were charged wrongly, you'll have to be exonerated anyway. And if you refuse to admit guilt, the farm authorities will assume you're refusing to repent. That's when your three years become difficult. Understand?"

I sat there staring at the regimented characters of print. "WHAT CRIME DID YOU COMMIT?"

"No," I turned to this reasonable policeman, "I can't write that I committed counter-revolutionary crimes, because I didn't."

"All right. Think it over for a couple of days." Officer Sun seemed finished, but not impatient. He opened the door and shouted into the foyer, "Fan Bin!"

The young man who had been sitting by the iron grille scurried over and stood at the office door with utter respect, his body rigidly straight, eyes lowered, arms close at his sides.

"Take Huang Longsen up to Room Three on the second floor."

"Yes sir," Fan Bin responded, his eyes still pointing toward the tips of his worn cloth shoes.

I walked behind Fan Bin to the grille. He was about twenty. His tattered overcoat came down to his ankles and was badly stained. He gave me one quick glance that took in everything, and sneered contemptuously. To street boys, I was a soft-boned bookworm. My defiance and courage suddenly seemed thin.

Fan Bin pushed the grille door inward, led me in, and latched it behind us. A gust of pungent lukewarm air tainted with a light pine aroma assaulted me. "Now that you're here," he said, his mousy eyes darting, "you'd better not step out of line."

His humility before Officer Sun had faded, exposing the personality of a street thug. I shuddered. Was I to live with thugs like him for three years?

The smell became stronger and more unpleasant as we climbed the wooden stairs and penetrated deeper into the building. The pine wood was overwhelmed by the stench of unwashed clothes and bodies. The long hallway was gloomy, lit only by what natural light oozed through the small transom above each door. Halfway down the corridor we passed a barrel stove and a wooden box full of sawdust. This was the source of the inappropriate fragrance.

Fan Bin stopped and pushed a door open. "Chi Fei! You've got another guest," he barked and shuffled downstairs to guard his lair.

2

At the Liangxiang Detention Center

Eight men, sitting on low stools in a narrow center aisle, turned to look at me. I saw menace in their eyes, beneath the pretense of docility. I stood at the door, confused and scared. One man stood up and walked over to me. "I'm Chi Fei: squad leader in this room. Hand me your luggage."

"I don't have any," I answered, wondering at the assumption that an inmate should have packed for the experience. Didn't the police provide uniforms and necessities?

Chi Fei seemed to read my thoughts. "A labor reform farm is not a prison. Everyone has to use his own things. I'll report this to the officer in charge and see what he says."

Then I remembered Officer Sun saying that my things would be brought.

"Well, then," Chi Fei said, "come over here. By the way, what's your name?"

"Huang Longsen," I answered dutifully.

I began to take in the features of my accommodations. The room was the size of a small classroom. The two windows on the right of the room were barred, and beneath them ran a platform the length of the room with eight tidy bedrolls. Across the two foot aisle was another bare wood platform, neither as deep nor as long, allowing space for the doorway and a cast iron stove and saw-dust box. The air was stagnant.

I stepped over the backs of the men to the far end of

the room. Chi Fei bent over, pushed a battered suitcase aside in the opening beneath the platform, and dragged out another stool. He set it down in front of me and handed me a piece of paper. "You're new here. First you read the regulations."

Chi Fei sat down next to me and picked up his little red book, "The Selected Works of Mao Zedong". The same book was on the platform in front of each man. I took the sheet, sat down, and let my eyes over the regulations. The printed words made no sense. Again, my mind was blank. Now, instead of stillness, a sense of apprehension, an unspecified fear filled the emptiness. Slowly, the eight figures cramped in the aisle became tangible. I stole a glance: they were all younger, mean, ugly, frightening – the kind of young men I would rather go around in the Beijing streets. They wore the clothes of construction workers. I held my eyes on the regulations and started to plan my strategy for dealing with the thugs who would be sleeping on either side of me. For the time being, keeping quiet and observing closely would be best. Fear would only make me more vulnerable.

My heart slowly settled down until I could concentrate. The police officers would likely require a recitation of the regulations to show their authority, like primary school teachers. Knowing that my ego would suffer more from humiliation than from physical torture, I had to be ready for their test.

A whistle blew sharply in the corridor. The men jumped up, overturning stools and banging against the platforms. "Nearly lunch time," Chi Fei said to me. It took me a long moment to stand up. The three men in their mid-twenties sat on the edge of the platform and fell backward, stretching their arms overhead and resting their feet on the opposite platform. The four younger men, eighteen at the most, rushed me with questions.

"What's your name?"

"Is this your first time in?"

"What are you in for?"

Chi Fei interfered. "No inquiry about personal

records. It's against regulations."

I pushed back my sleeve to check the time. It was ten to twelve.

"Are you allowed to wear a watch?" I asked

"Hey, it's Swiss! Good stuff! And it's new. Must be worth two hundred." My father had paid more than that.

They grabbed my wrist and examined it to see if it were genuine. Chi Fei brushed their hands off me and said, "We're not allowed to keep valuables. Why didn't they take it off you? You better give it to the officer to send home. It's against regulations. And you might not find it on your wrist tomorrow morning. You know what I mean?"

We had all heard stories of people losing hands as well as gold, but that was times past. I pulled my left hand further into the sleeve and moved closer to Chi Fei. He was twenty-two, half a head taller than me, well proportioned and handsome. His eyes were sharp and intelligent. I guessed he had been the ringleader of some street boys who played "civilized games" like shoplifting, picking pockets, and "moving house for folks." This type had several girls who traveled with them, and they were "respected" by neighborhood police because they never bullied others. They did not pick fights along the street, and when they took on rival gangs they observed some formal courtesies.

Their neighbors usually thought of them as nice boys. I could imagine Chi Fei smartly dressed, smoking expensive cigarettes, and walking proudly down the street. But here he wore a frayed cotton jacket, baggy trousers, and an old pair of cloth shoes. His hair was trimmed short.

I was starting to feel warm, more from nervousness than from the meager heat the stove emitted. I took off my overcoat and looked around for a place to put it, wary of intruding on anyone's territory. From novels I knew that gangsters, highwaymen, and street brothers took the issue seriously. I could not afford to offend these thugs. Chi Fei took it from me and placed it on the platform next to his bedroll. "You'll sleep next to me." I smiled with relief and gratitude.

The whistle blew again and a high-pitched voice yelled "Lunch is ready! Come and get it!"

"The hyena's howling again," Chi Fei said. "Watch out for that shithead, he's mean. He'll exaggerate anything you do just to keep the guards entertained. That's why they haven't shipped him out to a farm. He's been trying to catch me two weeks, but he might as well be digging for bones inside an egg. We'll see who's tougher. That son of a bitch!" He yelled toward the door in defiance.

"What the hell are you Room Three shitheads doing? I guess you don't want to eat..." the shrieks came nearer.

One of the boys flung open the door and screamed, "Quit crying, you baby! Mamma still loves you!" Then quieter, "Fucking pansy," he said as he spat at the ground.

Fan Bin thrust his head in. "Who's swearing at me? Do you want to die?"

Chi Fei said calmly, "I was. Come on in and kill me, you son of a bitch."

Fan Bin glared at Chi Fei who stared back steadily. Fan Bin let up and smiled wickedly, "Nah, you're too tough for me. In fact since you're so tough, I'm sure you'll make it without lunch." Two of the men on the platform picked up the bucket and wash basin from the shelf by the door and walked out.

I sat on the edge of the platform pretending to read the regulations. I had not been here an hour and already the tension in the air was irritating. I wanted to ask Chi Fei for advice on how to behave in this place, but was not sure if such questions were permitted, either by regulation or by stance. One man was leaning against the door, knocking out a tune with chopsticks on a coarse porcelain bowl. Buckets clanked outside the window and soon the corridor resonated with the sounds of metal and footsteps. Our men came in and set the bucket and wash basin on the empty platform. Thin mists rose from the food and from their clothes. The kitchen must be some distance away.

Chi Fei picked up a ladle, wiped it with a piece of newspaper and plunged it into the bucket. He filled each man's bowl with a ladle full of soup, careful to distribute the vegetables equally. The basin held steamed corn flour buns, two for each. "Huang Longsen, your turn," Chi Fei called. I stood up and walked toward the door. I had no bowl, no chopsticks, and no idea what to do. "Oh, damn," he said. "I forgot to get the bowls for you." He filled his own two bowls.

"Use one of mine for now, and I'll get you two from the kitchen this afternoon."

I accepted the bowl. He picked up the other bowl and the basin with four remaining buns, and walked to his spot at the far end of the aisle. I followed him and placed my bowl on the edge of the platform. He sat down on a stool. I sat down next to him. He bit into a bun, and with his chopsticks he shoveled the soup into his mouth. The room held no sounds but the whistling of mouths sucking soup.

I looked at the broth in the bowl. It was greasy. My three pieces of pork fat floated on top. The cabbage was dark gray. My stomach cringed. The corn buns seemed safer, but the impression of the cook's fingers offered the image of hands smeared with coal dust and other less appetizing substances. All I could remember eating in my native village was corn buns and porridge with brined vegetables. But since we had moved to Beijing, I had seen nothing this coarse.

"Aren't you hungry?" Chi Fei asked me. He had almost finished his meal.

"No, I'm not."

"You want to save it for later?"

I could go without such meals all my life. I shook my head.

"Do you mind if I have some?"

"Take it all." I pushed my bowl toward him, twisting my face into a smile so forced that it must have been transparent as hell.

He thanked me, swallowing the last of his second bun and attacking mine almost simultaneously. The others glanced at his mouth stealthily. Was it envy, or jealousy or something worse? I began to wonder if I had done the right thing by giving my entire meal to Chi Fei alone. If the others thought I was ingratiating myself with the squad leader, it would arouse antagonism. That was the last thing in the world I wanted to do at that moment.

I watched Chi Fei's vigorous mouth. And my mouth began to water.

Around four o'clock I was called to Officer Sun's. As I walked down the stairs, I observed that I felt less righteous. I lingered outside the door to collect a little dignity. "Huang Longsen reporting," I called. I wished I had never been born. Or at least that I could turn into a mouse and escape through one of the holes in the wall.

"Come in."

I straightened my back a little more and pushed the door open. Tang Wen had brought my things over. He stood up and looked at me. Was it sympathy, pity, or contempt? The confusion of the day was clouding my ability to discriminate the simplest expression. I stood, waiting for the last judgment.

"I brought your things. Have a look. If you need anything else, I'll send it over tomorrow."

I bent down, checking with deliberate care to hide the tears of shame that were rushing up. Quilt, pillow, blanket, bedroll; wash basin, toothbrush and paste, two towels, two mugs, face cream, some changes of clothes, a tin case with needles and thread, hot water bottle and two rolls of toilet paper. There must have been a requisite list. "These are enough," I said, raising my eyes, without raising my head.

"There are some books," Officer Sun said. "But they are in English. Regulations forbid reading in any foreign language. They will be sent back."

I nodded. Shalin must be thinking that a labor reform farm was like the state farms where office workers went to help during harvest.

"We must return now," Tang Wen said apologetically. "It will be dark by the time we get back to the city. If you need anything at all, don't hesitate to call. We'll send it right over."

My heart was touched by his words. They conveyed the respect of a colleague for an inmate at a labor reform farm. I hoped that Officer Sun had noticed.

"Please give my watch to my wife. And thank you for taking so much trouble for me." Tang Wen hesitated before going out. His instinct seemed to be driving him to shake my hand.

A car coughed alive outside the building and sped away. Driver Chang had not come in, which prevented some embarrassment. Sensitive Tang Wen would tell no one how humbly I was forced to behave toward a policeman. Driver Chang would certainly have remarked on it, destroying my reputation at the office as one unbending before coercion.

Once more I felt profound isolation engulfing me.

I longed to turn the clock back to happier times when I was a boy growing up in Beijing. I was isolated then, but it was a different, society-imposed isolation.

When I was eleven years old, my family moved to Beijing from a village on the southern edge of the coal mining center, Tangshan. My father had found work in the capital city as a electrician. Only three years earlier the Communist revolution triumphed, and Chairman Mao stood on the rostrum at Tiananmen Square to proclaim the founding of the People's Republic and establishing of the Central People's Government. His words rang out around the world: "Thus begins a new era in the history of China. We, the four hundred and seventy-five million people of China, have now stood up."

My mother, two younger brothers, and I had emerged from the railway station on the bustling and rumbling Qianmen Street. It was an overwhelming first impression being introduced to the most crowded commercial area in Beijing right off the bat.

Electric streetcars clanged on narrow tracks, their

poles sparking as they bounced off the overhead electric lines which were cantilevered from concrete poles along the streets. The air, though dusty, was still far cleaner and fresher than in Tangshan, where a perpetual pall of coal dust hung.

Although the dominant colors of Beijing clothes were still dark, the quality of fabric and the cut were distinct from those in Tangshan. And there were more solemn-looking people in uniform-style dress, the cadres of the new government offices.

We boys huddled around Mother who looked about bewildered. She was an illiterate country woman who had toiled in the corn field and vegetable garden and cooked for a family of thirteen until the very day we moved.

Father, who had come to the city earlier, called over two rickshaws one for our luggage and one for Mother and my two brothers. "I'll take Longsen with me on the tram," he said. He wanted to save money by hiring one less rickshaw. "Don't worry, I've given the address to the pullers. They'll get you there just fine."

The streetcar creaked for a long moment as it turned into Chang'an Boulevard. It moved west along the crimson palace wall. I saw a wooden archway with floral paintings, which reminded me of a smaller one at the graveyard of a landlord family in the village. We passed over, then under the archway at Xisi.

After that, stores were fewer along the street and the houses became lower and shabbier. We got off at Huguosi Monastery and walked half an hour through a labyrinth of side streets and alleys to reach our new home in a mean side street.

Three rows of three rooms each were set on the north, south and west, and a high wall on the east defined a tiny square courtyard. In the village, our front yard alone could have held fifty people easily. There were a set of millstones, the vegetable cellar and an ancient grapevine spread over the front gate. The backyard was even larger with the pigsty, barn, a vegetable plot, and several peach trees. This was a different story altogether.

"This is the best I can afford," Father said to Mother apologetically. "And this courtyard is much better than any other around this area."

The landlady, Mrs. Chang, told Mother not to let me play with the boys in the street. "They are wild," she said. "There are no decent boys around. Our two families are the only decent people in the whole alley. So don't let your children wander out after school to learn bad manners."

I don't know by what criteria she put us as her kind. We were not much better off than the rickshaw pullers, porters, vegetable venders, and scavengers who lived in the seven other courtyards on our short alley.

But Mother came to believe that we were different from the lowly neighbors. So I was confined to the courtyard after school.

All the families in the alley drew water from a pump in the courtyard next door. It was in a small room squeezed into the northwest corner of the courtyard. The tiny, dark room was the home of Dian Wen, a boy my age, and his elder sister and brother, and their parents. Wooden boards serving as a bed took up all the space in the room except a three-foot square around the pump. All their belongings were either hung from the ceiling or tucked under the boards.

Mrs. Chang hired Dian Wen to fetch water for her family. When I was sick he carried water for us as well. Mother paid him one fen for two buckets, the fee set by Mrs. Chang.

Dian Wen was tall and lean. I envied his freedom. His parents didn't stop him from going fishing or swimming in the moat or catching crickets in the vegetable fields along the railway tracks. He could play in the street all afternoon once he had delivered his water. His mother needed the dozen fen he earned to buy flour.

His father, a rickshaw puller, didn't put much heart into the business. He had several time-consuming hobbies: birds, crickets, and teahouses. He would forget to solicit customers once he began talking with other bird and cricket fanciers in the street, or when he sat in a teahouse listening to a storyteller. I often saw Dian Wen's mother standing at the gate waiting for her husband to return, so she could have money to buy corn flour for supper. She would carry it in an earthenware pot with a chipped rim whereas we used cloth bags and could afford rice and wheat flour.

The alley had houses only on the north side. To the south was a great stretch of wasteland bordered on its west by shacks, the ring of ghettoes at the foot of the city wall. On the south was the garbage dump. Women from those hovels swarmed over it scavenging rags, scrap metal, coal cinders, waste paper, anything they could use in their homes or sell to junk collectors. Dian Wen's brother and sister and several other older children raked the debris as well.

The boys living along the alley would play soccer in the afternoon, marking the goal with schoolbags or broken bricks. They would play cards or marbles when there weren't enough of them for a soccer game. I longed to join them. Playing with my kid brothers was boring.

My backwater country accent sounded awful and I felt ashamed of it. I was ashamed of Mother, too. She had bound feet and could not read. Fortunately, Dian Wen's mother and most of the grown-ups in the neighborhood could not read either. But other women had natural feet and that was more apparent.

The boys ridiculed me and refused to let me breach their exclusive circle. They played a game using small cards with colored pictures. They would put a pile of them on the ground and slap one palm very hard next to it to cause the jet of air to blow the pictures over. The winner got all the overturned cards. I bought a huge pile of pictures. Still they would not let me play. "Get out of here," one of them shouted at me as he waved his hand covered with dirt. "You country hick!" The boy was half a head taller than I was.

"Who's a country hick?" I demanded.

"You are," he laughed.

I punched him in his laughing face with all the force I could muster, and threw myself on top of him. He staggered and we fell in a heap on the street. I was on top for only a second. He grabbed my hair and knocked my head against the ground. "One, two, three," he counted. Tears of shame welled up in my eyes. I wasn't hurt physically as much as I was mortified.

"That's enough," I heard Dian Wen say. I stood up, looking around for a brick. "All right," he said to me, his hands inside the pockets of his tattered jacket, "you can hang out with us."

I perceived that he must enjoy great prestige in the alley. The boy I fought with even gave me a smile of conciliation.

Soon, Dian Wen and I were good friends, and he took me along when they went to swim or catch crickets or climb the old gate. He even introduced me to a ghetto gang and allowed me to go with him to watch a fight between two gangs behind the City Zoo.

I was brought back from my childhood reveries by a queer sensation. The detention center had become suddenly very quiet. There were no noisy steps in the corridor, and the men in our room lay staring at the ceiling. They did not look so fearful now.

Soon the sound of the dinner bell flooded the silence. Two men exited with a bucket and wash basin to fetch supper. Once again the dank room stirred to life.

I didn't eat supper that night either, though the kitchen served wheat-flour steamed buns instead of corn-flour buns. While Chi Fei was consuming my share, he took two lumps of chocolate from his jacket pocket and pushed them across the platform toward me. He tilted his chin up and down to urge me to eat them. I wanted to decline, but didn't want the others to notice what was happening.

I put one of the chocolates in my mouth. It melted in the saliva. I tasted no sweetness. Perhaps, the tears I had suppressed after Tang Wen left were still flowing into my mouth. The other inmates ate with enormous relish. I couldn't understand why these people became hungry so quickly. They had been doing nothing but sitting all day.

After supper, there was an hour of free time before the night study session began. We were not allowed to go out of the building. The corridor was noisy. I estimated there must be over fifty people on the second floor and more on the first floor. The third and fourth floors were waiting to be filled. Most of the men in our room played cards.

The smell in the room was that of stale air, bringing bile up from my empty stomach. The cracks around the two windows were sealed with strips of old newspaper to preserve the meager heat from a sawdust stove. Outside the windows, bare branches of poplar trees shivered in the wind. I could see two bits of newspaper floating erratically in the swirling air currents. I went to the latrine at the northern end of the corridor twice, and stood near the open window, trying to breathe in fresh air to suppress my queasiness.

Eventually I sat down by Chi Fei at the far end of the platform. I hoped he would give me more information about the detention center. We spoke softly.

"We have study sessions on two afternoons and every evening, except Saturday evening," he began. "The guards had a meeting this morning. That's why they kept us inside. It may be nice to be inside for half a day in bad weather, but a whole day inside is no better than solitary.

"Actually there isn't much work for us to do at the detention center. They only grow a few plots of vegetables, and now the ground's frozen. They know they can't keep us inside all the time. We aren't mindless robots. Political doctrines don't work on us. Long confinement will only make us edgy, which means more fights than they want to deal with. The guards have to think of something to keep us busy. They used to let inmates carry loads back and forth, but they don't do that any more.

"The center can hold two hundred men and fifty women. The women's quarters are in a separate compound to the east. You can see the roof to their quarters out the window. When the whole center is filled, they will empty it by shipping most of us to different work farms. They always keep some people here to do odd jobs and help look after newcomers.

"Fan Bin, that bastard on duty, has been here over a year. He doesn't want to be sent to a farm, neither do I. The work on a farm is hard, the food's bad, and the guards there are the worst. Not to mention, it's too far from home. Your family can only visit you on major holidays. I want to stay here at least three or four months before going to a farm, but this place fills up fast: sometimes in a week, sometimes in a month. It depends on how active the Beijing Public Security Bureau wants it to be.

"Did you say it was Officer Sun who checked you in?" I nodded in assent. "You're lucky to have met him first. He's okay. He treats us with a modicum of respect. The other guards aren't so reasonable. He is the only guard here with a high school diploma. The others are demobilized soldiers with families in country villages. They're a bunch fucking hicks. The only way they can think of to show their authority is to badger the hell out of us until we break. Officer Sun never does that. He tries to help.

"Just a week ago, they made us squat every time we talked to one of them . Those cowards were fearful that we were going to beat the shit out of them. So to retaliate, they would give us a beating at the slightest provocation, even if they were mad because their wives refused to let them hump before work. They put inmates in straitjackets and into solitary confinement for no reason, and used some other pretty nasty restraints, the kind you only thought they used in films.

"This, of course, has changed immensely since Chairman Mao himself gave the order to treat prisoners as human beings. Now the guards aren't allowed to beat inmates any more; we can stand when talking to a guard, and our food ration has been raised from eight to twelve yuan a month.

"You know how the Chairman learned about these 'inconveniences?'

I looked at him and shook my head.

"In the past couple of years, a whole shit load of former Party officials' children have been sent to prisons and labor reform farms, much to the dismay of their parents. When the fathers regain their positions, they get their children out. The children tell their fathers how terrible the prisons are, and the fathers report it to the Chairman.

"Liang Yu over there," Chi Fei raised his chin toward a young man in the far corner, who was reading something against his bed roll, "is one of these playboys. His father must be a big shot, since he and his wife come in a car to visit their son. Liang Yu is allowed to keep all the food his parents send him. All the guards are more tolerant toward him than to any of the rest of us. I'm sure that if his father was rehabilitated at 10a.m., Liang Yu would be out by noon. No one here dares to question how serious his case is."

Chi Fei looked at me, expecting some indignation, or resentment against such class injustice. I didn't have any. To me, my being here was enough proof of how unjust the world was. Right now my mind was functioning very sluggishly. For the past few days I had the feeling that not even a death sentence could have aroused a response from me. I had no real interest in anything. A fire for revenge had consumed my ability to feel. I just wanted to subsist and bide my time.

"Hey, I'll tell you something," Chi Fei lowered his voice further. "Officer Sun has his eye on a guard in the women's section. She's a piece of work: a real police school graduate. You can see her sometimes in the vegetable fields when she takes the female inmates out to work. I never saw a woman guard so pretty."

Chi Fei seemed to have realized my inertness and thought his lecture had been too long. He shifted to a more cheerful subject, and I forced a smile to indicate that

I was interested.

Chi Fei's face lit up. "On the outside, I'd bet you any amount that I'd have her in a week, tops. But here, you have to be careful. Can't so much as stare at her for ten seconds, especially when Officer Sun is around. If he catches you, you won't get off easy. When he's on night duty, he spends the night over there, in the women's quarters, not here. Somehow, they schedule their night duty together. We all know it. But no one dares to say anything. Piss him off, and Officer Sun can be meaner and harsher than any other son of a bitch in this place."

I shifted my position on the platform. I felt obliged to say something to Chi Fei, but failed to come up with anything worthy of telling or asking.

"Don't tell others about your background," he continued. "Nothing about your family, at least nothing that's true." Chi Fei was in a good mood tonight. I had noticed he had no interest in talking to the other inmates. He seemed not only to mistrust, but to individually despise each of them. He apparently took to me right away because I appeared to be better educated and therefore closer to his equal.

"People held here are cheaters, liars, and thugs. 'Social scum' is what the guards call 'em," he continued. I wondered why he didn't include himself and me.

"Don't tell any of them where you live. Some may get out earlier than you do, or get probation for sickness. They may go to your home and cheat your family out of money. This kind of thing happens all the time, so don't say I didn't warn you."

I tried again to smile, but felt the muscles around my mouth were too stiff to flex.

"When you want to know anything," Chi Fei continued, retrieving a piece of candy from under his bed roll. "Want one?" I shook my head. He stuffed the candy into his mouth. "When you want to know something, ask me. Now let's get ready. The night study session will begin any moment."

We slipped down from the platform and smoothed

the bed sheet where we had been sitting. The others stopped playing cards and got off the platform, too. Most of them went out to the toilet to piss. During the study session, going to toilet was not allowed, except for those who had running bowels so this was their only chance for awhile.

Along the northern wall of the latrine there were a dozen narrow gaps spaced out in a concrete flap. Under the flap was a trough where all the excrement collected. Once every half an hour, water rushed down from a tank made out of an oil barrel anchored onto the wall to flush away the accumulation. A narrow trough running along the southern wall was for the urine.

I followed the others in going to the latrine, where I shivered from the chill of the draft coming from the open window. Through its iron bars I could see the highway on which I had arrived, and empty fields to the south. Still farther, puffs of smoke from a speeding train rose and bent backward, seeming to freeze in the winter sky. I shivered more violently as I urinated. I should have eaten something to keep me warm.

After returning to the dormitory, I sat with the others in the aisle for two hours the study session. We were supposed to use the time for reading and discussing the "Quotations from Mao Zedong", but no one said very much. We just sat there.

By now I knew most of the quotations in the little red book by heart. We had studied them again and again at the Bureau and in neighborhood meetings. I had even been assigned as an instructor on the "Quotations" to a teen-age group of Red Guards who came to Beijing in the summer of 1968. They came from Guizhou province to participate in one of the many rallies that were being held in Tiananmen Square. They were proud to be in Beijing and looked forward anxiously to the day when they would be reviewed by Chairman Mao from the tower of the Imperial Palace Gate. I was one of six selected by the Bureau because I was young, politically reliable, and had little to do in the office.

During the five days before the parade, I took them to visit schools where big criticism posters were displayed denouncing China's biggest scab, renegade and capitalist pig, the former president Liu Shaoqi.

Every morning I gathered the fifty or so in my charge to begin the morning study session of the little red book. I chose several quotations and led them in reading in unison. I always considered such study sessions as a waste of time. It reminded me of my first year of schooling in my village. The old teacher led us in reading aloud from our text, "A man has two hands. There are ten fingers on his two hands..."

But I dared not laugh. Everybody was required to start the day by reading aloud some excerpt from that little red book. Refusal was an unforgivable act of profanity. However, the sincere and innocent expression on the children's faces made me wonder if I wasn't being disloyal to our great leader. I felt ashamed for the cynicism that was building up inside me. Their total devotion to the great leader was pure and noble. I shuddered at my profane thoughts; I was afraid I would one day say them aloud. Not a few people had been beaten to death by Red Guards for disrespectful remarks about the Chairman.

At the detention center, when the whistle blew again at nine o'clock, we ran into the foyer at the southern end of the corridor, bumping into each other. Fan Bin kept yelling "Hurry up!" to impress the officers that he took his duty seriously. Some swore at him, "Your mother must have fucked a dog to conceive you!" "You piss stain!" "Bastard!" and the more civilized "son of a bitch." But Fan Bin ignored the comments and kept shouting.

We squeezed into the foyer in an irregular formation according to room numbers. Officer Kuang read a list of names. We answered "Here!" one by one. "When there are more people," Chi Fei whispered to me, "the roll call will be outside."

Officer Kuang warned us to watch our behavior and not to think of running back home. "The highway and the nearest railway station are guarded," he said. "If we find out that anyone has plans to escape, we'll add another year or two of misery to his time."

The foyer was cold, and my overcoat wasn't doing the job. It was a light weight coat, more suitable for riding a bike between my home and the office. Most of the other inmates had cotton-lined coats that didn't look as nice, but were much warmer. Fashion had no place here. I wished I had a coat like theirs. I began to wonder where they collected these old overcoats. They probably wouldn't wear such crude gear on the outside. They probably kept them handy specifically for situations like this one.

My empty stomach gurgled painfully. I shifted my weight from one foot to another to generate some warmth.

"Hey, there!" Officer Kuang pointed a finger at me. The inmates in front of me turned their heads and leaned backward to expose me to the officer. "What's your name?"

I answered.

"Louder!"

I said my name again.

"Ah, it's you! Our great intellectual!" the policeman emphasized with sarcasm. "Don't think you're superior to the others in this place. They stole and fought all right, but they did much less harm to the country than you did. You wanted to overthrow the rule of the Chinese Communist Party. By the nature of your crime, you're considered an enemy of the people. The leaders of your work unit were lenient to send you here, instead of jail. You better always remember, you're a counter-revolutionary! You'd better behave. Otherwise..."

He didn't finish his threat, and so I didn't know what the "otherwise" would entail. But his scathing opprobrium was enough to scare me silent. I had been here only a few hours and had not yet met this Officer Kuang. How did he know so much about me? It meant that my case was serious. Before I was sent here, the police must have been warned about how dangerous I might be. But Officer Sun had said that the police didn't have my dossier when he checked me in.

I stopped shifting my feet, and didn't feel cold any more. In fact I began to sweat. The blood racing inside me stimulated all my internal organs to put out heat.

"Don't be bothered by that guard," Chi Fei whispered to me. We were undressing and slipping into the cold quilt slowly. "They give the same bullshit to everyone who they think might cause them trouble. Ever read *The Outlaws of the Marsh*? Remember when Lin Chong was banished to Cangzhou? There the governor gave each newcomer a hundred slashes with bamboo strips to make them afraid. He's using the same trick here: punishment in advance. Now go to sleep. Tomorrow we're going to be carrying coal. Now, *that's* punishment."

"Officer Kuang said that by the nature of my crime I was an enemy of the people. What does that mean?" I asked.

"Hah, bullshit!" Chi Fei grunted. "The guard called you an 'intellectual.' They hate people with too much up here." He tapped his temple. "To them, well-educated people are dangerous. Haven't you ever read Chairman Mao's, *On Contradictions*? According to the great Chairman, there are two forms of contradictions in the world: contradictions among the people, and contradictions between the people and the enemy. At present in China, the people's enemies include US imperialists, Soviet revisionists, and those Chinese who attempt to subvert the Communist Party's rule. People's enemies should either be shot or put in jail. According to the official dogma, labor reform elements like us are still in the category of the "people", not people's enemies. A labor reform farm is not jail. So we don't wear prison uniforms or shave our heads. It's all bullshit. We eat the same food as the jailbirds, and we get the same treatment."

Fan Bin pushed the door open, knocked it with his knuckles and commanded: "Time for bed, girls. Lights out, and keep the giggling down!" Then he shut the door quickly. He didn't want to hear what Chi Fei was going to say.

"Go fuck yourself!" Chi Fei shouted after him anyway.

I closed my eyes, not because I was sleepy but because I was afraid Chi Fei would continue to talk if I kept my eyes open. He would probably talk in even a louder voice to show his contempt of Fan Bin.

Yet I couldn't fall asleep. Hunger was taking its toll. The stinking air in the room was sickening. The room grew loud with a cacophonous symphony of inmates' snoring. It immediately grated on my already raw nerves. I began to regret the many statements I had uttered against Bureau officials. If I had kept quiet, swallowed my pride as many others had done, I wouldn't be here.

My neighbor, Mr. Duan, was right when some months ago he tried to dampen my soaring righteousness by saying, "Pride is not food. You can survive without pride, but without food you'd surely die. There are fools who, in the face of danger, think first how they will look after death when they should be thinking of ways to survive. When you stand under the eaves of someone else's house, you must bend your head."

But I had responded to him in the words of our ancestors that, "Trees have bark to live for; men have dignity to live for." This touched off memories of heroes in ancient times who died gloriously, without compromising their integrity. Now, lying among street thugs, I could no longer feel so righteous. Officer Kuang had crushed my pride as the fifty-some pickpockets, rapists, burglars, brawlers and who knows what looked on in amusement.

The damp sweat in my underwear was now making me chilly. I curled my knees into my chest, tucking the quilt tighter around my neck. I had not had many thoughts of Shalin since the morning I was taken away from the dining hall. Now I missed her terribly. Our tiny, rundown, dark room in the old neighborhood now seemed very dear; I would give anything to go back to it so I could sleep next to my wife.

The snoring rose and fell more regularly and was becoming more tolerable. Chi Fei slept soundly, his face turned to the wall. The dim light that came from a single bulb near the door shimmered. Around midnight I heard steps moving up and down the corridor. The night duty officer was checking heads.

Finally, I fell into a fitful sleep, only to awaken soon thereafter from a horrible dream. It was pitch black outside the barred window, and very quiet. I heard none of the usual night sounds to which I was growing accustomed. Piercing waves of cold air attacked my feet, and crept under my quilt. I began to wonder if I should ask Shalin to borrow a cotton-lined overcoat from one of my brothers, or someone else, so I might keep warm in the future.

I couldn't go back to sleep any more. The dim electric light from the other end of the room began to get on my nerves. I lay on the hard wooden platform, my eyes dry and stinging from staring at the ceiling for so long. I closed them to alleviate the stinging, but they popped open by themselves. When they were closed I experienced an intense feeling of anxiety in my heart. The feeling became so strong that I just had to open my eyes. It was like the description I once read in a medical text of the period just before a heart attack. So I had to keep my eyes open and stare at something, trying to put the fear of a heart attack out of my mind.

Through the window, I watched the eastern sky turning fish belly white. Weak spines of light began to stripe the sky as the sun rose from under the horizon. It expanded, framing the poplar trees and roof of the women's sector in silhouettes. I wondered what it was like there.

Chi Fei had said that the women inmates were kept inside most of the time to sew baby clothes or paste cardboard boxes. The center later sold these to factories. Some must have left babies at home, but I doubted if many did. Most of them were too young to have married yet. I wondered why girls stole or acted like their male counterparts. Wasn't hooliganism an exclusively male institution? Their gender should have protected them from this predicament.

I wondered how Shalin was doing now. How worried

was she? Was she going from place to place appealing my case? Before I came in here, the wives of several confirmed counter-revolutionaries had started a writing campaign of petitions to higher authorities. I didn't wholly approve of this. It was the kind of political activity that might inevitably bring repercussions.

During a political campaign in 1957 many well-educated professionals landed in disgrace. The central authorities, at that time, required each unit to designate a certain number of counter-revolutionary Rightists among their staff members. Those leaders who couldn't meet the quota were branded as Rightists themselves. The same thing happened during the Cultural Revolution. At that time, the purpose was to keep the class struggle going and to prove the correctness of Chairman Mao's theory: "As long as there are people, there will be class struggle."

If I wasn't designated a counter-revolutionary, someone else would have been taken in my place. So I believed it was silly to appeal to higher authorities and I always complained that the lower authorities had done injustice to me. I had strongly opposed Shalin's plan to join with the other wives in their petition-writing campaign. Now I was away from home, and she would probably go ahead and join them. She was naive to the complexity of politics.

I was getting more restless. I felt I had to get up and take a walk to calm my fluttering nerves. But I couldn't get out of bed to walk in the room. That was against the regulations. I tried to concentrate on other things to calm myself.

Eventually my thoughts turned to what I could do now that I was confined with street ruffians. I searched my memory for ways I had long ago dealt with the wild youths and gang members I had known as a boy. I tried to remember how they talked, what phrases and slang they used, and how they acted.

At that time, curious and adventurous, I had learned their language and their way of brotherhood. I got along well with them and enjoyed their excursions outside the city walls. At times I even gained the fleeting respect of some of the older street boys because I often behaved more bravely than they did. Actually, I was quite scared when I pretended to be brave. But that was twenty years ago. During my six years in the army and six years after I left it, I had refined my behavior and moral values. Now I desperately needed my childhood experiences to help me cope with my new situation.

My childhood friends would say, "You got a full tank?" when they wanted to know whether you had eaten. They called cowardly types, "piss stains." I would have to greet my new roommates with the terms "pals, guys or brothers." I wondered if any new street jargon had been invented. I had to find out.

At the same time, I reminded myself, I had to be careful in using their language. My appearance must have suggested to them that I was more of a bookworm than anything else. If I adapted myself to their way too suddenly, they would be suspicious. There had to be a period of transition for me. Keeping quiet would be the best strategy for the time being. The most important thing, I decided, was not to show weakness. I mustn't be brought down to my knees psychologically. Otherwise I wouldn't be able to ward off their bullying.

Chi Fei slept soundly, peacefully. This young man held power over the others, even some of the guards. I wouldn't have trouble with them if I could maintain a friendly relationship with him.

3

Loading Coal and Manure

The streak of gray light over the women's sector became larger and rose higher. The sound of a metal object being struck cut through the stagnant air, vibrating high and low. In the next moment, a whistle blew and Fan Bin's nagging voice filled the corridor, "Everybody up! Rise and shine. I don't envy your miserable asses today."

The men bolted from the platform bed and began to throw their clothes on. "Hurry up!" Chi Fei said to me. His urging was unnecessary. I could handle this particular situation better than any of them.

Instinctively I had slid down the bed and skipped out of the aisle before any of them could stand in it to block my way. I waited for Chi Fei to get ahead of me. The corridor and stairway rattled and rumbled with running feet. Fan Bin was still yelling, unmindful of the curses thrown at him from the mass of shadows tumbling down and out of the gate. He had only his tattered cotton-padded overcoat on. His legs and feet were bare. One boy stretched his foot sideways and brought it backward in an arch. Fan Bin staggered but caught his balance. "Out, quickly!" he yelled, refusing to be distracted from his duty.

I sneezed from the chilly morning air and shivered, feeling goose bumps creep up my arms, over my chest and back, down to my legs. Reaching into my jacket pocket, I found no handkerchief. I put the thumb and forefinger of my left hand on the two balls of my nose and blew it. The diluted snivel shot out of my nostrils down to the ground and froze. I tried putting my hands into my pockets to keep them warm, but then took them out and folded them into the sleeves of my jacket. This country villager's way for getting warm was more effective.

Officer Sun walked out of the building. "Fall in!" he shouted, not very stylish in the military sense. I could do better.

We scrambled to form three columns. Then began our morning drill of aligning, turning about, marching, and running. We passed the women's quarters when we ran along the pebble road. The women inmates were also drilling. They began to shout louder when they saw us: "One, two, three, four!" We upped our volume to drown them out.

Breakfast that morning reminded me of the feed Mother gave to the pigs back in my native village. Corn flour porridge splashed and slopped in the bucket, forming stains at the edge and side like dripping paint. As Chi Fei ladled out the thick porridge, it congealed in the bowls. I gulped the porridge down in big mouthfuls as fast as I could, and chewed on a big chunk of salted turnip to disperse the raw taste of the corn. I then pushed two corn buns down my throat, feeling the coarse grains scrape my gullet.

I needed the food. We inmates of Room Number Three were assigned to carry coal dust that day, a dirty and heavy job.

Back home in the office I was generally regarded by my colleagues as inferior because of my limited schooling. Now, at the detention center, I was seen as inferior by the police officers because I came from a white collar job. In a socialist society white-collar workers were often viewed as parasites, and only people working on machines or behind a plow were seen as true producers of social wealth. My fellow inmates showed disrespect because I had no "street record." I had to show both the guards and the street boys that my intellectual look and deplorable physique could stand up to any kind of work they could do.

The distance between the coal heap and the yard where the coal was pressed into cakes by machine was half a mile. Each load weighed 150 pounds. Two men shared a shoulder pole from which hung a wicker basket that held the load. I had expected Chi Fei to work with me, but he assigned Liang Yu, that son of a disgraced big official to himself, and Black Head, a boy of about nineteen years of age, to team with me.

I didn't get a good feeling from Black Head on the first day. Half a head shorter than I, but robustly built, he had a constant sneering smile that was both sinister and mischievous. A vicious scar across the upper corner of his left eye emphasized his boyish looks. His cotton-lined jacket had only two buttons on the lower part. The rest was open, revealing a worn sweat shirt that bore a random design of holes and tears.

Normally, the shorter person would be under the fore end of a pole when carrying a two-person load. But Black Head picked up the rear end as I filled the basket and tilted his chin, ordering me to pick up the fore end. Then, as I bent down to reach for the pole, he jerked his end high and put it on his shoulder. The rope holding the basket slid downward to my end.

I said nothing to him, knowing the trick. To myself, I said, "Son, you are too young to make fool of me. I didn't waste the ten years of food that I ate before you were born so don't underestimate me."

I placed the pole on my left shoulder. I had intended to rise suddenly to throw Black Head off balance. But a sudden thought stopped me. It was just the second day of my being here. I knew it would be better to make friends before making enemies. So I waited for Black Head to stand up, and then we walked forward.

I had done every kind of heavy manual work in my six years in the army. A basket full of coal wouldn't have bothered me at all in those days. But my muscles had atrophied from sitting all day long in the office during the past six years. Black Head kept pushing the rope toward my end, and I felt the 150 pounds of coal in the basket become heavier and heavier as the morning progressed. Soon, my underwear stuck to my thighs and spine, my lungs ached for more oxygen, and the tendons of my calves twitched and convulsed like the vibrating strings of a cello. I swallowed laboriously to moisten my parched throat and gulped down air by taking deeper breaths than I exhaled.

"I have to show the street thugs I can be tough too," I urged myself. I saw that the shoulder pole of Liang Yu's end was also shorter than that of Chi Fei. Liang Yu staggered dangerously as he crossed over the open sewage ditches by the roadside. In less than an hour, Liang Yu seemed exhausted. He sat down on a plank and refused to rise when the basket was filled again. Chi Fei grabbed the collar of Liang Yu's jacket and said coolly, "Get up, you spoiled son of a bigwig. Remember where you are. You must remold your rotten ideas by working hard!"

Liang Yu whimpered, "I can't walk another step."

"You can, you playboy!" Chi Fei didn't raise his voice, but the tone was threatening. "Get up and work! We have to fulfill our quota today."

Liang Yu bent slowly to pick up the shoulder pole and placed it carefully on his right shoulder underneath a blackened towel which cushioned his raw shoulder. Chi Fei walked swiftly, pushing Liang Yu so that he had to lean forward.

As I felt my legs buckling and ready to give way, the section of steel rail hanging near the gate was struck to announce the morning break. The ringing was music to our ears. You could hear the sigh that emitted simultaneously from each man. I found a wall and slumped down at the foot of it. My whole body ached, threatening to fall apart. Chi Fei walked over and sat beside me. He fished out a pack of cigarettes and raised it toward me. I shook my head. He knocked a bottom corner of the pack with his thumb, and a cigarette jumped half way out. He drew it out of the pack with his lips and lit it, inhaling contentedly. The fragrance was tempting.

"You're tougher than I thought," he said with an amused tone. "I was afraid you wouldn't last an hour, let alone the whole morning."

I smiled weakly.

"That good-for-nothing, Liang Yu, has had his fill for the time being," Chi Fei said, wiping his forehead with a clean handkerchief.

"It must be from playing around with one of his girls," I mused. The handkerchief was smaller that the usual size for men and delicately embroidered.

"You and he will work together after the break. You don't have to carry full baskets. Two thirds full will be fine. I'll see to it that the guards don't chew you out."

Chi Fei sounded condescending, and I definitely didn't want this kind of patronage.

"No," I said. "Don't worry. I can do worse jobs than this."

"Do as I say," Chi Fei said. "It'll take several weeks for you to adapt yourself to this kind of life."

"You don't bother," I said. "I said I could manage, so I can do it. I won't die from it!"

Several heads turned toward our direction. I was startled by my raised voice.

Chi Fei looked at my face closely for a moment and said, "All right, whatever you say." Then, rising abruptly, he shouted, "Break's up! Everybody get to work!"

I picked up a shovel and filled the basket one-fourth higher. "Let's go!" I said to my partner Black Head, who looked at the hill of coal in the basket and at me and grunted, "Do you want to kill us both?"

I thrust the pole onto my shoulder. Black Head placed his end on his shoulder. This time he didn't push the rope toward me.

The morning ended. On our way back to the dormitory for lunch, no one had energy left to joke or talk. The same stuff, a bowl of cabbage soup with several pieces of fat pork floating on top, and two steamed corn buns. But they tasted better. There was an hour and half for the noon break. We all lay down to take a nap.

The steel rail was struck too soon. Muffled by the wall, it sounded mournful and remote. I picked myself up from the platform bed. All of my joints were creaking and scraping, and it seemed as if every muscle was sore. I stumbled out of the gray building. The sky had become darker. The others of Room Number Three didn't seem in much better condition than me. I stiffened the pulsating sense in my calves and locked my knees so I could walk more upright.

"Huang Longsen," Liang Yu came to me, dragging a shovel and a basket. "Chi Fei wants me and you to work together."

I picked up a shoulder pole and walked over to the coal heap. Liang Yu followed behind. I set the basket down and he began to shovel coal dust into it. The shovel was unsteady in his hands. Several times it overturned before it reached the basket. The coal spilled onto the ground. I took over the shoveling and filled the basket.

"You ahead, or I ahead?" I asked him.

"I'll be ahead," he said. "I can't keep the basket balanced from behind."

So I took the hind end of the pole, pulling the rope a little away from the middle toward me. Liang Yu smiled. The black smears around his eyes were like the black rings around the eyes of a giant panda. He hadn't washed his face before lunch. He held the pole with both hands, trying to reduce the pressure on his shoulder. I walked steadily, careful not to swing. Crossing the ditches, I gave an upward pull at the rope to lighten the weight of the basket on the pole. On the next load, I walked a bit slower and filled the basket one-fourth less, as Chi Fei had suggested in the morning.

The blessed ringing of the steel rail brought the afternoon break. Liang Yu and I found a sunny corner in the yard to sit down. Chi Fei looked in my direction, but went to sit with others to smoke.

Liang Yu was about twenty-three, thin, and half head taller than I, but he weighed less. His protruding shoulder blades propped up his black-silk, floss-padded jacket. His face was thin and long. His eyes were large but unfocused. His skin was delicate and fair, revealing blue veins on his hands. He needed a haircut badly. As he sat down, he seemed to shrink into a size smaller than mine. If he were to perform in a Peking Opera, he would certainly be cast as a ghost with no need for make-up.

"I know you're in for political reasons," Liang Yu said. I kept my head bent and eyes closed, to save as much energy as I could. "Officer Sun told me. His father and my father used to work together." I didn't feel any sense of challenge in his voice. "I don't agree with what that woman Jiang Qing is doing either," he said. "She has brought down many good people."

I was scared by his mentioning of Jiang Qing's name. She was the wife of Chairman Mao and now the leader of the Cultural Revolution. Even Premier Zhou Enlai had to wish her eternal health at public meetings. I looked around. No one was listening to us. "Don't talk like that," I said in hushed tones. "You may get us in trouble."

"I joined a group to correct the mistakes she has made," Liang Yu said, as if he had not heard me. "They arrested all of us, sent most to prison and several to state farms. I'm the only one that was given two years on a reform farm. I'm not afraid, and as soon as I get out, I'll be fighting again."

I shifted my butt uneasily. Liang Yu's father must be very high in the Communist Party echelon. Otherwise he would have been given much more than two years on a reform farm. Such cases as his would be sentenced to at least ten or fifteen years in prison, and perhaps even death during the height of the Cultural Revolution. His group was apparently a genuine counter-revolutionary organization. It was unlike ours in the Beijing Foreign Trade Bureau. Ours was denounced as a counter-revolutionary gang only because of the beating of small fish and the cursing of some top leaders.

Liang Yu's group on the other hand aimed to overthrow the whole regime. I shouldn't have had anything to do with Liang Yu for my own safety, but he piqued my curiosity. I had never talked to one of the children of very big officials. He must know a lot of inner-circle secrets.

"Don't mess with those street thugs," Liang Yu said, raising his broad forehead and his large, lusterless eyes a little to sweep the pack of rowdies nearby. "They are social scum," he flipped his head toward them. "The shame of mankind. Their only chance for reform is hard labor."

I chuckled silently. Here was an inmate talking about the reform of social scum, while he himself was suffering the most by the means to reform them. "Don't lose faith in yourself," he said, "and believe that the majority in the Communist Party are devoted to our high ideals. Be prepared to contribute your ability to the Party and the country."

I was fed up with Liang Yu, who was not only dangerous to talk to, but he was also stupid. I hoped the section of the steel rail would sound soon. It did. I rose and began to shovel coal into the basket. This time I filled it to its rim, and didn't give an inch of leeway to Liang Yu.

"He must be preaching again," Chi Fei said as we walked back to the dormitory. "He preaches to everyone, teaches us to be more refined and to abandon our bad manners. Something must be wrong in his mind, or he is just an idiot. Who knows? Those big shots in Beijing can't produce intelligent children. Their brains are clogged with too much fat, and their semen is thin and weak from screwing too many women."

I grinned in appreciation of his humor.

"He's a miser, that good-for-nothing Liang Yu," Chi Fei twisted his nose in contempt. "He came from Shanxi province, and Shanxi people are all misers. They wipe their hind ends with their fingers and suck at them so as not to waste anything. Liang Yu's mother embroiders a mark on everything she sends over: towels, sheets, clothes, handkerchiefs, socks. So nobody will steal from him. Every week his parents come to see him. No one here is allowed family visits that often. They bring him tons of food. He keeps the food in a locked tin box under the bed. Every once in a while, you can catch him as he opens it and takes out a little bit to eat. He never offers any to anyone, the miser. The damned box is full. Most of the cakes have probably gone stale by now. That Shanxi bastard."

"By the way," Chi Fei continued, "don't get too close to that jerk. He can say what he wants. He's protected by Officer Sun, whose father is a bigwig too. When his father is put back in office, everything he did before will be forgotten by the authorities. But I guarantee, they'll remember everything you say." He poked me lightly in the sternum. This gesture reminded me very acutely just how mortal I had become. I nodded my head.

Most of us were dispatched to deliver manure to the vegetable plots during the next five days. It would be two months before the field was planted. There was nothing else for us to do at the detention center, but they wouldn't let us stay idle for long.

Comparatively, the job was easier than transporting coal, and it was cleaner. Although it was smelly, particularly when we raked open the compost heap where garbage, last year's crop stalks and human and animal excrement, had been sealed up with a layer of mud to ferment through the winter.

The men's quarters were almost full now. We would be sent to Chadian after the Spring Festival.

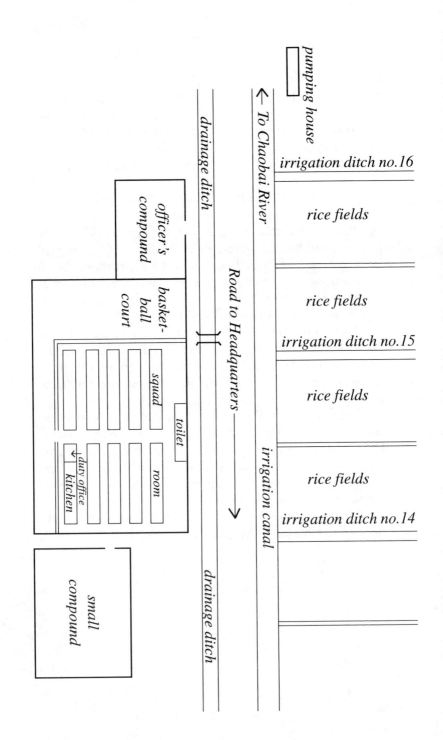

4

On Our Way to Chadian Farm

We were lined up on the basketball court in front of the gray dormitory building for a final inspection before being trucked to the Yongdingmen railway station. From there we would go to Chadian Farm by train.

"Huang Longsen!" Officer Kuang bawled. "Fall out!"

I shuddered from the surprise summons and stepped forward to stand in front of the others. While I was frantically thinking of some reason for which I was being picked at this particular moment, I noted how ridiculous it was for the policeman to use military terminology among this batch of city thugs. I wondered if he had ever had a high enough rank in the army to have allowed him to shout this command. If he had made corporal during his army service he wouldn't have been in this lousy job, guarding this hole in the ground.

"Step forward!" the guard barked again, louder, for the benefit of the nearly 200 inmates. I moved three steps further. He took three steps to meet me, brushed open his cotton-padded overcoat and retrieved a pair of handcuffs. "Put out your hands!"

I stared up at him with a look intended to make him realize how contemptible it was to show off his authority on a helpless person, and I stretched out my hands with as much defiance as I could muster. He cuffed me, intentionally snapping them shut too quickly. I felt the sharp edge of the metal on my wrist bones.

Then he turned to address the inmates. He had to shout in order to overcome the howling wind that always heralds Beijing's dusty spring, "Watch out, all of you! Anyone who refuses to repent will be dealt with like this one. Huang Longsen, we're sending you and all of your friends to Chadian. You're going to have to learn to behave yourselves, work hard, and strive to turn over a new leaf in your lives so you can become contributing members of the society."

He went on to lecture us about what we should and shouldn't do. I heard pairs of shuffling feet behind me, the insidious sound of a flock of locusts gnawing on corn leaves, stealthy and ugly. The sound also reminded me of a village latrine with millions of maggots wriggling in the open pits and flies bustling against the thatched walls. The inmates were cold and impatient. With the cuffs on, I couldn't withdraw my hands into my jacket sleeves to get them away from the lashing wind. But I didn't feel the cold. My whole body sweltered in helpless rage.

Everything, every word and gesture added to the enormity of this indignity. In a historical context, my family, my whole lineage, had been dealt a severe blow. As far back as I knew, my forefathers had been upright and proud farmers who owned land and tilled it themselves. In my native village the Huang clan was known far and wide for its honesty and its being law abiding. My grandfather taught us children not to pick as much as a single melon from a neighbor's field. No one through the generations had ever before been entangled with the law.

When police came to check the family registration book, my grandfather would gather us, thirteen all together, including my parents, two uncles and their wives, and me and my baby cousins, in his room so the policemen could count heads. Such checking would make us very nervous, as would any minor summons to the police station.

In our village, when a thief was caught, the villagers would bind him up and exhibit him in front of the village temple. Now I was being treated just like a thief, but I was not a thief. In fact, I had never done any harm to anybody, as my father taught me.

My anger rose, as did my feeling of shame. I began wondering if I should not have heeded the advice of Officer Sun and Chi Fei to fill that registration form and plead guilty to counter-revolutionary thinking. If I had done so, Officer Kuang wouldn't have handcuffed me. But now it was too late. My only hope was that Officer Kuang would end his sermon soon and send us on our way.

Two dozen policemen in blue uniforms, complete with red collar pins, cap badges and side arms, came out of the gray building. I recognized some of them as being from the detention center. The others must have come from the Chadian Farm. They swaggered over to us and stood there as if they were watching some idiotic monkeys at the Beijing Zoo.

Seven trucks that had arrived the afternoon before started their engines and were soon roaring loudly, unnecessarily consuming extra gasoline. It was time for our departure.

I was ordered back into the ranks, conscious of the stares and sneers from all around. I stood in my place and looked vacantly ahead. Black Head moved half a step toward me, nudged my elbow and winked. I nodded to assure him I was all right.

Chi Fei was not among us. He had succeeded in ingratiating himself with the detention center police and had made them believe he could help in maintaining discipline among the unbroken newcomers. When we departed, he was left behind and was thus spared the heavy labor and harsher guards at the Chadian Labor Reform Farm.

I somehow missed him, but not as much as I would have if I had not learned quickly how to deal with the unpredictable and often dangerous characters around me. I could protect myself. I didn't know what the life would be like in Chadian, though I was looking forward to it. There, Chi Fei told me, the inmates were kept working in the fields most of the time. As long as they finished their daily quota of work, the police would leave them alone no matter what crimes had brought them to the farm.

One squad after another was herded into the open trucks. Black Head gave me a pull as I struggled up the short ladder that extended half way to the ground at the rear of a truck. He and I had become friends. His nasty sneering grin had grown into a childish, innocent smile. I half-suspected that Chi Fei had asked him to take care of me. He had been trying to do so over the past week.

Another street veteran, one who arrived at the detention center a few days after the Spring Festival, also became a bodyguard of sorts for my time at Chadian. This new boy was nicknamed Tiger. He was Black Head's old buddy from the busy streets around Qianmen. Tiger was also nineteen, solidly built, the same height as Black Head, and with the same mischievous smile. They were much alike in temperament and appearance, twin brothers of evil.

Our cavalcade roared out of the steel-plate gate of the detention center. As we left, I saw the figure of Chi Fei in the window of the latrine on the second floor, an arm stretching out to wave good-by to us. Black Head and Tiger waved back cheerfully. "Smart devil," Black Head said to me. "And a stand-up guy."

We sped along the highway to the Yongdingmen railway station. Two policemen, each sitting on a front corner railing of the truck bed kept an alert vigil. A third armed policeman was in the cabin beside the police driver. A marked jeep with a red flashing light on top led the way. Another jeep brought up the rear. They took the matter, and themselves for that matter, too seriously, I noted. We were not dangerous political prisoners or organized gangsters. None of us was about to break his neck jumping out of the speeding truck, and none of us had the wherewithal to coordinate a breakout by our friends on the outside. Who would risk death by intercepting an armed cavalcade, anyway? Of course, there were those among us who boasted that they would "wade in a sea of fire or climb a mountain of knives" for friends. But we all knew this was just idle chatter. Talk was cheap.

I felt warm, squeezed among my fellow inmates, and I felt cold for the two policemen braced against the rushing wind from the north. Their upturned collars flapped in the gusts, and their hands tightly grabbed the upper wooden strip of the truck railing. "Poor saps," I whispered to Black Head vengefully.

"Fuck 'em. Serves them right," he answered loudly.

"Who's talking there?" the policeman on the right yelled. "Shut up and be quiet!"

"Yes sir!" Black Head shouted playfully.

A tremor of laughter rose among the inmates.

"Shut up, you smart ass!" both police guards shouted over the wind.

"Yes sir!" several more responded.

The enraged guard on the left seemed to forget he was sitting on the corner railing of the truck. He jumped up and fell down. The inmates near him caught him and heaved him up to his perch again. "Better use a bit more caution there, sir," they reproached. Laughter rose again, louder.

"Be quiet!" the other guard shouted menacingly. "We'll see how much laughing you do at the Farm."

The road was desolate, completely devoid of people. Occasionally a bus passed by. Passengers in it looked out at us from the closed windows. The inmates made faces at young women in the bus, causing the police guards to shout at us again. After we entered the urban area and traffic became heavy, the two police guards stood up, their hands on the pistols hidden inside their overcoats. They reminded us in menacing yells: "No talking and stay still!"

All of us fell into total submission. Even Black Head and Tiger kept straight faces now. These two street boys knew that the police guards would really do something at this moment if they were not careful.

Our trucks pulled up in front of the Yongdingmen railway station and parked next to each other. They ordered us to get off the trucks and line up in a long queue.

Yongdingmen station was reserved for the short-haul trains whose destinations included Beijing's rural counties, and for slow freight trains. Not many passengers from the city used it. The hundred or so people in the open lot in front of the station building began to gather around us. I stood sideways so as to hide the handcuffs from their view. A gate was opened especially for us to get into the boarding area.

A section of the platform had been cleared of passengers and station workers. Policemen formed a lane with their bodies as we were escorted toward a waiting train. The swelling crowd swarmed over to have a good look, pushing against the police cordon. Young spectators cheered and hooted, and many inmates shouted back and waved. Policemen barked orders to maintain order.

Black Head and Tiger carried my bedroll for me. I still had difficulty holding the net bag with my wash basin, other personal effects, and two pairs of shoes in it. I pulled its cord tighter and heaved my shoulders to pull the bag higher on my back. My face burned. I hoped desperately that no one I knew might be at the train station and recognize me.

I knocked my right knee on the steel step at the door of the car as I tried to board the train. An attendant, a young man in a blue railway uniform, guffawed and stepped aside to let me fall sideways. The net bag slid off my shoulder and crashed against the side of the train. The wash basin, the two metal mugs, and two enamel rice bowls clanked loudly. The cord holding the bag tugged at my handcuffs. I winced as the metal edge of the cuffs cut deeper into my wrists. I was only 110 pounds in weight. Between the skin and bone at my wrists were only tendons and blood vessels.

Black Head gripped my waist belt through the jacket from behind and gave me an upward push. I stumbled onto the dirty, square, steel-plate floor inside the door of the car. The train attendant laughed. I dragged my net bag with the clanking utensils into the narrow aisle.

I heard a voice in the dark shout, "you, over to that

seat!"

I didn't look up to see which seat he was directing me to, but hurried over to one at a window and sat down. Black Head and Tiger followed. They put their bedrolls up into the overhead rack and net bags under the seats. Leaning over me, they put their heads out of the open window to smile at the crowd on the platform.

"Close that window!" a policeman shouted.

The two boys withdrew their heads reluctantly and pulled down the window slowly, waving their hands while they did so.

"Sit down!" the same voice shouted. "You two want handcuffs?"

The boys mimicked panic and sat down next to me. Our train started slowly. The crowd on the platform stared at us. I stared back, but at no one in particular.

I had taken a window seat so the other passengers wouldn't be able to see the handcuffs on my hands. It was unnecessary since the police had reserved the car exclusively for their prisoners, and we were the last car of the train. The door linked to the car in front of ours was locked. No regular passenger could come in. Still, I was ashamed.

The train attendants were probably happy to have us. They stayed in their small cabin to play cards all the way because the doors were not opened at any station, not until we reached our destination. They didn't bother to serve us boiled water as the other attendants did for the regular passengers, because we were social scum. The policemen fetched water from the boiler for themselves. I didn't move from my seat all the way, not even to relieve myself in the toilet. The others found any excuse they could to stand up and walk the length of the car so as to loosen up and get the restlessness of youth out of their systems in preparation for the farm, I guessed.

The landscape outside the window was bleached by the early spring winds and dust. The dull rhythm of the wheels cranking against the rails went on and on. From time to time, a policemen would stand up to count heads.

At such times everyone was required to remain at his seat.

It seemed the train engineer knew he was carrying some two hundred street thugs and was unhappy about it. As the train slowed down to approach the Chadian station, he put on the break roughly. The train quivered in small jerks as the brakes gripped the wheels.

The platform at Chadian station was too short to accommodate the long train, so our car stopped beyond the end of a wooden fence. The attendants yanked the two doors open. The steel door frame and steel steps clanked sharply. "Hurry up!" they yelled loudly. "Train's only here for two minutes!"

The police guards shouted from many places in the car, "Open the windows! Open all the windows and throw your things out!"

Our car quickly turned into pandemonium. The boys stopped making dirty whispered jokes and scrambled to get bedrolls down from the overhead rack, pushing them out through the windows. I dragged my net bag out from under my seat, looked at it for a moment, and then decided it wasn't worth the struggle to carry its contents through the aisle and down the door ladder. I raised it with my cuffed hands and pushed it over the window sill.

"What are you doing?" Tiger yelled at me. "All your stuff is going to break."

"To hell with it," I announced.

The basin, the mugs and the bowls struck the gravel at the track side pitifully and protestingly as the bag rolled down the embankment. I got into the aisle and climbed down the steel ladder. Unable to support myself with my hands, I lost my footing and rolled down the incline from the tracks. Several others had fallen before me, and the accompanying laughter had become dimmer and less irritating. I stopped myself up in time to avoid a puddle of melted snow.

The windows on the cars in front of us were all open and heads were popping out, looking at us with amusement. I looked back at them. Strangely, my feeling of shame had disappeared. I had arrived at a labor reform farm, a place I would stay for three years, a time long enough to become my home. I belonged here, so I was the master. From now on Beijing, where Shalin and our son lived, would be another world.

The train puffed out several angry whoops and jerked forward impatiently. The attendants watched us from the open doors. One of them leaned out dangerously with one hand gripping a side handle of the door while waving toward us with the other hand. I recognized him as the person who had laughed at me when I was trying to climb the ladder into the train. "Bye fellows! Enjoy your time!" he shouted. At that moment, I hoped he would fall out of the train and be crushed to death.

Seven trucks from the labor reform farm were waiting for us in an open lot by a small pond, covered with rubbish and dead reeds, that stood below the tiny railway station. We were packed into the trucks, which then climbed up a steep bank, onto a roughly-paved asphalt road, and sped toward the west. I could feel the damp, chilly air flowing from the east. A police guard came over to me and took the handcuffs off. He then walked away without saying a word. It was no longer necessary to take rigid measures now that we were in the bounds of the famous Chadian Labor Reform Farm.

The tension in our police guards disappeared. The two guards on our truck no longer remained aloof, but rather stood among us to ask our names and ages. They even chatted among themselves, and shouted greetings to acquaintances riding bicycles on the highway.

Forty minutes later we stopped at the general headquarters of the Chadian Farm. It was lunch time. Many people were going in and out of the kitchen with enamel bowls or aluminum lunch boxes. Boys and girls of primary and middle school age were also there. They spoke with a perfect Beijing urban dialect and dressed much the same as their counterparts in Beijing. The dilapidated auditorium and other structures, as well as the rustic surroundings and grown-ups who dressed and looked like backwater village types and talked in strong provincial accents made the children seem another species, one to which, we felt, we belonged. But we knew the children must belong to those grown-ups.

The aroma of food in the air was tormenting. My mouth watered. I swallowed hard, and, with others, got down from the truck to go to the latrine to relieve myself. Returning, I climbed back up into the truck and waited.

Thirty minutes later, our trucks pulled out the yard of the general headquarters and sped further westward. The dozen policemen from Liangxiang were not with us. There was only one guard on each truck.

The gravel highway ended abruptly at a wooden bridge over an irrigation canal, and gave way to two unpaved roads. Four trucks turned onto the northward road, the other three turned onto the southward road. I was on the first truck going north. Our group was assigned to two of Chadian's nine sub-farms.

The trucks lurched, jumped and slid over frozen ridges and ruts that became slippery when the surface was melted by the sun. There were also many potholes filled with melted snow. We drove between an irrigation canal, with its banks raised five feet above the ground, and a drainage ditch four feet wide. A short time later we again turned west, still flanked by the irrigation canal and drainage ditch.

Paddy fields divided into large strips by irrigation ditches stretched neatly away from the canal toward the North. On the southern side of the irrigation canal were vegetable plots and orchards. Rice crop stumps protruded out of melting snow cover. Willow and locust trees stood sparsely and pathetically on the irrigation canal banks, along the drainage ditch, and along the edges of the fields. The land was flat and lifeless.

A village-like community appeared ahead of us and soon we passed under an arch built of raw wooden poles that served as the entrance to its single street. Strung horizontally over the arch was a paper streamer, its red color fading. The broken, unreadable characters in black ink must have been painted for the celebration of the

Spring Festival. Red brick row houses on the northern side of the road were family homes. Several of these on the southern side of the road were likely used for a grocery store and some other commercial service facilities.

Children ran out of the houses to shout: "Another batch of labor reform elements are coming!" Their accent was a mixture of several provincial dialects with that of Beijing the most prominent. Their clothes were shabby. Some of the women, no better dressed, were cooking lunch on brick stoves in the courtyards. The stoves were fueled with burnt crop stalks and tree branches. The women looked up at us indifferently.

The inmates around me didn't show any interest in either the children or the women, as they had those at the general headquarters. Some of the younger inmates hooted distastefully at the children who ran close to the roadside to chant insultingly, in unison: "Labor reform elements, labor reform elements!" They threw lumps of earth at us.

Someone in our truck cursed, "Bastards!"

This caused the police guard to turn around and bawl, "Who's swearing? Don't you know where you are?" No one said anything else as our trucks drove through the street. Later, we learned this was a residential area for the families of lower ranking policemen, and we came to call it the Officer's Village.

Soon we saw another village ahead, but it contained a much larger cluster of row houses of red brick. As we got closer, we saw that the houses were constructed in three parts. The main part, in the center, was enclosed by a high wall mounted with barbed wire from which hung red electric lights.

In another ten minutes our trucks drove into the steel plate gate of the main part and parked in an open lot that contained three basketball hoops. Their rings were unusable because they were either quite crooked or missing. A dozen men in civilian clothes were waiting for us. They were local police officers assigned to be our overseers.

When we lined up in formation, these guards came forward, each with a pad in hand, and called names from the list on it. Smoke rose from two chimneys of the kitchen and I smelled the flat odor of food cooked without oil and spices, typical of poor-village fare. Still, my stomach ached for it.

"Take your things inside. Meal's in ten minutes!" an elderly officer announced. The officers in civilian clothes took us into a smaller compound on the northern side and directed each squad to its room. The compound on the southern side, across the open ground, was apparently occupied by another group of labor reform elements.

Lunch was composed of two corn flour buns that were getting cold and a bowl of cabbage soup. The corn buns tasted much like those at Liangxiang, and the cabbage soup was barely edible – boiled in plain water and salt, with rotten leaves of cabbage in it and without a single drop of oil. Supper was the same. Breakfast next morning was even worse. I missed the nasty looking, greasy slices of pork fat that floated in the cabbage soup at Liangxiang.

I should have expected this. Chi Fei had warned me that the food at a labor reform farm was bad.

5

I Set Myself Up at Farm 583

Farm 583, one of Chadian's nine sub-farms, was located in the middle of the sprawling Chadian territory. Its 1,700 hectares of fields were bordered by the Chaobai River on the west, the moat-like main drainage ditch on the north, and Farm 586 on the east. A dirt road ran eastward, beside the irrigation canal, to a wooden bridge where it joined the asphalt road leading to the general headquarters.

The living quarters of Farm 583 were divided into three parts: the Big Compound, the Small Compound and the Officers Compound. The Big Compound, where the labor reform inmates were kept, was further separated by walls and an open ground with two basketball courts that subdivided it into two smaller compounds. All the newcomers joined the remaining inmates in the northern compound. Black Head, Tiger, and I were assigned to Squad Two of Team One.

There were four squads in each of the four teams. Each squad slept in one room. Each of the eight rows of one story houses had two squad rooms. The eight row houses stood neatly in two columns on either side of a pebble-paved path.

On the northern end of the path was a lavatory with a thatched roof and brick walls. At the southern end was the gate to the northern compound. On the right side of this gate was a long, unfurnished room which served as a meeting room. On the left side of the gate was the inmates' kitchen and the duty office. This also served as the watch house to the gate.

The doors of both the kitchen and the duty office opened toward the south, which meant that inmates had to first go out of the gate to reach them. Two small windows in the back wall of the kitchen provided an opening through which food was handed to the inmates. The small windows were protected by thick wooden boards when it was not meal time.

Our squad room was in the first row house, just behind the kitchen. Three young men, the remainder of the original Squad Two, were taking a noon nap. They were wrapped in dirty cotton quilts, their cotton-lined jackets over their heads. None of them even stirred when we entered.

Finally one of them, in his early twenties, pulled the jacket down to reveal his gaunt face. He nodded his head as a way of greeting. "Cold, ain't it," he grunted. "We're out of coal, and the crop stalks are wet. The fucking bed stove don't give no heat, It just smokes. No point lighting it, I guess."

"There aren't very many of us in this place," Black Head said to the young man. "You the only ones left?"

"They split us up," the young man grinned. He took an immediate liking to Black Head. "The others were sent to Farm 586. I'll give you one guess as to why." He gave Black Head a nod.

Black Head said he knew. It was just like the practice at the Liangxiang detention center. The police used a few of the "old hand" inmates to be the backbone for the newcomers, to stick around and show them the ropes.

"The name is Ah Ming," the young man said.

The other two men on the bed still didn't move.

The squad room was much the same size as the rooms at Liangxiang, except for the ceiling. The beams and rafters of raw timber were blackened by time and smoke. The reed mats that formed the inner lining of the roof had holes in them from which powdered lime and sand fell in tiny cascades when a sudden gust of wind rolled over the roof outside. The platform bed was made of bricks instead of wooden boards. It took up half the room space lengthwise. The reed mats were torn in various sizes and shapes.

A square, low stove made of bricks attached to the platform bed looked strange to the city boys, but not to me. Such an arrangement was commonly used by country folk in north China for both heating the bed from underneath and cooking during the winter. The stove was fueled either by burning coal or crop stalks. This one mostly burnt crop stalks. The peasants had plenty of crop stalks from the autumn harvest. Coal cost money and was probably not even a consideration, though it could produce much more heat.

A cast iron cauldron sat rusting on the stove. The film on top of the water in the cauldron shimmered with hues of gold and blue. Another stove had been placed in the middle of the room. It was also built of bricks, and was also unlit. To say that the room was cold and gloomy would be to understate the utter feeling of desolation which pervaded these four walls. All the things in the room were of dark, dirty colors.

Two small windows looked out at the row house behind. Two large windows looked out at the courtyard in front. There were cords, with clothes hanging on them, strung between young willow trees. The clothes seemed to have been carelessly rinsed in soapy water, without being washed properly.

The windows had no iron bars over them. The door had no lock. That meant we would be allowed to move around freely within the courtyard. That was a promising prospect for me. In the three weeks at Liangxiang, I had developed a fear of being inside a room with other prisoners when we were not working.

Each of the two smaller compounds was occupied by one squadron of about two hundred labor reform elements. The high wall around the Big Compound was mounted with electric wires. Although there were red bulbs strung at intervals, the wires were not alive, Ah Ming told us.

The whole of north China was desperately short of electricity. It didn't have nearly enough to meet the needs of China's growing industries and expanding areas under irrigation. Accordingly, power to Chadian was cut off most days and almost every night during farming seasons. Even if the wires had been connected to an electrical source, they would've been useless. Furthermore, the red bricks of the high wall were pulverizing. It would've taken an inmate less than ten minutes to put a hole in them. The wires seemed to serve only a symbolic function to remind those living in the Big Compound where they were.

The Small Compound was located outside the eastern wall of the Big Compound. It contained the sleeping rooms of three workers, persons who used to be Rightist inmates and had been retained on the farm after they had finished serving their terms. The Small Compound also had a storehouse where they kept farm tools and fertilizer bags, a stable with five horses and two oxen, and a cow shed with five milking cows. Several gaps in this compound's run-down wall of bricks and rammed clay had been mended with tree branches to prevent the cattle from getting out. In a corner of the Small Compound was a tiny, neat plot fenced off with locust tree branches. I assumed it must be the private vegetable garden of the three ex-inmate workers.

The Officers Compound was on the western side of the Big Compound. Within the Compound were the Officer's Canteen, their office rooms, and a guest house where relatives of the inmates stayed overnight when they came to visit. The houses and walls were better maintained than anywhere else. The path was paved with bricks, and the glass on all the windows was intact.

A pumping station sat right under the dike of the Chaobai River 500 yards down the road from the gate to the Big Compound. The superstructure housing the machines was built of blue bricks instead of the less durable red bricks. A long channel led the river water into a deep pit at the pumping station. The irrigation canal began from behind the pumping station and ran east in front of the three compounds.

Beyond the river dike and blocked by it, was a wide expanse of flood plain with the river some distance away. It was said that none of the police officers, during the past two decades, had ever seen the river water reach the dike. So it had become somewhat of a relic. The flat, wide top, however, served conveniently as a section of a highway. Trucks, jeeps, horse- or ox-drawn carts and occasionally cars, pumped along over the many dents and cuts made in it by rain during the summer. After the rainy season, there were always some people available to patch up the rain damage to make it serviceable again.

Because Farm 583 was too close to the outside, non-criminal world, it had never been used to house persons serving formal prison sentences. When Rightists were assigned jobs in the Chadian factories during the early 1960s, Farm 583 was used for them, but they hadn't been sentenced to terms as criminals. The five electricians at the pumping station, all grown-up children of police officers, had been given an extra duty to keep an eye on the inmates from the Big Compound. Without an officer escort, no inmate was allowed to pass over the wooden bridge that crossed the channel, beyond which the dike rose fifteen to twenty feet along an easy slope. To us, the river dike seemed much higher than the wall of the Big Compound.

I was one of a few labor reform inmates who ever got a chance to cross the wooden bridge, climb up the dike, and walk over the half mile of flat land to reach the river. It happened three months after I arrived at Chadian. Along with several others from Squad Two, I had been taken by Officer Niu to dredge the inlet of the channel. The river water was getting lower and lower each year, and the inlet had to be deepened in the spring before rice field flooding began.

I felt quite liberated when I stood on the broad top of the dike, looking over at the river which shimmered in the bright sunshine. For a moment, I forgot all my grievances against the bureau officials back in Beijing, and the injustice of society in general.

The dike ran south to north. If one continued along it toward south, Officer Niu told me, one could reach Beijing. Officer Niu had said these words in such a tone that I felt for just a moment the hope that I might achieve my only goal in life, to be free once again.

The three months at Chadian had so far been like a bad dream, and I wished it were no more than that. My ambition to become someone of merit in society had been shattered. In the beginning, the police officers at Farm 583 were suspicious of me. To them, I was a "political criminal who harbored a profound hatred for the Communist Party and its leadership." I was assigned to do the dirtiest jobs, such as cleaning the cow sheds, pigsties, and latrines. I didn't hate the police officers. They were not my persecutors. They were hard on me because they genuinely believed that I was a dangerous saboteur of the Communist cause. It was their duty to treat me accordingly. There was no point in my hating them.

I did every job quietly and thoroughly. Once I even overheard Officer Wang saying to Han Jen, leader of Squad One, that "Huang Longsen never complains or asks questions when he is given a job. But he can always do any job better than we expect. I just can't figure out what kind of a person he is. He's difficult to fathom." When I heard this, I wished I had been that tight mouthed and prudent back in Beijing.

I was not particularly anxious to win trust or sympathy from the officers. Knowing that the Liangxiang guards thought I was too educated, I further deduced that they would have passed this information along to the guards here at Chadian. Also since I was older than most of the inmates, I was inherently dangerous to them. They had to be sure I wouldn't incite trouble among the arrested street thugs who were strong in brawn but weak in brain.

People who read books, as I did, would have difficulty convincing the simple-minded police officers at the

Farm that I was innocent. I had to prove myself in action. I wanted to convince the policemen, in time, that I didn't intend to make trouble. Thus I might gain comparatively more freedom and make the confined life at Chadian easier.

Officer Niu was not as simple-minded as Officer Wang, who was Officer Niu's partner in charge of Team One. I had a feeling that Officer Niu, if given a chance to talk with me as a free man, might come to see eye to eye with me on most political and social matters.

We arrived at Chadian after the coldest days of winter had passed. This was when one of the hardest periods of the year began in the fields. At the end of February the ground was thawing. We were all sent to dig, repair, and deepen the drainage and irrigation ditches.

But on the first day, right after lunch, two inmates from each squad were sent with handcarts to fetch loads of worn-out, rubber knee-high boots that had been discarded by the local coal miners. We paid two yuan for each pair. We each had to buy a tube of glue with which to patch the holes in the boots. Since we were not allowed to keep cash, everything we bought went into an account book. Expenses for daily necessities were deducted from the twenty yuan monthly allowance mailed to the farm by our original work units, or by the Beijing city government for those who hadn't had jobs to begin with.

The next morning we were marched through the gate of the Big Compound to the drainage ditch canal. The ditch was six feet wide. Silt, over many years, had almost filled it up. We had to clear it. We dammed and drained it, section by section. Each of us was assigned five square feet to dig five feet deep. This took two days of hard work, and we were told that, because we had just arrived, we were given only half the regular quota.

We gawked at the filthy bottom of the ditch. Dead, rotten reeds matted the top, and long, thin reed roots lay underneath in tangles. It seemed we would never be able to scoop up so much mud, spade by spade, even in the two or three years of our terms.

"Get down there and start digging," Officer Wang yelled.

I walked down the slope and tentatively stepped in the mud. I had patched the dozen holes in my pair of rubber boots with meticulous care and was rewarded for the effort. Many others were swearing at their boots. Water had found its way in and wet their socks. The water was freezing to the touch. Officer Wang yelled at us and urged us to get to work.

Mud began to fly onto the bank. I was not strong physically, but could think, and I planned to beat others by wit. Supporting my body weight on the handle of the spade to keep my feet from being sucked deeper into the mud, I speculated, conscious of the watching eyes of Officer Niu from up on the bank.

I first dug a small, deep square hole in a corner of my assigned area and guided the remaining water into it. Then I began digging from the other end of the area, carefully minding that as little loose earth as possible dropped off the spade. Each time, before inserting the spade into the earth, I wet the spade's surface so that the mud wouldn't stick to it. I pushed the spade into the mud, jerked the handle to detach the chunk of mud from the earth, tossed my right hand with a quick gesture, and sent the mud flying high in the air. Each chunk of mud made an arch before it fell to the bank, leaving a three-foot clear space from the edge of the ditch. Thus I wouldn't have to climb up the bank to remove the mud to make room for more as I went deeper.

After I dug half way down, I walked over to the corner of the next layer and dug another deep square hole so it would drain any water that had oozed from underneath. This was the only moment I straightened my back to take a breath. I had also anticipated the reeds and roots by sharpening my spade on a granite rock. It cut through the tangled mess without much resistance.

Near the morning break at ten o'clock, my legs began shaking and my heart fluttering, more because of hunger than exhaustion. Every chunk of mud seemed to be the last I could throw up on the bank. I had to grab the spade handle tightly in order to stiffen the piercing pain of broken blisters on my palms. I couldn't give up, I urged myself. Not until I dropped dead!

For a while the digging became totally mechanical. My brain became as numb as my overexerted muscles. Then the pain and exhaustion returned. I even toyed with the idea of thrusting the spade against my foot. Its sharp blade would probably cut off one or two of my toes without my feeling much more pain. Then the officers would have to send me to hospital. No. I vowed at that time that I would never do such harm to myself again.

For a distraction, I began digging in frantic succession for several minutes. It worked. My brain went blank again. I felt nothing as my nerves directed my arms and hands to toss the spade in and out of the silt deposit.

That day I dug five cubic feet, a record for Farm 583.

When the whistle blew, we were marched back to the Big Compound. I dragged my heavy legs, tapping the last drops of energy I had, just to keep up with the marching pace. I didn't even go back to the squad room to wash. I couldn't move my legs another step. Sitting down under one of the two small windows at the back wall of the kitchen, I asked Black Head to bring my bowl over.

The two steamed corn buns and bowl of boiled turnip soup had no effect on my aching stomach. As I later lay on the platform bed, my stomach was still screaming for more. From a cloth bag hidden behind my bedroll, I took two candy pieces which I had preserved from the Liangxiang Detention Center, stuffed them into my mouth, and sucked on them slowly. Saliva in my mouth began to flow like a fountain. All the joints of my body were now getting loose, my back was painfully sore against the uneven, hard brick surface of the bed. Black Head kindly brought a basin of water so I could wash myself.

"Were you trying to kill yourself out there today?" he asked.

I had no energy to answer.

"It would have been okay if you had, I suppose. But since you didn't, you're going to have to start thinking of the others from now on. If you keep working like that, the guards are bound to increase our loads, because you've proved that we can dig more. You'd better go easy tomorrow. Now, wash up. The evening study session starts in a couple of minutes."

I wouldn't dig more tomorrow, I had already decided. I didn't tell Black Head because he wouldn't understand my strategy which was to show to the officers that I was not a "soft-shell egg."

The book-cultivated half of myself also rationalized my suffering by recalling the great sage Mencius: "No one fulfilled a great mission and played a role in history without first undergoing a hard process of tempering, a process that exercises his mind with suffering and toughens his sinews and bones with toil, exposes his body to hunger, subjects him to extreme poverty, thwarts his undertakings, and thereby stimulates his mind, tempers his character and adds to his capacities."

But the natural half of myself retorted: "I don't have any great missions to fulfill in my life! To hell with all the hypocritical bastards!"

Just as I had predicted, I was appointed the leader of Squad Two a mere three and half months after I had arrived at Chadian. Squad leaders enjoyed the privilege of taking their men out of the Big Compound on individual assignments without an officer's surveillance. Under me, there were eleven people. All except Pockmark were in their early twenties or under.

I remained close to Black Head and Tiger through all my stay at Chadian, though I wouldn't call them my friends. They were not my type, or, as the cliché goes, we were not birds of a feather. There was the age gap of thirteen years between us, and there were differences between us in other ways. For example, life for the two boys was nothing more than the excitement in a fight, the thrill in "pilfering a wallet from a rich guy," and the expanded image of themselves they experienced when they sat in a fancy restaurant with an eight course meal. As Black Head described the pleasant sensation of pilfering a wallet from someone's pocket: "It's just like fishing. You know, when the float sinks, you jerk up the rod and, voila! You've hooked a big fish!"

I said they were too young to grasp the complexity of life. They said my philosophy of life was foolish. I argued with them a couple of times and gave up. I knew I wouldn't make them understand that the worthiness of one's life was based on being useful to society. "Your life is boring and tiring," Black Head concluded after listening to my high-sounding lectures.

Actually the two boys and I had little in common to talk about. Still, we were known among the other inmates and officers as being "as thick as thieves." I was not worried about such an impression. Though the two boys were known as troublemakers and many in the Big Compound were afraid of them, I believed that as long as I could keep them from doing excessive things, the officers wouldn't blame me for "patronizing bad elements."

Black Head and Tiger had grown up together in one of the oldest, poorest, and most intellectually backward neighborhoods in Beijing. The side streets and narrow alleys are hidden behind the grand facades of silk, fur, jewelry, and clothing stores. The area also boasts the Quanjude Beijing Duck and Gongdelin Vegetarian restaurants on Qianmen Street, half a mile south of the Old Imperial Palace. It used to be inhabited by small vendors, rickshaw pullers, railway station porters, deck hands who worked at the Qianman railway station, and prostitutes.

During the early 1950s, shortly after the founding of the People's Republic of China in 1949, the Communist police rounded up hordes of gangsters, street thugs, opium addicts, and prostitutes from this notorious Qianman district. Truckloads of gangsters were taken out of Yongdingmen, the southern gate of the old Beijing outer city, only one-third of a mile to the south of the glorious Qianmen city gate tower. There many were shot in the wasteland. Some of the gangsters shouted a brave farewell to the crowding spectators: "In another twenty years, I'll be a man again!" Opium addicts and prostitutes were sent to reform centers, from which, after their addiction and venereal diseases were cured, they were sent to join land reclamation brigades in the frontier provinces.

As China became more and more modern, the local residents were elevated to the position of attendants in the many stores that the government took over during the nationwide socialist reform drive in 1956. Some also became lift-truck drivers at the Qianmen railway station, waiters and waitresses and cooks in many of the restaurants in the vicinity, factory workers, and office clerks. The area itself, however, didn't become modern. On the contrary, the houses built of broken bricks became even more downtrodden, and the courtyards became even more crowded as lean-tos and sheds were added to accommodate the fast growing population. The youngsters, though with some years of schooling now, inherited the neighborhood tradition of libertinism.

Black Head and Tiger were both the youngest of three brothers, who were, in turn, buddies commanding dozens of boys in the neighborhood and at school. Their mothers pleaded with the older brothers to lead normal lives, failed, and then gave them a desperate order: "not to involve your youngest brothers in your wild life." The two aging women needed at least one son to remain with them in their later years. They knew that their older sons would be killed, or land in jail sooner or later.

The older brothers obeyed their mothers' order. They excluded their youngest siblings from everything they did; they didn't take them to "play" or eat out. The two younger boys, however, organized their own gang without their older brothers' patronage.

Blackhead and Tiger were thirteen when the Cultural Revolution began in 1966, and fifteen in 1968 when

China was plunged into the chaotic fighting between political factions all over the country. The call from the great Chairman Mao "To rebel is right" suited the two boys fine. They converted their street gang into a Red Guard group and named it "Turning the World Red."

At school, they smashed windows and desks in the classrooms, and beat up teachers, all in the name of "knocking down the revisionist education system." Back home they marched old neighbors who had served the former regime as policemen, as well as gatekeepers and errand runners for the rich, through the streets for public ridicule. They had a great time when older students and young workers were painting Qianmen Street in red revolutionary slogans. All the stores and restaurants gave them free drinks and food, and praised them for their creative work.

By 1968, Red Guards were traveling all over China to "exchange revolutionary experiences" at the encouragement of Communist Party leaders at the top. They were provided with free train, bus, and ship transportation; free meals, and free lodging. Black Head and Tiger took this opportunity to see other parts of China. They visited Shanghai, Hangzhou, and Guangzhou in the south; Changchun, Shenyang, and Dalian in the northeast; and Huhhot and the grasslands of Inner Mongolia. "We would have gone to Tibet if we were allowed," they boasted.

They "graduated" from junior middle school in 1969, without taking any formal exams. The Communist Party Central Committee was urging city youngsters to go to the countryside to "receive education from the peasants." But this time Black Head and Tiger didn't follow the call.

"Bullshit!" the two sworn brothers said, and refused to leave Beijing. The neighborhood committee and the police station put them on the list of "educated youth waiting for job assignments," a term that was to become a fig leaf used by the government to cover up the huge unemployment problem among city youth several years later.

Loafing at home, Black Head and Tiger didn't have to learn shoplifting or burglary – they were born with the expertise. Twice they were sent as juvenile delinquents to the Tiantanhe Labor Reform Farm near Beijing. Each time for six months. The police finally decided they were old enough for Chadian.

Chi Fei, whom we had left behind at the Liangxiang Detention Center, had been a "big brother" to Black Head and Tiger. This "big brother" had told the two boys to look after me. They acted as loyal friends, much as righteous outlaws did in olden times. I had read about such friends in my younger years in many novels about outlaws, such as the *Outlaws of the Marsh, Seven Swordsmen and Thirteen Knights, Eight Senior Righteous Men and Eight Junior Righteous Men,* and *The Romance of the Three Kingdoms.* I used what I could remember from these books to deal successfully with these two street players. Soon I could stand on my own without my two "younger brothers" as my protectors and on equal terms with any tough in the Big Compound.

I gradually took it as my obligation to see that Black Head and Tiger didn't go beyond the limit and thereby get all of us in trouble. I maneuvered delicately, however, so as not to give the police officers the impression that I had become one of them. I wanted the officers to treat me as a man of intelligence, hard working, law abiding, and always willing to help wild boys back onto the correct road of life. On the other hand, I didn't want the inmates to call me a "guards' bootlicker." So I kept a respectful distance from both the boys and the officers. At the same time, I did my best to build up a moderate degree of respect for myself from both sides.

Despite my precautions to keep my distance, I did make two friends before the first four months had gone by. One was Officer Niu and the other was an inmate named Han Jen.

6

A Sympathetic Officer

I had been conscious of Officer Niu's watching me all the time. He would measure the depth of my section of the irrigation ditch or test the bank of it with a kick to see if I had built it with any clever deception – that is, only looking good but unable to stand the flowing water for an hour. He would do this after I moved to another spot. On his tour of night duty, or during a break in the fields, he would call for one or two inmates over to have a "talk" to give us an educational lecture on how we should behave. Over the first three months he must have talked to all forty-eight inmates of Team One, except me. He apparently was not yet ready to deal with a man as "unfathomable" as me.

His eventual talk with me took place during a morning break, when we were flattening fields and building ridges after tractors had done the plowing. It was done during a time when, in another month, the fields would be flooded with water for rice transplanting. It was early May, a relaxed period for the inmates. All the irrigation and drainage ditches had been repaired, the sprouting wheat didn't need much care, and the sowing of corn and sorghum had not yet begun. This period allowed time for the inmates to loosen up before the busy season, which would last through the spring sowing of sorghum and corn, then the rice transplanting, then the summer wheat harvest, and finally, autumn harvest. After that, there would only be short intervals of repose before the whole cycle began again.

The mid-spring sun was warm, and the work was not hurried. The morning and afternoon breaks often lasted half an hour instead of the regular fifteen minutes. Officer Niu must have been lonely sitting on the bank of the irrigation ditch bank to oversee us in the fields. He blew the whistle ten minutes before the ten o'clock morning break time. Each of us found a soft spot in the field and lay down against the ridge.

It was then that Officer Niu called out from his vantage point, "Huang Longsen, come over here!"

I had expected this summons for a week and had prepared my strategy for this audience which was to take no initiative in talking, but to give willing answers. I smiled at Black Head and Tiger, and winked to tell them there wouldn't be trouble. They smiled back.

"Sit down," Officer Niu said, as I climbed up the five-foot-high bank of the irrigation ditch. I chose a spot three feet away from him and sat down on the ground, turning my legs at an angle of forty-five degrees from his direction but keeping my face toward him to show my respect for an officer. I could feel the pricking stumps of dead grass under me.

The young willow tree, under which Officer Niu was sitting, had turned tender green. Its soft, thin twigs drooped down in a lovely manner. The drainage ditch under the bank of the irrigation ditch was half filled with clear, deep-blue water. The water table was rising now that spring had come. Shoots of reeds were emerging through the earth. Several months earlier inmates were required to keep their heads bent when talking to an officer. But this was no longer the practice. I wondered how I would feel if I had had to talk with Officer Niu that way.

"You've been here for three months?" Officer Niu asked, as if looking for words to begin his talk.

I was disconcerted despite my readiness for it. The officer shouldn't be so polite in his tone. It might mean that he felt uncomfortable treating me as an ordinary inmate. In the beginning, I had feared the officers who treated me with suspicion because they thought I was dangerous. Now they treated me with remote politeness. I feared this kind of attitude, too, because this might end in their resentment against me because they were unable to treat me as an inferior.

I moved my buttocks uneasily to avoid the grass stumps and said, "Yes sir, three months and twenty-one days."

"Have you adjusted yourself to the life here?" he asked. "It can't be easy for you to live in such a place. I mean people like you who have never known street life, but now have to stay with these thugs day and night."

I smiled and said nothing.

"You've been doing all right. I can see you aren't soft. I would say you're tougher than most of the street boys. I supervised some Rightists several years ago. They were book-reading types, too, but none could carry themselves as well as you have. Many broke down physically or mentally from hard labor and plain old depression."

"I am not a book-reading type," I said, "if you mean by that term those who have gone to college. I joined the army when I was in my third year of middle school. In my six years in the army I did every kind of farm work. The work here is not much harder. I like reading," I added, to disperse any notion I might have given to Officer Niu that I was trying to place myself in the "common ranks."

"I've been learning English by myself for over five years," I continued. "But back in the office I was still taken for a country bumpkin by those intellectuals."

"Oh?" Officer Niu looked me in the eye.

I liked the relaxation I could now see in his face.

"So you're not some college educated bookworm." He laughed lightly. "No wonder you can deal with the rabble so cleverly. These people here are not easy to handle, even for some of our tougher officers. Among them there are some reckless men who don't care about the consequences of what they do. Some are cunning and deceitful. They think of every kind of dirty trick they can play on inexperienced or soft-hearted officers. Last year, one young officer, just out of the army, was stripped of his pants in the field. He cried in front of the mob."

Officer Niu burst out laughing, but checked himself immediately. He explained, "The young officer believed that, if he treated the street toughs with sincerity, he might move them to correct their bad habits. But a kind heart won't work in a labor reform farm. I have never been to a police school, but I have heard that the school teaches the students there how to keep a straight face. That's the only way to deal with people who intimidate, and cheat others."

He asked me about my parents, my wife, and my job in Beijing. I told him about the circumstances in which I got entangled in the power struggles during the Cultural Revolution.

"I hope you won't get too chummy with the street boys," he said. I nodded my head. "I know you won't. I can see you're a person with high aspirations. Don't get disillusioned by your present plight. Things keep changing. The Cultural Revolution is changing all the time. One day certain people are acclaimed as vanguard revolutionaries, and the next they become arch enemies of the revolutionary cause. During the past two years, seven people I know of have returned from the Chadian Farm to their original jobs in Beijing. Before that, all the labor reform elements were expelled by their working units and kept on the farm or sent to remote regions after they were released. Now your jobs are reserved for you until you return. You're much luckier than those Rightists were. So don't lose hope. You're still young. Thirty-two? There will be many chances in the future. Who knows what will happen in China next year? Are you still reading English?"

"No," I said. "The farm regulations forbid inmates to read in any foreign language."

"Well," Officer Niu thought a while and then said, "I'll talk to the general headquarters and see if they can make an exception in your case. At present, people seem to do nothing but struggle against each other. Political slogans are not food. One reason we Chinese are looked down on is that we never unite to do anything. We are like a bag full of crabs, clawing, grappling, and snatching at each other, and getting nowhere."

I wondered if he hadn't gone too far to talk like this to me, a labor farm inmate. I didn't really want to be so friendly with an officer, especially when political issues were involved. I looked up at Officer Niu and around toward my fellow inmates, who were lying scattered against the newly built ridges, smoking or cat napping, comfortably. Officer Niu saw my uneasiness and said, "All right, that's enough for today. You can go now."

He blew the whistle to start work. I returned to the fields. Our conversation had lasted through the whole morning break.

"Got a scolding?" Tiger asked.

"No," I said. "I've done nothing wrong. Why would he give me a scolding?"

"But it took so long," He said suspiciously.

"He gave me a lecture on Marxism and Mao Zedong Thought," I said.

"Bullshit!" he grunted.

Secretly I was happy. If I could handle the relationship with Officer Niu carefully, I might be secure.

Officer Niu was senior among the dozen officers on Farm 583, and his words carried much weight. Even Political Instructor Feng had to "discuss" matters with him when he planned to give new orders. Once we heard Officer Niu countering Political Instructor Feng's order dividing the labor force. "He doesn't know anything about growing crops," Officer Niu told Officer Wang within our hearing. With Officer Niu as my patron, I expected an easier life for the remaining two years and eight months at Chadian. He might even exert his influence to get my early release.

After that day, whenever Officer Niu was on Sunday duty, he would call me to the duty office so we could have a friendly chat about many things. Apparently he was quite lonely. I had suspected this much since he didn't have much in common with the other officers. He was too intellectual for them. Though he had little formal schooling, he read a great deal and was sharp in his thinking and observations. Like me, he was cynical, refusing to submit to authority. We had our own ideas about how things should be. Because of this, he had remained an officer of the lowest rank through his twenty-two-year service at Chadian.

I came to discover many other things about him in the ensuing months. For instance, he originally joined the Communist army in 1947 at his native village in Shandong province. He fought in the nationwide war of liberation all the way to the conquest of Beijing, and stayed with the army until 1951. Then he became a guard at Chadian. He had escorted Kuomintang officers, officials, and secret agents, both captured and surrendered, to the detention center. From then on, he seldom left the farm except on occasional errands to Beijing to bring back a new batch of convicts or labor reform elements.

He returned to his native village every two years for a home visit, and in 1957 married the girl his parents had chosen for him. He brought her back to the farm and together they raised two boys, now going to high school at the general headquarters. His ambition was to send the boys to college in Beijing. The two boys were doing well at school and the prospects for them going to Beijing was promising. This was his greatest consolation, because he knew it was hopeless for him to rise any higher in the police force.

Officer Niu was a tall man, half a head taller than average. He had a slim body and firm features. I think that if he were to wear the woolen uniform of a section chief, he would be able to carry himself much more elegantly than many of those in the Beijing bureau offices. He read real books, not the children's picture books or cheap novels most other officers read. The gap in intellectual level between Officer Niu and his partner, Officer Wang, was almost as great as that between heaven and earth. In contrast, Officer Wang was trifling in build and raw and coarse in his manner. He would shout and swear at the inmates, but could talk to us in the most casual way too when he was in a good mood.

Officer Niu kept a stern expression, and wasted no words. Almost everyone in the Big Compound feared him. He would give orders to inmates of other teams, without worrying about causing antagonisms with the other officers. Once he ordered us to clean the cow shed. A squad of Team Seven was repairing the side road to the Small Compound. Their officer must have gone to have some tea or to play a chess game somewhere else. The inmates of the squad were sitting around chatting and smoking. Officer Niu stopped and looked at them. Most of them quickly stood up and began to work. Two boys, however, ignored his stare. Officer Niu walked over and said, "Get up and get to work!" The two boys, both around twenty years of age, looked up at this officer who was putting his nose in another officer's business, and remained sitting.

Officer Niu didn't turn around but called out, "Han Jen, tie them up!" Han Jen, leader of our Squad One, came over to take the rope from Officer Niu. Han Jen had the reputation of a good martial arts master and had learned to tie people up in the police way. The two unfortunate boys, who must have been new to Chadian, struggled vainly for a few seconds in the hands of Han Jen, and then yielded to the powerful tugs and pulls of the "penalty rope."

Shortly before I was sent to the Liangxiang Detention Center, the government had outlawed the physical torture of prisoners. But Chadian was too far away from Beijing. The order came slowly. Also, Chadian officers had their own interpretation of what constituted physical torture. They still occasionally used the "penalty rope" to tie up inmates, as a warning to other troublemakers.

The "penalty rope," only half as thick as one's thumb and about twelve feet long, looked innocent enough. But used by a clever hand, it would cut off circulation in the arms within two minutes. The more one in penalty struggled, the tighter the rope would become, thus cutting deeper. We watched the two boys' faces whiten and moisten as their sweat began to flow. The others in their squad averted their eyes. In about three minutes the two boys began shaking. Their eyes had lost their brave defiance and their heads drooped in submission. In another minute, one dropped to his knees, followed by the other.

"Untie them!" Officer Niu ordered.

Han Jen and another inmate undid the ropes as fast as they could.

"Now, go to work!" Officer Niu ordered the two boys, "and don't let me catch you again!"

As we marched down the road. I turned to see the two boys, trying to pick up their spades with great difficulty.

"In the past," Han Jen told me later, "some would lose the sensation in their arms for more than a month after being tied up for ten minutes. They say the maximum one can take without losing the use of their arms is fifteen minutes. I don't like to do it. But some of the guys actually need to be taught hard lessons."

One day Officer Niu told me in the duty office, "I stopped trying for promotions a long time ago." He had had a drop too much over a lonely supper that he brought from the officer's kitchen to the duty office. The room was premeated with the stale smell of cheap alcohol. "But I still don't feel it's fair. Just because he has several more years of schooling than I do, doesn't give him the right to lord it over me." He was referring to Political Instructor Feng. "When I was fighting the Kuomintang army, he was still a goddamned toddler in split trousers. Now *he* gives *me* orders? No thanks!" He picked up a small plastic bag from the desk, thumbed out some crushed tobacco, arranged the crushed leaves on a piece of paper cut from stationery and began to roll a cigarette.

Many inmates had learned to smoke these "Big Cannons" from the officers. They found raw tobacco more satisfying than cigarettes, and much cheaper. They couldn't afford to smoke cigarettes all the time on their twenty-yuan monthly pittance. So they bought tobacco leaves and made them from scratch.

Officer Niu was a meticulous man, doing everything quite neatly. His Big Cannons looked better than any other's. Biting off the paper knot at the top, Officer Niu struck a match to light it, then inhaled deeply. Puffs of grayish smoke spread throughout the room. I didn't smoke, but I liked the smell of it. I had once tried a Big Cannon and vomited, bringing all my supper up.

"Well, forget the instructor." Officer Niu waved his hand to ward the smoke away from his face. "You know, Huang Longsen, I've been thinking about putting all the inmates under twenty into one squad with you as the squad leader. Then they can live and work separately from the older inmates. This place is no good for young people. They only learn how to become worse here. They exchange experiences of stealing and playing with women, and they brag constantly. They brag so often they begin to believe they can do things they never dared to do before. I'm sure Tiger and Black Head will return here, or go to jail, just as soon as they're released."

I was amused to hear him using the inmates' nicknames.

"That's a good idea," I agreed, careful to be sure that my tone sounded respectful. "People as timid as Pan Rong have learned to be boastful. With Ah Ming backing him up, he tries to intimidate others. The other day, he picked a fight with Millstone. It was ridiculous for him to pick a fight with a man that big. Millstone could twist Pan Rong around his little finger if he had a mind to do so. Pan Rong provoked the big man because he knew he wouldn't dare to fight back. He called Millstone some of the foulest names he could think of. Millstone stood there with a red face. I hate people who bully others when they only do so if they have the backing of friends. I went over and pushed a spade into Pan Rong's hand and told him, 'You're a great fighter, aren't you? Why are you calling names instead of really fighting? Come on, boy. Give it to him.' Pan Rong looked at me and then at the spade. He put his hands tightly against his sides. I said to him, 'Get back to work, you brave chick.' So the fight was over."

Officer Niu joined me in laughing, and laughed heartily.

"You did the right thing," Officer Niu said. "Well, Huang Longsen," he hesitated and gave the Big Cannon two deep draws, inhaled deeply, withheld his breath for several seconds, and exhaled the thick smoke slowly through both his nostrils and mouth. "You keep on like this. I can't guarantee, but I will see that you get every chance to be released sooner."

Officer Niu wouldn't expect me to show gratitude, so I said nothing.

"But one thing I should tell you," he said, examining the tip of his Big Cannon. "Be careful what you say when Political Instructor Feng is around. You should be stricter with those in your squad. When there's a quarrel again, don't hand out a spade. Others may accuse you of inciting blood-letting. The instructor is not a man of humor and may not understand your tactics. Be careful with what you say at squad meetings, too. Someone may report on you and distort what you really mean. As the saying goes, 'Don't harbor harmful intentions against others, but be on guard to protect yourself.' You're too outspoken. I've suffered a great deal myself by being outspoken. If I knew how to follow the tide, I would now be much higher in rank than just a policeman guarding several dozen petty criminals. You have only three years in this damn place and then you can go back to Beijing. No matter how low a job they give you, you'll be far away from all these cutthroats, pickpockets, and rapists. I'll be here the rest of my life, even after I retire. I have nowhere else to go. If I am not burnt to ashes after I die, I'll be buried not far from those who have died as criminals here."

Officer Niu fell silent. I didn't know what to say and felt awkward sitting there. I wanted to return to the squad room and while away the rest of the evening playing cards with the others. But I couldn't possibly leave without Officer Niu dismissing me.

"Don't let the boys sneak out to the village store again," Officer Niu said, as if suddenly remembering the warning. His Big Cannon was burning his fingers, which were stained yellow from long years of smoking. His penetrating eyes were losing their usual sharpness. "I don't worry that anyone will escape under my charge. I know they let you know every time they wade over the drainage ditch to the village. But that makes you answerable for the consequence. You know what I mean?"

I, of course, did and said so. The paper wrapping of the Big Cannon was now blackening his fingers. I wanted to tell Officer Niu he should drop the cigarette, but refrained from doing so. That would indicate too much concern for a police officer coming from a labor reform element.

I looked around. The officer's duty room was in no better condition than those of the row houses we lived in. The rafters were black with soot and badly cracked from the many years of use; there were spider webs in all four corners and over the rafters; the walls were scarred by water stains. Worse, there were spots of missing plaster where rain leaks had cut through to the bare bricks beneath.

I congratulated myself for not having been here in 1958 with the Rightists. The three workers of the Small Compound had been here for over a decade and had to remain here until no one knew when. But the government now had a new policy about labor reform elements. We were given a definite term to serve and were then allowed to go back to our old working units.

Through the window I caught a glimpse of Political Instructor Feng crossing the basketball court and coming toward us. I shifted my position so he wouldn't see my face. He was walking toward the duty office. I didn't know whether I should stand up or not. To sit in a chair while talking to an officer was against regulations.

Officer Niu snuffed out his Big Cannon and crushed the butt between his thumb and forefinger. "You can go now," he said. "And put the boys to sleep."

The boys were still making a lot of noise. I shouted through the row houses, "Time for bed! Stop playing and wash your feet before you go to sleep!" Then I went into our squad room, picked up a towel, and went to the tap in the front yard to wash my feet under the water.

7

Han Jen, Leader of the Inmates

Han Jen was a veteran at Chadian of one year and two months, and he was *the* inmate leader of the Big Compound. He was looked up to by the majority, feared by some, and begrudged by a few. He had ten months left in his two year sentence. His factory in Beijing had reserved his job and continued to pay him sixty-two yuan a month while he was at Chadian. That pay was more than any of the officers at Farm 583 got. The monthly pay for Director Feng and Officer Niu was a little more than fifty yuan.

Officer Niu relied greatly on Han Jen to prevent disturbances in Team One until I arrived.

Han Jen came from a family known for its ability in kungfu. His great grandfather won the first place in an imperial contest for military commander candidates during the Qing dynasty, and his grandfather and two granduncles fought kungfu matches north and south of the Yangtze River against anyone who would dare to challenge their family prowess in the kungfu world. Han Jen's father didn't enjoy that kind of glory because China had become a republic, and modern warfare demanded army commanders who knew how to direct battalions of big guns, tanks, and airplanes. No matter how good a kungfu master he was, he couldn't stop a flying bullet. But Han Jen's father thought he might let his ancestors down if the family tradition was ended with him, and so he passed on the tradition to his only son, with nostalgic remorse and a foreboding.

Han Jen seemed born with the family heritage. Before he started school, he had learned the movements of the All-Style Composite Boxing, which his forefathers had developed by assimilating good points from all the best boxing styles. Yet he carefully followed his father's warning not to show off. He seldom met other kungfu practitioners in public parks, and he never talked about his skill among fellow workers.

In 1967, his father was accused of being involved with gangsters in the old society and was taken away by Red Guards to a prison somewhere outside of Beijing. Han Jen, twenty-three that year, quietly lived on in the city with his mother. The next year, his mother died of poor health and a broken heart. While receiving no news of his father, and suffering from loneliness, Han Jen had taken to drink. Within a year his neighbors began to say he had changed into another person.

One night, drunk in a small tavern, he beat up a customer who had been verbally assaulting an elderly man. Han Jen had apparently forgotten he could exert unusual force from long years of kungfu practice. The man he struck was injured so severely that he almost died.

Han Jen, at the time, was not on good terms with his factory superiors because of his rebellious nature. The officials would have liked to put him away forever. His neighbors, however, pleaded on his behalf, and the police eventually decided two years in a labor reform farm would be enough to make Han Jen obedient to authority.

After I won the trust of Officer Niu, I was careful not to encroach upon Han Jen's "territory." When Officer Niu asked me to rouse the team for work or for roll call, I would go to the Squad One room and say, "Han Jen, Officer Niu wants me to tell you that it's time for work." He would then walk out and stand in the central path between the two columns of row houses and shout, "Time for work. Come out, quickly!"

One day as I "relayed" Officer Niu's order to gather the men together for work, Han Jen said, "One of my shoe laces is missing. You get the men together." His tone was friendly, so I shouted the order. I could shout the order better than he could because I had served in the army and had been a sergeant for my last year of duty. From then on, Han Jen and I shared the honored duty. I soon found in him a good friend, whom I could talk to and trust.

One day our team was resting during a short morning break while working in the fields. The sun was warm in the southeastern sky, and I lay comfortably on the soft earth, my head on a tuft of dry grass. I imagined my wife's face in the changing forms of white clouds. Others lay scattered in various positions, some of them smoking Big Cannons.

"Hey, Huang Longsen," Black Head nudged me on my shoulder and directed his eyes toward a young woman walking on the road. "That's Officer Wang's wife. See she's looking our way. You know whom she wants to find? Han Jen. I bet my balls there's something going on between them. Look! She's smiling."

I looked up at Han Jen, who lay ten yards away in another plot, instead of at the woman on the road. He was roused from his dozing by the sudden jabbering among the other team members, and he raised his head to look in the direction toward which everyone's eyes were fixed. Then he lay down again, his head on a ridge and his left leg curved to reveal a huge tear in his trousers at the knee.

"Don't imagine things," I said to Black Head. "Be careful not to let Han Jen hear you. He'd crush you for sure."

"I'm telling the truth, whether you believe it or not," Black Head said, and smiled with an ugly grin.

The woman was wearing a pink, woolen sweater and trousers made of some light material, with the legs cut short ten inches above her ankles. She wore her hair short, not the way country women did but in imitation of the city style. She looked quite fashionable against the surroundings and compared to the other officers' country wives. She reminded me of a monkey back in my native village that was brought by a traveling entertainer to perform on street corners. The entertainer would dress the animal up in an imperial court official hat and garments so that it could imitate human movements.

Seeing the gawking and dirty looks that came from our direction, the young woman picked up her pace as she moved toward the Officers Compound.

"I noticed it as soon as we arrived here," Black Head continued eagerly. "The woman comes over to the Big Compound often and her staring at Han Jen is unusual. I can see what's happening at one glance. That woman is not bad, uh?"

I turned my head the other way to make myself more comfortable.

"Don't tell me you don't like women," Black Head persisted. "That woman is not bad looking, particularly around this damn place, though she's a little too plump. I'll mark her for sixty points. How much do you give?"

"I told you don't talk about women," I said impatiently. "You're too young for that kind of thing, anyway."

"Hah, hah," Black Head laughed and raised his voice, "I had three girls in one year before I was scooped up and taken here. How many have you had in your life?"

Others now turned their heads and perked up their ears, expecting a savory story.

"Stop it!" I pretended to be angry. I never believed what they said about how many girls they had or how many restaurants they visited in Beijing. They would boast about anything to win admiration or envy from others.

Life on the farm was always tedious and the food was poor. With a half-empty stomach and a dulled mind, I found in their boasting, or "spiritual banquet" as they called it, a temporary relief from my boredom and homesickness.

Though I doubted what Black Head said of Han Jen and Officer Wang's wife, I began to speculate about the matter.

Han Jen was an electrician. Very soon after he arrived at Chadian, the officers learned that he could fix any kind of electrical appliances on the farm. His name would often be boomed over the single loudspeaker on top of a pole on the other side of the wall that separated the Officers Compound and the Big Compound: "Han Jen, you are wanted at the warehouse to check the feed cutter," or "Han Jen, you are wanted to help at the pumping station."

The officers would exploit the free-of-charge electrician to repair their radios, clocks, flashlights, and many other things. Their wives also found out that the labor reform element was an excellent carpenter as well. From time to time, they asked their husbands to bring him to the Officer's Village to knock together a table or a cabinet that had fallen apart, or to shave a chopping board out of raw planks. If their husbands allowed, they would have asked him to build furniture for them, too.

Thus Han Jen became the freest man in the Big Compound. He could go out of the gate at any hour on any day, and he had many chances to go to the Officer's Village. The officers were away from home the greater part of the day and often had night duties. If Han Jen wanted to seduce a young wife, he wouldn't have much difficulty doing so. He was handsome and relatively young. But I doubted Han Jen would have an eye for Officer Wang's wife. She was too rustic for him.

But how could I be sure that such things didn't happen? Without seeing a woman for many days at a stretch, any one might be desirable, as a saying goes: "A starved man is not choosy about the food he eats."

Soon Officer Wang's wife emerged from the Officers Compound and walked up the bank of the irrigation ditch toward where Officer Niu sat. The morning break had exceeded the regular time by at least ten minutes. Officer Niu still sat there dozing, leaning against a young willow tree.

The young woman stole glances toward where we were, which aroused more snickering. Now, at closer range, I could see that she really didn't look bad: her skin was fair, her eyes big, and her mouth sensitive. But she had the most prominent characteristic of country women: roundness everywhere. She had round ankles, round calves, round hips, round waist, round shoulders, round arms, round wrists, round elbows, round cheeks, and a round forehead. If I could have gotten nearer, I ventured a guess that I would have probably also seen a round nose.

She talked briefly with Officer Niu for a minute and then they walked together back to the Officers Compound. As soon as they disappeared behind the officer's kitchen, there was a loud burst of guffawing among the inmates, accompanied by a deluge of dirty jokes.

"She must have very nice tits," Pan Rong said gleefully. "See how high they are. But she has too much fat around her waist. She looks like a barrel." He laughed.

"Don't belittle her beauty just because *you* can't get her," Tiger teased. "I bet her belly is as soft as a down-stuffed cushion."

"Ah, must be very satisfying to lay her in this nice weather," Pan Rong talked on joyfully. "Old people say fucking in spring is good for the health of men and women. The man's masculine energy and the woman's feminine energy supplement each other. In spring *yang*, or solar energy, rises and *yin*, or earthly energy, sinks. Men are dominated by *yang* energy, and women are dominated by *yin* energy. By fucking, both men and women can achieve a balance of the *yang* and *yin* energies within their bodies. I feel the *yang* energy in my body is too high right now, and needs to be balanced."

"You need to be fucking a woman," Pockmark said coolly. "There's one for you. Go and do it."

"I would be willing to stay here for another year if I could lay that chick right now," Pan Rong said.

Others guffawed loudly, and Pan Rong's spirit was further boosted.

"Go ahead!" Tiger shouted happily. "If you are man enough, stop your empty talk and go over to have a real feel of her. I'll give my Sunday meal to you if you dare do it."

Han Jen had been looking into the sky all this while,

chewing a dry grass stem. I was waiting anxiously for Officer Niu to return so he would blow the whistle to end the break. The air was getting charged to an exploding point. Officer Niu seemed to have forgotten about us.

I said to Pan Rong, "You'd better shut your filthy mouth. Talking won't satisfy your cravings. Let's get to work."

"Who are you?" Pan Rong said to me. He had been carried away by his show of bravado. "Don't you even think for a moment now that you're in favor with Officer Niu that you can order us around. Remember, you're still one of us. You still eat two corn buns and a bowl of boiled vegetable for lunch and supper, the same thing we eat and the same stuff we shit."

Several others sneered at me and cheered for Pan Rong. My face burned. I wished I could beat these skunks physically, and hoped Black Head and Tiger would intervene on my behalf. But they didn't this time.

I took up my spade and walked away.

Han Jen rose slowly, spit out the grass stem, and walked over to Pan Rong. I walked further away.

"Then who are *you*?" he demanded.

Pan Rong turned and looked at Han Jen sheepishly. He didn't realize that what he did had offended Han Jen, the irrefutable leader of the Big Compound. He had been intoxicated by his own show of bravado, but Han Jen's threatening stare had dissipated this glorious feeling.

"I didn't say anything against anybody. Did I?" Pan Rong looked around and at his patron Ah Ming, who looked down at a big clump of earth, too compacted to be good for sowing.

Having failed to solicit aid, Pan Rong readied himself for a fight. He couldn't yield to unreasonable bullying. "Han Jen," he stated, "if you want to pick a fight, you should at least find another place and another time. Besides, Han Jen, why me? Why would you want a fight with me?"

"No reason," Han Jen said. "My hands are just itching for a fight. That's all."

Seeing no way out, Pan Rong made one last mistake by saying, "All right. Everybody is afraid of you. They believe what you boast about your kungfu. I don't. Even if you dared to try and cut my head off, there would be nothing more than a hole in my neck."

"I am not going to cut your head off, you bastard," Han Jen said quietly. "You keep it on your shoulders so you can eat chicken shit with it. I'm going to hit you once. Only once. You can fight back with anything you want."

Pan Rong straightened his back, moved his left foot half a step outward to get a better balance of his body, and thrust out his chest. "Go ahead and see if you can knock me down with one punch, as you say."

Smiling coldly, Han Jen placed his hands on either side of Pan Rong's shoulders and said, "If I can't throw you down on the ground with one push, I'll let you hit me as much as you want." Then he relaxed his arms and breathed evenly. Suddenly his shoulders heaved and his elbows jerked straight. An invisible flow of force seemed to be transmitted from the ground through his legs, spine, shoulders, arms, and into his spread hands.

The spectators saw Pan Rong jump off the ground and fall backward three or four feet, falling into the drainage ditch with a splash. Five seconds passed before someone cheered, "Bravo!" Several swarmed over to Han Jen to extend their congratulations, "That was great!"

Pan Rong climbed out of the drainage ditch and shivered, either from the cold water that was dripping off his trousers, or from humiliation. He walked to a higher spot and sat down on the edge of the field to empty the water from his rubber-soled shoes. He looked as pitiful as a stray dog caught in a sudden downpour.

After supper I was waiting for my turn to wash my bowls at the only tap. Han Jen came over and said, "Do you want to go for a walk?" Seeing my surprise, he added, "I was told to fix a switch at the pumping station. Those good-for-nothing offspring of guards can't do it. I'll tell the duty officer I need an assistant, if you want to go. It won't take more than half an hour. Then we can go up to the dike."

"All right," I said, suppressing my eagerness to get outside of the compound.

The guard at the gate had a list of inmates who had been approved by their officers to go out alone. He smiled at us when he opened the small sub-door cut in the gate to let us out.

Han Jen and I spent twenty minutes at the pumping station. He was impressed with my familiarity with electric machinery. I told him I learned about such matters when I was a ground crew member of an army airforce squadron that maintained electric meters and instruments.

Leaving the station, we walked over the wooden bridge that was also the sluice gate for the channel directing Chaobai River water to the pumping station. Over many years a path had cut deep into the easy slope up the broad top of the dike. Weed and shrubs on both banks of the dike were pleasantly green. The river glistened in the glow of the dusk toward the west. We walked one-third of a mile in one direction along the dike and back, then one-third of a mile in the other direction and back. Then we sat down on the slope facing the farm side so that we would be visible to the electricians in the pumping station or any officer down below. We didn't want to cause unnecessary suspicion.

"You may have heard something," Han Jen said. "I mean about something going on between me and Officer Wang's wife."

Caught in surprise by his question, I didn't know what to say. But I turned my head to look at him in expectation.

"I don't know how much is known among the guys in the Big Compound," he continued placidly. "I hope not much. It's true that she and I have an affair going. She offered herself to me. It was last year, about late August. It was getting cold, but still warm enough. Officer Wang brought me to his house to fix his wife's sewing machine. She cooked me a bowl of noodles as a reward. You know,

I really want to throw away any bowl of noodles or rice that the wives of the guards give me after I do something for them. I am a man, not a beggar. But I have to say thanks to them and eat it. Otherwise they would tell their husbands and I would get into trouble. Well, the following week, Officer Wang told me to fix his wife's radio. This time I went alone. He was on duty that Sunday. His wife had on a short sleeve shirt and light trousers. She kept brushing herself against me. Then she undid two top buttons of her shirt. When she bent over, I could see her breasts. I am twenty-eight and know such tricks. Why not? I told myself. They put me in this damn place for two years to suffer, I might get some revenge by fucking a guard's wife. That was how it started."

I felt obliged to say something in appreciation of his trust in me. So I said, "Aren't you afraid you may be found out?"

"I was afraid in the beginning. Sometimes I still am. But she wants me to come over from time to time. Now I am afraid more of offending her than of being exposed. When I think of it, sometimes, I don't really care about what will happen to me. You watch the clock when you fuck, try to enjoy every second you can. One's life is worth nothing at all. When they want to throw you into a pigsty, you have no right to fight. If I had the cheek to lick the boots of those bastards in the factory, they wouldn't have sent me here, just for beating a drunkard.

"They hated me. I knew all along they would find fault with me one way or another. They couldn't fire me because one of the best things about our country is the guarantee of a job for everyone. But they found a way to put me here for two years. They wanted to teach me what reward I would get for my disobedience. Before they shipped me to the detention center at Liangxiang, the Party secretary had the gall to give me a kind-hearted piece of advice. 'Han Jen,' he said in the nicest tone, 'you must understand that we really didn't want to send you to the labor reform farm. But we have to maintain discipline, nothing personal. Two years hard work will do you a lot of good. We are sure that you'll return a good worker.' I wanted to tell him to go fuck his mother. Instead, I put on a nice smile and said to him, 'You've been very nice to me. It's all my fault getting into this mess. I'll do my best to reform myself through hard labor.' You see, I had already learned to be smart, and be quiet.

"Now I have a record. When I return to the factory, they won't be very nice to me. They may assign me to sweep the floor or clean the latrines. So why should I care about my future?"

I wanted badly to convince him I understood, but couldn't think of any words that might be appropriate. So I just looked at him with more intensity.

"Her parents live in that village over the main drainage ditch." He pointed over to the north. "I mean Officer Wang's wife. She used to be the best looking girl around and felt it would be a waste to marry a country boy. The villagers are poor because their land can grow only sorghum and it yields very little. We can grow better crops because we can afford to wash the alkali out of our fields by pumping river water into them. The villagers can't afford the electricity. When the reeds grow to two or three feet high in the drainage ditches on the farm, the village girls come to cut them for fodder. The animals in those poor villages have the worst luck. They have to eat reeds instead of grass. The soil has too much alkali for good grass to grow.

"The girls wade in the ditches, water reaching up to their breasts. In early spring, the water table rises fast. The water in the drainage ditches has not been exposed to the sun for long, so it is harmful to the young women. But they are in it ten hours or longer each day, cutting the young reeds. Do you know how much they earn for the work? Eight cents a day! Eight cents can't buy an egg in Beijing. You'll see what they have for lunch. Steamed buns of sorghum flour. Have you ever had sorghum flour buns?

"The type of sorghum they grow here is not the kind from northeast China. The kind from northeast China is white and tender. You have to buy it in special stores in Beijing. The kind grown here is composed of small grains and has a dirty scarlet color. Ugh! Made into steamed flour buns, it tastes tart and tough, looks like coagulated blood and is damned slippery when you swallow it. You feel the lumps go down quickly through your stomach and bowels directly toward your anus and then it stops for a moment. You feel like there is a balloon inside your belly and a dead weight in your ass. Makes taking a shit very difficult. The stuff isn't even fit for animals!"

"I bet the animals don't like it, either," I commented. "What lousy luck to be born around here. For men and animals."

"They don't have big animals, such as horses and mules," Han Jen said. "They are too poor to afford them. The whole village has only seven donkeys and two oxen. Most of the time the farmers pull the plow by themselves."

"That's good," I commented. "I mean fine animals such as horses shouldn't live on only reeds."

"Human beings shouldn't live on only bitter sorghum grains," Han Jen said, as if rebuking me.

"That's right," I said quickly. "Both men and animals deserve better."

"Last year some young devils here tried to take advantage of the village girls," Han Jen continued. "Pinching their arms and making dirty jokes, that kind of stuff. They wouldn't dare to do more than that. If the girls didn't pay attention to them, they wouldn't let the young women do their work. Finally I got sick of watching such shameless display of hormones. I knocked one guy into the ditch and shoved another guy so hard he stopped breathing. Looked like he was going to snuff it right then and there. I told them to leave the girls alone. Those girls' lives are wretched enough without some shameless thugs bullying them!"

"Good for you," I pitched in.

Han Jen neglected my praise and went on, "Some villagers took me to be one of the guards because I can move around freely, and my clothes are even better than those of some of the guards. They asked me to let them live inside the Big Compound and work for the farm. I asked them why they wanted to be kept like animals."

"Why?" I asked.

"They said it was because they could have steamed buns of wheat flour and rice for meals. We have meat every Sunday. They have meat only once or twice a year. That's why they envy us."

"Oh," I said.

"I told them only those who have broken the law are taken in. They said they would do something to break the law. I told them the farm takes only those from inside the city of Beijing, not villagers nearby."

"What did they say?" I asked.

"They were disappointed. You see, lives here are cheap. I would rather die than spend my whole life in such a village."

I was about to say I agreed with him, but he didn't give me the chance.

"Well, Chulan, that's the name of Officer Wang's wife, didn't want to marry a village boy," Han Jen said in a tone as if talking about his own wife. "She waited until she was twenty-one, an old girl according to village standards of betrothal. She and her parents were getting worried when, just in time, a batch of fresh, young guards were then assigned to the Chadian Farm. Officer Wang was among them. Her parents asked an older guard they knew to make the proposal. Officer Wang accepted at once. He, himself, came from a country village in Henan province and likely wouldn't have a chance to marry a Beijing girl. All the guards want to marry their daughters to men in Beijing."

Once again I felt I should contribute something to the conversation. But Han Jen didn't let me.

"Chulan now feels Officer Wang is not up to her standards," he said. "She thinks he's too coarse. Officer Wang is coarse, indeed, and his looks are deplorable."

"Indeed," I said hastily.

"Since she doesn't like Officer Wang, she apparently

makes use of me as a substitute, or else she really likes me or hopes that when I return to Beijing I can take her along. Anyway, I don't want to worry about it right now."

I waited for a minute to see if Han Jen had more to say. He didn't. He bent his head down between his knees in order to draw lines on the ground with a dead twig.

His silence made me want to say something that might put him at ease and assure him that all he had told me was definitely off the record. His affair with an officer's wife was very dangerous, and I felt I should tell him so.

"You're still young," I said. "Why ruin your future on a country woman? She's not worth it."

He looked up at me. I found something resentful in his eyes. My words might have been too ungracious to the girl. "Maybe she is really in love with you," I added quickly.

"You may be right," Han Jen shifted his stare toward the picture he was drawing on the ground. "I've realized that I can't go on like this forever. Sooner or later they will find out. I've been trying to put distance between her and me, but I have to be very careful not to rouse her suspicion that I want to cut her off. I want her to know, in time, that there's no chance for her to go with me to Beijing."

"You be careful," I urged sincerely. "Although a labor reform farm record is already bad enough, it's not shameful in your case. Discovered adultery on the labor reform farm, however is not as easy to explain to others."

Han Jen nodded his head. "Somehow, I'll manage to get out of this mess," he said.

The dusk deepened. Smoke was no longer rising from the two chimneys of the officers kitchen. I was getting nervous. It was my first time to be out after supper without an officer beside me. So I said to Han Jen, "It's getting chilly. We'd better go back."

8

A Visit to the Officer's Village

From outside, the houses of the Officer's Village looked much the same as those of the Big Compound, except that there was no wall enclosing them. There were five identical rows evenly spaced from south to north on the northern side of the dirt road and irrigation canal. Between the rows were vegetable plots that each family fenced off with barbed wire, sorghum stalks, sunflower stalks, or willow twigs.

The officers came from country villages before they joined the police force, and they knew how to make use of the tiny spot of land attached to their houses. Those who didn't know, persons such as Officer Wang, learned how to grow vegetables in no time. Harvest from each plot provided a good supplement to the forty or fifty yuan of the monthly income on which the officers depended to support their families.

Officer Niu's house was in the third row, the middle one of five families. The two rows in front muffled traffic noises from the road, and the two back rows served as a buffer zone against noises in the fields caused by frogs, toads, and rats.

Officer Niu was a neat man. So were his wife and two sons. Their three rooms and the kitchen were kept clean and orderly at all times, as were their vegetable garden and chicken coop. Their fence was built of sorghum stalks woven together with barbed wire, and cut even on top.

Officer Niu was a great vegetable grower, the best in

the Officer's Village. In early March, as soon as the ground defrosted, he dug up the earth in his plot and planted garlic, which they had run out of by the end of summer last year. In one month they would have green garlic sprouts on their meal table. This planting was followed by leeks, squash, ripe tomatoes, eggplants, string beans, cucumbers, and finally cabbage and turnips. Before the winter set in, Officer Niu and his two sons would dig a small cellar under the vegetable garden to preserve the supply of cabbages and turnips. These two items would last through the greater half of winter until the Spring Festival.

Of course, their tiny plot couldn't produce enough to meet the needs of the whole family the year round. But at least the Niu family could write off from their annual budget two or three hundred yuan for the vegetables they grew.

Officer Niu was nostalgic whenever he talked about the earlier years. Sometimes when he was with inmates, and having a good day, he seemed to forget whom he was talking to for a moment. At these times he would talk about all sorts of things, but he had a special place in his heart for fishing.

He was a great fisherman. He owned five fishing nets of various sizes of mesh. Unfortunately, chemical fertilizers had killed too many fish and crabs, and the marshes were now dried up because of land reclamation. Chaobai River water had long ago stopped being a flood threat. Actually, the Chadian area had become a place of constant worries about drought. Officer Niu's large-mesh nets were useless. On a whole Sunday morning, Officer Niu could catch only enough small fish to cover the bottom of a basket. This usually caused him to swear. He missed those years before the mid-1960s when the ponds and river of the Chadian area teemed with fish of all kinds.

In those years, the Chadian Farm didn't have so many inmates and families of police guards. A great part of the farm land still lay in waste, and chemicals were unheard of. During those times, Officer Niu could catch as many fish as he wanted from early spring until all the drainage ditches became frozen. Fish as large as two feet long lived in the drainage ditches then. During the winter, he would go on his bike to the Chaobai River or one of its tributaries in order to cast his net. He wouldn't bother with small fish in those days. And often in the summer, fish in the drainage ditches that were suffering from lack of oxygen in the water would jump out for fresh air. Some would land on the roadside. He could pick up several big carp in the early morning on his way home from night duty.

Crabs used to be the scourge of rice and other crops. Their powerful pincers were like sickles, chopping off rice and sorghum ears. In those days, one of the duties of the Big Compound inmates was to catch as many crabs as they could every day, which the farm then took to the Beijing market. In September, the crabs became fat on the ripening crops. Local inhabitants were so spoiled by the abundance that they ate only the delicious roes and the tender meat from the upper part of the crabs' pincers.

Now the ditches were devoid of fish and crabs, Officer Niu had to go to the main drainage ditch to cast his net. Fish in the ditch came from the Chaobai River when water was high. Even during the height of summer, when the Chaobai River was at its highest level, he could catch only one or two large fish. It now seemed that fish in the Chaobai River were also on the brink of extinction.

Han Jen and I had been brought to his house to fix his radio, which crackled too loudly from static. Han Jen had told him I was familiar with such things also, and Officer Niu gladly allowed me to come along. Han Jen fixed the radio in no time and we then sat around the dining table in the hallway. The open door to the kitchen showed a cast iron stove for burning coal and a brick stove for burning crop stalks. The pots, pans, jars, and bottles were arranged in strict order and clean.

Another door, closed, must have been one of the three bedrooms. There were two doors that opened to the front courtyard. Along the sorghum stalk wall, on the east-south corner of the lot, was a strip of string bean plants whose vines were vigorously climbing up the sorghum stalk fence. A low table and several small stools scattered on the hard-pressed dirt ground. The low table was similar to the one my family used to eat our summer meals in the courtyard.

This was my first time to be in a family environment in the four months since I had left Beijing. Officer Niu's wife, in her early forties, of medium height, with gray hair showing at the temple prematurely, and a kind face, served us tea as if we were her husband's younger colleagues. I would have felt ill at ease in another officer's house, but not there.

"Life in the Big Compound was very different several years ago," Officer Niu said. "The Rightists had thoughts they kept within their own heads. I didn't blame them. They wouldn't tell their true mind to anyone, because they were sent here for speaking their thoughts too loudly. Still, I had a tacit understanding with some of them. Inmates today are not as learned. They are much easier to deal with. But for the incompetent officers, the Rightists were easier to deal with because they didn't fight back or play tricks. These officers didn't know that the Rightists looked down on them and only showed total submission on their faces.

"The street boys haven't lived long enough or read books enough to be that smart. As I have said to you two, this place is no good for them. They only learn bad things here. The problem is the low quality of the officers. They don't know how to handle the street boys correctly. I used to give suggestions to those higher up, but have stopped doing so. They won't listen to me and they think of me as being a pain in the ass. Now, I don't think much about it and save a lot of my breath."

But, I thought to myself, he still did.

Mrs. Niu came in to pour more tea. As she did so, she said to Officer Niu, "Director Feng asked if you were home moment ago. He wants you to go over there for a talk."

"What does he want to talk to me for?" Officer Niu said with irritation. I could sense a sudden anger welling up in him. "I don't want to have anything to do with him. Tell him I have too many household chores to do. This is my day of rest!"

"Why offend him over this trifling matter?" Mrs. Niu said quietly. "You go over and listen to him for half an hour and then you leave. That won't do you any harm."

"I just don't like to see his face," Officer Niu said bitterly. "It's only because he stayed in a Beijing office for a couple of years with the big shots and got in their favor, now he can order me around! How much does he know about running a reform farm? He's lucky to have come here so late."

Mrs. Niu looked at her husband with concern. He had not been treated the way he deserved. Many of his former comrades-in-arms were now sitting in offices either at the general headquarters or in the Beijing public security bureau. But he was forgotten, stuck in this mud hole for over two decades without any hope of ever getting out. He was intelligent and creative, but his curse, like mine, was defiance of the authorities. She had become more worried during the past two or three years as he was getting old and several younger policemen had been transferred from Beijing office to be the leaders of the farm.

If we were not present, he probably would have said in a more unseemly manner, "Don't be bothered by that greenhorn of an instructor," Mrs. Niu coaxed her husband. "By the way, I have your uniform ready."

"I'll ask to be excused from tomorrow's meeting," Officer Niu said, now having checked his sudden explosion of anger. "I don't want to listen to any more empty talk. It's a waste of my time."

Police officers at the Chadian Farm, except those in general headquarters offices, didn't wear uniforms for daily duty. The uniform was saved for times when they went to Beijing on official errands or when they attended formal meetings at the general headquarters. The present director of general headquarters came to the farm from Beijing with Instructor Feng, and Officer Niu all but cherished his resentment against both of them.

Mrs. Niu looked at us and saw our uneasiness. "Well," she said. "You two have more tea."

"We have had plenty," Han Jen said as he stood up. I did too. "If you don't have anything more for us to do," he said to Officer Niu, "we'd like to go back now."

Chulan called out from behind the house, "Is Mrs. Niu in?" She entered the backyard through the sorghum-stalk gate. Mrs. Niu opened the hallway door to let her in. She glanced at Han Jen and then said to Mrs. Niu, "I saw them come. Have they fixed your radio? My sewing machine got stuck again. I would like to have Han Jen to see what is wrong with it."

"You go and have a look," Officer Niu said to us.

"I'm not going," I said. "Han Jen can do the job alone. I'll go back now."

"You're coming with me," Han Jen said. "It won't take long. Then we'll go back together."

He stood there waiting for me to come. I knew he wanted me to be with him to abort Chulan's scheme. I hesitated, not sure if I should go. Chulan would hate me for that. She looked at Han Jen, urging him to move. Han Jen looked at me, begging me to come with him. He was like a small boy who had done something mischievous in the street and hoped a grown-up neighbor would accompany him to his home so that his parents wouldn't punish him too severely.

"It won't take long," Han Jen said again.

I looked at Officer Niu, who said, "You go with Han Jen and then go back to the compound together."

Chulan's face registered displeasure. She said "thank you" to the Nius only after she stepped outside of the hallway door. Han Jen followed her, a naughty boy in fear of facing a scolding.

As we entered Chulan's backyard, I could see that it was as neat and clean as that of Officer Niu, though the vegetable plot was not fully exploited. There was a chicken coop in one corner. Half a dozen hens pecked along the base of the sorghum stalk fence. A huge rooster, with a bright red crown, raised his head to look at me suspiciously. He croaked from deep in his throat.

All the houses at Officer's Village were of the same size and layout, regardless of the size of the family or the rank of the officer. Higher ranking officers lived in apartment buildings near the general headquarters. Since there were only Officer Wang and his wife in this family, Chulan had made the two extra rooms a living room and a guest room. Her mother stayed there from time to time when she visited.

The bed room was decked out in a poor imitation of the urban manner. Instead of the platform-like bed that other officers' families slept on, a double wooden bed was placed under the window facing south. Bright sunlight shone on the floral bed sheet with its pink background. The chest of drawers against the wall near the door was of modern design. But another chest, a table, and two chairs were old fashioned, no doubt the dowry from Chulan's parents.

Two New Year pictures, one depicting peony flowers (a symbol of nobility), and the other a large gold fish held by a plump male baby (a symbol of wealth and fertility) hung on the wall near the door. The floor was paved with red bricks.

The sewing machine was directly under the New Year picture depicting the plump baby with the large gold fish in his arms. I watched as Chulan helped Han Jen raise the top lid, lift the machine head from its cradle, and align the belt to the wheel. Chulan made intimate contact with Han Jen at every opportunity, much like an ardent lover. Each gesture was full of youthful vigor.

As she bent down to pick up the screwdriver Han Jen had dropped, a great part of her breasts showed through the open neck of her shirt. They were smooth and round. The color, brought up to her face by the exertion, enhanced her attractiveness. I found her quite desirable in her plumpness, and felt jealous of Han Jen for having such a young woman so eager to offer herself to him. At the same time, I was sympathetic toward Chulan. It was a pity for her to have married a man as coarse and trivial as Officer Wang.

My mind wandered, imagining why they had not had a baby. With country folks, it was taken as a disgrace for a woman not to have given birth within two years of marriage. If Chulan's parents were not worried, Officer Wang's parents certainly must be, and they must have questioned their son as to the matter. They might have even demanded that he divorce Chulan because of this. I didn't think Chulan was so modern in her thinking that she didn't want a baby. Either she or Officer Wang must have had trouble conceiving. That might be the reason she felt no compunction in sleeping with Han Jen.

What was it like when she was in bed with Officer Wang, I wondered. That man, small in build, had features converging toward the middle of his face around his nose like a meat-stuffed bun, the folds brought up to the top. "A flower stuck to a pile of cow dung," I murmured aloud.

"What did you say?" Chulan looked up at me with her round eyes.

"Nothing," I said and returned to reality.

Han Jen had riveted his eyes to the machine in a way too focused to be comfortable. He must have been very ill at ease, for he dropped the screwdriver several times. Sweat appeared on his forehead and forearms like fine dew drops on the finely polished surface of a new tractor. He had said nothing except, "Hand me the pair of pliers," or "Hand me the bottle of lubricant."

It was not me but Chulan who implemented his orders. So I had nothing to do but keep my eyes on Han Jen's hands, with an occasional glance toward the ample exposed calves and half-revealed breasts of Chulan.

The machine was new. Its parts had not meshed well yet. Han Jen readjusted the tightness of several screws and then the machine ran perfectly. He worked the peddles of the machine for a while, fed thread into the needle, and tried it on a piece of rag. The machine whirred and clicked merrily. He slipped off the belt from the wheel, lifted the machine head, and tested the nuts and screws

with the screwdriver once again. This was entirely unnecessary. He was procrastinating, afraid of finishing the
job too soon and thus offending Chulan.

In another five minutes, he put the belt back on the
wheel, and peddled the machine for another testing. Finally he said to Chulan, "You shouldn't have any trouble
with this sewing machine for at least six months." Then,
straightening his back, he said to me, "We'd better return to the Big Compound. As it is, we'll only have time
to play two or three matches of chess before afternoon
meal."

It might have been my imagination, but Chulan's face
seemed to lose a shade of pink, gain a tint of whiteness,
and become longer and colder. She looked prettier when
she was angry.

"Don't you want to stay for a cup of tea?" Chulan
asked.

"No, thanks," Han Jen said politely, giving Chulan
the hint that now he had an inmate with him he had to
be careful.

"Then at least you should wash your hands before
you go." The woman seemed to have gotten the hint and
was reluctant to let her lover leave her so easily.

"I'll wash my hands in the ditch," Han Jen said.

Before Chulan could say anything more, we walked
out the gate of the front yard and onto the path leading
to the road. Han Jen was literally fleeing.

On the way back to the Big Compound, we didn't talk.
I guessed that Han Jen felt a bit uncomfortable after
this most awkward encounter. Not wanting to exacer-
bate the situation in any way, my attention drifted to the
trees which lined that desolate road.

There were only two kinds of trees in Chadian that
could survive the high content of alkali: willow and locust. The willow trees grew mostly on the banks of irrigation and drainage ditches, while locust trees could be
found by the ditches, along the road, and in spots of waste
land. The willow trees always looked young because they
couldn't grow thick and high, much like Mouse in my

squad who was usually thought to be under fourteen years of age at the first glance. Actually he was already nineteen.

Winter at Chadian was a longer season than it was in Beijing. In late May, when the locust trees had already shed their blossoms in Beijing, those at Chadian were at their blooming height, with a profusion of tiny white flowers growing in strings. The flowers gave out a pleasant scent that spread in the air far and wide.

My grandmother told me locust flowers were sweet and edible, especially the stamens and pistils. I remember her chewing a mouthful herself to show me that they were not poisonous. Every spring we children would sneak out of the gate of our backyard to twist off strings of flowers from the locust trees on the edge of a small pond. We chewed on them with relish. After we moved to Beijing, mother could afford to buy fruit for us. And I hadn't eaten the childhood delicacy since.

Since the locust trees at Chadian grew lavishly in high bushes, their flowers could be plucked just by reaching out one's hand. By now, Han Jen's face was beginning to relax a bit. The tenseness had all but dissipated. I picked off a string of them and chewed on the flowers to demonstrate to Han Jen, as my grandmother had done for me, that they were delicious. "Here, try some," I offered.

Having nipped at a couple of the pistils, Han Jen picked a cluster of half-open flowers off a higher branch and started to eat. "Not bad. Not bad at all," he said.

I was hit by a feeling of guilt. If I had not been with him, Officer Niu might have given him a bowl of noodles. If he didn't, Chulan would surely have given him something nice to eat. Now he had to eat tree flowers instead.

I plucked off another large string of locust flowers and stuffed them into my mouth to show Han Jen that I was really enjoying this special food.

I shouldn't have drunk so much tea at Officer Niu's house. The water was gurgling inside my stomach, and the caffeine in the tea had stimulated my digestion. With hardly any animal fat in our diet, the caffeine played a negative role on my system. My heart ached from hunger.

"Back in my native village we ate many things that grew wild in fields in the spring," I said to Han Jen. "A kind of herb, we call it bitter sprouts, is quite tasty when mixed with fermented soybean paste. I saw some by the irrigation canal near the Big Compound the other day. We could stop there and pick some of it. I still have half a jar of fried soybean paste left."

Han Jen chewed on the flowers contentedly. I nipped off some more and chewed them. However, I couldn't relive the sweet taste from my childhood. The gurgling sound in my stomach became louder and was tormenting. If only there were meat-stuffed cakes! I could consume a hundred of them in no time!

The sun was now past its zenith toward the southwest. We sat down on top of the canal bank. The road was deserted of traffic as the whole farm was at rest on Sunday. Occasionally, an officer or an ex-inmate worker on a bicycle would pass us and look in our direction with a quizzical eye. If we knew the officer, we would call out respectfully, "Good day, sir." The officer would nod his head in acknowledgment – austerely, solemnly, condescendingly, or smilingly depending on how much service Han Jen had given him in the past.

"Bastard!" Han Jen would curse under his breath with a smile, as the officer returned his attentive gaze to the hard-edged ruts in the road.

"There are four cardinal causes of trouble among human beings," Han Jen said. "They are drinking, women, money, and temper. When you get stuck in one, you just can't pull yourself out. Confucius, you know him? The guy with thick glasses that keeps the accounts of things we buy against our monthly allowance? He's a college graduate and was the editor of a magazine before he was sent here. He can recite whole sections from ancient books by great sages. That is why he was nicknamed Confucius. Still in spite of his great learning, he was arrested for stealing. Imagine that! Him stealing..." He shook his head and smiled slightly. "He tells me he can't help it. When he sees something another may have left lying around, he has this need to take it. Otherwise, he says, he feels as if *he* has lost something of his own. He's over forty, has a good job and a family, but still, he steals.

"Another example: Teacher Sun of Squad Four. He's a middle school teacher. I saw his wife during the Spring Festival when she came to visit him. She's very pretty. But Teacher Sun seduced a young fellow teacher. You see, as I say, when you get caught in one of the four cardinal causes, you just can't get out.

"I got in for beating people when I was drunk. But drinking is not my problem. I drink all right, but not that much. To tell you the truth, before my father was taken away and my mother died, I never touched a drop of alcohol. I was not interested in women either. I am not now, though I've got this damn affair going on with Chulan.

"I'll tell you another truth. Back in Beijing, girls in my factory lined up to marry me. I never accepted any of them. I wanted to wait until I had established myself in my career. Ah, to hell with my career! Money? I never thought of it seriously. My father left enough to make up the shortage from my monthly salary. That was all I wanted. My philosophy about money is that it's not good for one to have too little of it; but too much of it will bring trouble.

"The saying that 'birds toil to their death for food; men toil to their death for wealth' is true of many people. I detest those who are like greedy monks: the more alms they are given, the more they ask. I don't want to be a slave to money. Only one cardinal cause of trouble is left for me, my temper. My temper is too short. I can't stand seeing the weak and old bullied. I often wish my father had not taught me kungfu. Then I wouldn't come forward whenever I saw a bully."

He stuffed a handful of locust flowers into his mouth.

"I would like to have the strength and skill you have," I said earnestly. "Whenever I meet a nasty man in a store, one who knocks his way ahead in line, or one who rides his bicycle fast in the street to scare others, I wish I could give him a good beating. But I never dare say a word of protest, and I feel ashamed for that. I have to excuse myself because I'm not built for fighting."

"You're built for giving orders," Han Jen chuckled good-naturedly. "The first time I saw you I knew you weren't ordinary. You have this way of dealing with everyone."

I was flattered. "That's been my biggest problem," I said. "You know what crime they accused me of? They said I was the Chief Advisor to a counter-revolutionary clique. My friends would come to me for advice about the present political situation and I would tell them things the authorities didn't necessarily want to hear."

"Then you'd better not become a political advisor to the boys in here," he warned half-jokingly.

"I may want to one day," I said.

Han Jen looked up at me.

I restrained from telling him that when I was called names at the office meetings, and when I was forced to "confess", I had thought of raising a resurgent army to kill all those hypocrites who made innocent people suffer. My face must have been flushed with anger because Han Jen quickly changed the subject.

"I don't understand why Officer Niu put that skunk Chan Wen as head of Squad Four. You know how he got in?"

I nodded my head, but added, "Not in detail."

"He was a Communist Party branch secretary in a workshop of the Capital Steel Company, with a lot of power to wield. He made eyes at all the young women under him and hinted that, if they would agree, he would raise their pay or assign them easier jobs. It was a pity his short, stocky features were not appealing. He couldn't lure any of them into his bed, no matter what he promised. On one summer night, he slipped into the room of a woman worker and hid under her double bed. He listened to her and her husband making love. After the couple had gone to sleep, he came out from under the bed and seeing the woman there stark naked, he couldn't control himself. He fished out his cock and rubbed it against the woman's thighs. She didn't wake up even when he turned her legs around so he could push his cock in. But then – man, oh man – she woke up and about screaming.

"The husband gave Chan Wen a good beating in front of the neighbors, all workers from the same factory. You see, women can drive a man out of his senses. Just for half a minute's pleasure, Chan Wen lost his Party membership and got three years here."

"There must be something wrong with his mind," I offered an explanation, not entirely believing the story though I knew there were many cases among the inmates that were too strange for fiction.

"In a large forest, you can find every kind of bird," Han Jen quoted a Beijing street idiom, and then he suddenly laughed loudly. "You know, Huang Longsen, I was talking about Chan Wen. If I were caught being with Officer Wang's wife, what story would there be about me? They might say I dragged Chulan off the bed to fuck her while Officer Wang was sleeping on the bed, Hah, hah..."

His laugh was hysterical. I looked at him puzzled.

"Well," he quieted down, "let's stop talking about others. We have too much to be concerned about for ourselves. Officer Niu told me the other day that two squads from our team will be assigned to look after the rice paddies this summer. That's a job with some freedom. It doesn't demand hard work every day. I learned, last year, from some of the workers in the Small Compound how to do the job, and Officer Niu has given me the hint that my squad will be chosen.

"He thinks pretty highly of you. You should try to let him know you're interested in the job. After you get it, you can be alone almost all the time because each person is allotted several plots to take care of by himself. It is impossible for the guards to watch all those working in rice paddies. Because of this, they always choose those who they don't expect will try to escape.

"The questionable people in your squad are Black Head and Tiger. But I doubt if they would mess things up for you, now that you're their squad leader. If you can put Officer Niu at ease about those two, you won't have any difficulty in getting the job. If you don't get it, it'll go to Chan Wen. I hate to think of my squad and his out there together. Chan Wen is notorious for spying on the men from other squads, and reporting the smallest infractions to the guards.

"You know, there are fish, frogs, eels and hedgehogs in the fields. Away from a guard's eye, you can catch them and roast them in the fields. We need the protein."

This was an attractive prospect, and I immediately felt a desire to get the job.

"Also, there is not much hard work," Han Jen continued, showing his own wish to get the job for me. "The application of fertilizer only has to be done a day or two every month. Between fertilizing intervals, the only work you have to do is to maintain a certain level of water in the fields. The trick is to build an inlet and outlet in the ridges of each plot so that when you open the sluice gate in the irrigation ditch, the water flows automatically into each plot through the inlet. The outlet releases the surplus water. You sit by the sluice gate to watch, that's all.

"The rice is ripening in early September, and doesn't need the water. We'll have practically nothing to do but lie on the irrigation bank to rest. It's just about then that the fish in the drainage ditches begin to swim downstream to seek deeper water in preparation for the coming winter. We can build small dams in the ditches, with a gap in the middle of the dam. If we put a sieve under the flow, we could trap as many fish as we want.

"Last autumn, every morning I collected quite a few fish, and sometimes even a couple of big ones. We ate boiled fish every day. I didn't have to eat that pig slop of boiled vegetables from the kitchen for nearly half a month." He sucked in air and swallowed the saliva that came into his mouth.

"Let's go back now," he said. "It's nearly time for the second meal. Fucking cooks! They must use the cooking oil for tea because I can't find a single drop of it in the vegetables. Someday we're going to have to teach them a lesson. They're inmates too, so they shouldn't be so hard on us. Fucking bastards!"

We stood up. Han Jen stopped me from walking down the irrigation canal bank onto the road. "Let's go along the bottom of the canal," he said. "I don't want to see the face of a single fucking cop *or* any of their children."

We slid down the other side of the bank and walked along the dry bottom. Locust bushes blocked the sight from the road.

Upon returning, we informed Officer Wang that we were back. He was playing chess with Officer Gao, and waved us out impatiently with a flick of the wrist. "Bastard!" Han Jen cursed.

Officer Wang didn't have a good reputation among the inmates, nor among the officers either. Besides serving as the partner of Officer Niu in charge of Team One, he was the supervisor of the inmate's kitchen. He had chosen the four cooks. Rumors went around that the cooks stole the inmates ration of meat to provide night snacks for Officer Wang. But I didn't believe he could be so ruthless as to eat the meager ration of meat allotted for the pathetic inmates. Yet some radicals claimed they had seen him with their own eyes eat at the inmates' kitchen.

Officer Wang was coarse and often acted viciously toward us, but at the same time, he was very simple-minded and played no treacherous games behind our backs. When he felt like it, he was known to extend the work breaks in the fields for over an hour. When he was in good mood he even engaged in some harmless rough-housing with us, and when he was in bad mood he sulked or took a long nap in a sunny spot. He sometimes swore at us with the foulest obscenities, and occasionally would kick one of us for no reason. I did my best to avoid meeting, or talking with him.

Near the single tap, just around the corner from the duty office, there were several wash basins filled with clothes standing in soap suds. The electricity had been cut suddenly so the pump in the water tower couldn't deliver water. There were several card games going on between inmates of the row houses. I looked around and didn't see Black Head and Tiger. Mouse was sitting alone outside the door to our room. His tiny body seemed to have shed another layer now that he had taken off his tattered cotton-lined jacket.

"Where are they?" I asked him.

"They're inside," he said in a high-pitched whimper, like the weak yelping of a puppy at the mercy of a cruel boy.

I entered the room and was almost choked by the overwhelming cloud of strange smelling smoke.

"What the hell is going on here?" I shouted.

"Hey, keep it down," someone among a cluster of heads in the smoke said angrily.

"Oh, it's Huang Longsen." Tiger stood up and smiled. "Come and have a bite."

I walked closer and saw an aluminum lunch box being licked by black smoke and pink tongues of flame. Chunks of pinkish meat simmered in a foam of slow boiling water. The smell was fishy and sour, mixed in an aroma of Chinese prickly ash and aniseed. Tiger offered a pair of chopsticks to me and urged me to pick up a piece.

"What's it?" I asked suspiciously. Several weeks earlier someone from Squad Three stole a hen that had wandered into the fields and cooked it in the squad room. He was caught by the duty officer and placed in solitary confinement for three days.

"It's cat meat," Black Head said, munching greedily. "A wild cat we caught just by the wall outside our room. We didn't steal it, so they can't punish us for cooking it."

"That's right, we didn't steal it, Huang Longsen," another joined in. "The guards can't punish us for eating a wild cat. The most they can accuse us of is violating the regulation of no fires in the room."

Han Jen had told me that some of the guards kept their eye half-closed when the inmates cooked frogs, fish, or eels they caught in the fields. Now that I learned it was only a wild cat and wouldn't bring trouble to me, I squatted down by the lunch box, took the chopsticks from

Tiger's hand and picked up a small piece. The meat caused a queer sensation as I put it in my mouth. Only an overdose of salt and spices stopped me from spitting it out. The others looked at me. I swallowed the slippery lump quickly. It must be a problem of my sense of taste, I told myself. Nothing was wrong with cat flesh.

"Not bad, eh?" Tiger watched me happily. "Another piece?"

"No, thanks," I said. "You'd better finish it quickly and clear up the air in the room. Officer Wang may make an inspection tour any minute."

That was a bluff. Officer Wang wouldn't sacrifice his joy in the middle of a chess game to attend to his official duties. I said this in case anyone might report on Squad Two for building an illegal fire and cooking in the room. I would then be able to attest that I stopped them at an early stage, so that no harm would be done. The officer would do no more than warn me not to let it happen again.

"Have you given some to Mouse?" I asked. "You let him keep watch and you eat all the meat. It's unfair."

"Mouse," Black Head called out. "Come in. There are two big pieces of meat for you."

Mouse scurried in, rummaged in a blackened cloth bag, fished out his chopsticks, and squatted down by the lunch box. "Careful, it's hot!," Black Head said to Mouse. "But you'd better hurry up. Officer Wang will be making his rounds pretty soon."

Mouse picked up the larger chunk and stuffed it into his mouth. "Ah..." he exclaimed painfully, but didn't release his grip on the meat. He sucked in air to cool it, and started to chew it with his lips wide open. His eyes were already riveted to the other piece of meat in the lunch box.

I lay down on the far end of the platform bed, the privileged spot reserved for the squad leader in the room, and waited for the whistle to blow for the second meal at four o'clock. The tea I had drunk at Officer Niu's house gurgled more violently in my stomach. The lump of cat meat had only made me more hungry. I regretted that I had eaten only one piece.

9

My Squad Is Assigned to Grow Rice

One week later Officer Niu announced at a roll call that Squad One and Squad Two were assigned to tend the rice paddies until harvest time. Several young men in my squad forgot we were in the midst of a roll call and shouted, "Hooray!" That drew many hostile, jealous glares from the men of the other two squads of Team One.

I smiled at Han Jen who winked back at me, and I looked at Chan Wen who kept his eyes coolly and respectfully on Officer Niu. But his left leg shook noticeably with irritation. Everyone had expected Han Jen to be given the job because he was a veteran of the farm for more than a year and "had risen step by step." But no one expected me to get it. I had been at Chadian only four months.

As soon as roll call broke up, my men swarmed around me in our room and gave me three cheers. I told them not to make loud noises and to get ready for the evening study.

"We got the job," I said, as all of them sat down either on the edge of the platform bed or on small stools on the floor. "You're all happy about it, aren't you? But there's something I want to make clear: I want you to make a pledge not to play any tricks on me."

I put much stress on the word "me", implying that I would take any wrong doing among them as a sign of their trying to destroy my leadership, and that I would retaliate. I had to imbed this warning deep into them. Otherwise I would have a full pot of trouble on my hands. Any misstep I took or any serious problem that happened with them would not only ruin my advantageous position in the Big

Compound but also my chances at gaining an early release.

Because I had been sure that Officer Niu would give me the job, I had planned for several days how to handle the new situation. I was determined to finish this assignment to the satisfaction of the officers.

The top priority for me as a squad leader, in tending rice fields, was to see that no one under my charge would escape. So I added, "And no one will make a break." We inmates didn't use the word "escape," because it sounded like a bad word to our ears when the guards used it.

"We won't make breaks," Pan Rong said flatteringly. "We won't do anything against the regulations, not even so much as take a potato from the kitchen supply."

Since Han Jen pushed him into the drainage ditch half a month ago, Pan Rong had become less insolent. He still bragged about his family wealth and influential connections. But his audience had dwindled. His several "buddies" were more interested in his food than in his bragging. Realizing that my reputation had risen to an undeniable height among the other inmates and that Han Jen and Officer Niu would back me up in almost every situation, Pan Rong had begun to ingratiate himself with me. He started by applying his most successful means – food.

One afternoon Officer Wang sent him and me back earlier than usual to repair our spades. By the time we finished, the others had not yet returned. We were alone in our room.

"You look pale," Pan Rong said to me with great concern. "You need more nutrition." So saying he climbed up on the platform bed and dragged down a small suitcase hidden behind his bed roll.

The suitcase was well-known in the Big Compound. Called the "Treasure Trove," it was always full of beautifully prepared comestibles. Pan Rong's mother and sister were the most frequent visitors among relatives of the Big Compound inmates, coming nearly every two months despite the farm's rule that regular family visits were allowed only on major holidays. Every time they came they would bring Pan Rong great quantities of food.

Between visits they sent him food by mail.

Officer Niu became impatient with the two women and warned them that they were spoiling Pan Rong. "You're not helping him correct his bad habits," Officer Niu told the tearful mother after he threatened to send her food packages back to Beijing. But the two women continued to send them, and Officer Niu did not follow through on his threat because it was impossible to get the post office to take them back.

Throwing a package into Pan Rong's arms, Officer Niu would yell, "Tell your mother, it's all her fault that you're here!"

Pan Rong locked his precious suitcase with two locks – one was a combination lock – and used its contents to win friends. He would usually open it when he was alone. Many inmates looked at it with longing, and some even had tried to break into it.

Now he opened it in front of me. The strong aroma of food cooked in rich oil assaulted my nostrils. I stealthily took a deep breath, and averted my eyes.

"Take what you want, and as much as you want," Pan Rong offered.

Instead, I went over to the shelf, took down my wash basin, and walked out. "You keep it yourself," I said.

I later told Han Jen about this. He replied, "Seems pretty foolish to me. After all, your top concern here is to survive. He offers. You didn't ask. He can't eat that much anyway. Further more, it's a waste for him to eat all that great food. No matter how well he eats, he will still be a stupid pig. Next time he offers you food, take it. If you feel it's too filthy for you to eat, give it to me. I sure as hell won't mind."

From then on Pan Rong, from time to time, would offer me a cake, or several chocolate drops, or several pieces of dried meat. Although I now took these gifts, I never was able to warm up to him. For one thing, his his cheap flattery made me sick. For another, I didn't want to give anyone the impression that I was his buddy, because then he would feel like he could intimidate the others.

One evening during a study session Pan Rong was

sitting on a small stool at my feet. His pancake face turned up toward me, to reveal a disgusting smile which sliced his face in two. I deliberately ignored him by looking the other way. I refused to acknowledge his presence.

"Even if I lent you some of my guts," Tiger said to Pan Rong, "you still wouldn't dare to make a break, you chicken shit motherfucker."

Pan Rong immediately fell quiet, and hunched his shoulders.

"Don't worry," Tiger said to me. "Whoever dares to cause trouble for you, I'll put a white knife in him and draw it out red."

"Tiger," I said sternly. "This is a study session. You'd better behave yourself. We are here to be reformed of our bad habits through labor. But you talk like you're in a street fight again."

I then said to the other men, "From now on, we will have to be on our own most of the daytime in the fields. I want you to give me a pledge not to make a break for it, not only for my own sake but for yours too. Officer Niu asked me if I wanted to replace some of you. I said I would like to keep you all on the squad, and I pledged to him we would do an excellent job."

I looked around to see the gratitude in some of their eyes. "In addition to more freedom," I went on, "to be on our own has another advantage. If we do well, we'll have a better chance to get our terms cut, because that is proof that we have learned to handle ourselves correctly. Tomorrow we are to check all the sluice gates on irrigation ditch Number Fifteen. Our plots are on the western side of that ditch. Squad One has the eastern side. It will be easy to see which squad does better. Repairing sluice gates is a meticulous job. If we don't make sure that all the sluice gates are strong and secure, we'll suffer afterwards when the irrigation ditch is filled with water. They will leak like hell, and we will have a hell of a time trying to rebuild them. Tomorrow we'll know if anyone cheats in their work."

Someone shouted, "Whoever cheats is a son of a

bitch!" Another joined in, "We'll give the cheater a good beating!" Followed by "We'll make him suffer all the rest of his days here!" This group of men were in accord over very few things, but this was definitely one of them.

I wanted to make sure now that I wouldn't have any difficulty in the initial stage of the work.

That night, the men in our room slept fitfully in anticipation of their new job assignment. All of them felt lucky, and showed their appreciation to me for being a decent squad leader. Even Pockmark offered to empty my wash basin. He didn't seem to mind that I had soaked my feet in it. I declined courteously, of course. I detested the street gang practice in which junior members gave free service to senior ones. But, for his show of respect, I kept him in the squad, even though Officer Niu had suggested that I replace him with someone from another squad. Officer Niu was afraid Pockmark would become a burden to me, but I felt his loyalty far outweighed the physical burden he might represent.

"The old devil must have read many books," Officer Niu said of Pockmark. "No officers can win an argument with him. He has ten answers to every question. Officer Wang sometimes kicks him when he refuses to do his quota in the fields, but I don't like to waste my energy on him as long as he keeps himself within a limit. No point trying to squeeze blood out of *that* turnip."

Pockmark was the oldest man in our squad, fifty-one, lazy, and often unreasonable. Besides the nickname "Pockmark" he was also called "Knotty Meat" – a substance that a sharp knife can't cut it through. He masturbated, and demonstrated this to the boys. For that, he had been put in solitary twice before I came to Chadian. The second time he was in solitary he told the guard how enjoyable it was.

"Ever had a taste of opium?" he asked the guard, or so the self-proclaimed story went. To which the guard replied, "Sure, but only a few puffs." The Communists wiped out opium addiction in Beijing in the early 1950s. In the Kuomintang times, opium pushers were buried alive, at least those who had no official connections. The

Communists shot them. You can't find opium in Beijing now. "I had it when I went to the Northeast. Deep in the mountains there are many villagers who smoke it."

"Listen, young man," Pockmark had continued. "I'll give you a lecture on the opium history of China. The British brought it to China in the early 1830s. Near the end of the Qing dynasty at the turn of the twentieth century, bandits began to grow the poppies in remote areas of Yunnan, Guizhou and Sichuan provinces and in the Northeast. They stole from each other and fought with guns during harvest time. Then the Kuomintang government grew the poppies under the protection of regular troops. The profit from selling opium was a large chunk of their revenue.

"After the Japanese occupied the Northeast in 1931, they took over the opium fields, expanded them, shipped the raw opium back to Japan where they refined it into heroin, then shipped the stuff back to the Northeast and sold it to the Chinese. They turned all the locals into opium addicts. After the Cultural Revolution started in 1966, the Communists became too busy to fight against their real political enemies. Many villagers in remote mountains have begun to grow the poppies again and more and more smoke the stuff. Ah, wonderful stuff.

"Young man, I tell you, masturbating feels like smoking a pot of opium. After doing it you feel as wonderful as an immortal. If you don't believe me, you should try it yourself."

He would go on to say that on this occasion, the policeman rushed angrily into the cell and kicked him too many times to count. This a story Pockmark would tell anyone within earshot, whether they wanted to hear it or not.

The officers eventually couldn't do anything but let Pockmark out of solitary and leave him alone. I cured him by suggesting to the boys that whenever he was found masturbating in the open again, they should play a trick on him.

One evening, before the night study session, I was lingering in the courtyard. Mouse scurried over and whispered into my ear: "He was doing it!" I coughed to catch the attention of those playing cards in a corner and gesticulated with my head toward the room. They jumped up and charged in.

Pockmark was sitting on the platform bed at the western end, his pants stripped down to his knees. Baldheaded, fat, sitting there with crossed legs, his head bent over his fluffy bare chest in total concentration, Pockmark looked like the clay statue of a benevolent Buddha in a temple.

Four boys climbed up the bed and pinned him down. Black Head lit a cigarette, puffed at it hard to make the tip glow, and spit out a chain of smoke rings onto Pockmark's face. Then he raised the cigarette up to let the fat man see it, slowly traced it down over his chest and abdomen along the central line, and put its burning end on his penis. Two other boys anticipated Pockmark's scream by spreading his quilt over his head.

Pockmark clawed and kicked frantically, tearing the reed mat under him. His cries were muffled by the cotton-lined quilt. When he finally quieted down, the boys took away the quilt. His face was so red with anger and pain that it looked like an over-ripened tomato.

He didn't fight back as I had expected. He must have known I was behind it. Before I came, the boys had cheered him when he masturbated publicly. He didn't dare to challenge me because I had Black Head and Tiger as my body guards. According to Pockmark, they were the "only men in the Big Compound who were really willing to die fighting."

I had told the boys not to actually hurt him. But Black Head literally crushed the cigarette head on the big man's penis, which had gone limp from fear. From then on, Pockmark was never found masturbating in the open.

I had another reason not to let Officer Niu replace Pockmark. I wanted to show Officer Niu and the other officers, that I could deal with any kind of street players, old or young, treacherous or tough, better than they could.

I had figured out how to take care of Pockmark in

the rice fields. I would assign him the four plots between those of Black Head and Tiger, and tell them to see to it that Pockmark did the most necessary work to his plots. Though Pockmark was not afraid of the guards, he was afraid of these two boys. They had many small ways of teasing him, such as putting a toad in his quilt or a beetle in his shoe. Pockmark had an unnatural fear of insects.

I wasn't worried about his escape either. He had no wife, no children, and his relatives wouldn't have anything to do with him. "I like it here," he once told me. "Life in Beijing is too troublesome. I had to worry about food, about clothes, about the money at the end of the month, and I had to get up very early to go to work. Here, you walk fifty steps to get food from the kitchen, and the guards take care of everything else."

"Most people are hypocrites," he asserted. "They live for appearance's sake. They want a glorious job, a good house, good clothes. I don't care about all that. I would like to stay here the rest of my life. When I die, I wouldn't mind if they buried me over in that graveyard for criminals at Farm 586. I wouldn't even care if they fed me to the pigs. There's really not much difference once you're not around to see it. When I die, what am I going to worry about..."

The next morning, I proudly led my squad out of the steel-plated gate of the Big Compound, the first time we had done this without an officer trailing behind us. The guard at the gate counted heads against a list and didn't make any fuss. Instead, he nodded to me to let me understand that from now on we were acquaintances. I nodded back and smiled at him in a friendly way.

The guard, who looked to be in his late twenties, was neither an officer nor the child of an officer. He used to work in a town nearby. No one knew why he took the lousy job at Chadian, with its low pay and long distance from the civilized world, and a potentially "normal" life.

As soon as we crossed the wooden-plank bridge over the irrigation canal which led to irrigation ditch number fifteen, the men burst out shouting. They threw themselves down the bank which was blanketed with soft grass. Then, they vaulted over the drainage ditch, and somersaulted along the bottom of the irrigation ditch. I allowed them to enjoy this freedom for several minutes as it was one of the few moments of elation I had witnessed since arriving at the Farm. Finally, after everyone had adequately reveled in their new location, I assigned them to their specific jobs. I added a warning: "We'll be using the sluice gates to accomplish our task over next three months. If you do a good job now, we won't suffer down the road."

They responded enthusiastically with, "You can count on us, Huang Longsen. Rest assured that we'll patch up every mouse hole and ant hole around the sluice gate. You won't find a single flaw with our work at the end of the day."

Han Jen's squad arrived soon thereafter. They, too, celebrated before starting their work. I had the four plots on the southern end of the strip of land, on the western side of the irrigation ditch, directly opposite to those of Han Jen.

Master Chao and Master Huan, two of the three ex-Rightists living in the Small Compound, came to give us pointers on consolidating the sluice gates and building inlets into the smaller ditches to lead the water directly into the fields. They were to be with us through the rice growing season, teaching us how to attend the rice nursery, transplant rice seedlings, harrow, weed, apply fertilizer, and maintain the water in the fields at a proper depth.

Both in their early forties, Master Chao, short and solidly built, had been roughened through the years away from his office work in Beijing, where he was the editor of a literary magazine; and Master Huan, almost a head taller than Master Chao, fair skinned and steady, had preserved the scholastic look of a medical intern when he was branded as a Rightist in 1957. Master Chao was liked, but not much respected; while Master Huan was liked and respected. I had talked briefly with both of them a bit earlier when I was assigned to stock fertilizer in the Small Compound's storehouse. Generally, I got a good feeling from both of them. They must have liked talking to me.

The two veterans came over and patted me on my upper arms. "Glad you got the job," Master Chao said happily. Master Huan smiled to let me know he was glad too."Whenever you need help, you let us know," Chao added.

"I sure will," I said.

The air in the fields tasted fresh that morning. The work felt less tedious and tiring, though I did much more than was usually assigned to me on other days. The loudspeaker hanging from a pole in the Officers Compound cracked sharply to announce the morning break. It then played for fifteen minutes a song of revolutionary zeal or a high-spirited number from a Beijing opera, eulogizing the great deeds of the Communists. This went on throughout the break. Three boys came over to me to report they had dug up two eels from the ground, and invited me over to have a bite.

"I caught one this big!" Mouse said excitedly, gesticulating the length and thickness of the eel with his tiny hands. "It was very slippery. I couldn't get hold of it with my hands. So I grabbed it with my teeth. Come, I'll give you the middle part."

I told them to enjoy the booty themselves. My stomach still felt queasy when I thought of that piece of cat meat I had had one week ago.

We often dug out snakes, frogs, and occasionally eels when digging ditches. These creatures, in hibernation, were not very active. The boys would skin, gut, and roast them over a fire built with dead twigs or grass. The animal's fat dropping onto the fire would cause small sizzling sounds and boost the flames. The white flesh would turn pink, then white again, losing the bright luster of freshness, and then become blackened by the smoke.

The boys would bite a section off a charred spot and find blood still oozing out of the fine vessels. They would then roast it further, and bite again until the whole thing was swallowed. Our kitchen fare was so short of protein, that many of the inmates would eat any living thing, including scorpions they found under shady shrubs and in wall crevices. At first, I couldn't stand the sight of a writhing reptile held over a fire.

I called the morning work to an end at around 11:30 – ten minutes later than Officer Niu would have done so, and no one complained. Officer Niu didn't show up at all. He wanted me to know that he trusted me without any reservations. I had made special efforts to see that everything went smoothly by walking back and forth twice along the ditch of two-thirds of a mile, and in between I did my work.

Officer Niu had specifically assigned Han Jen and me to the plots at the head of the fields. I understood his purpose. No officers of a higher rank liked to walk far into the fields to inspect how the crop grew there. By early summer, the grass would grow high enough to reach one's calves. The dew would wet the trouser legs. If the ground was wet, the mud would be very sticky, sucking at the soles of shoes with great force. Most of the officers would just climb up the irrigation canal and look northward. The distance they could see clearly enough to make correct judgment was about a quarter of a mile. Farther than that, the crop and weed looked the same.

Directors and Party secretaries of the general headquarters would come in a jeep. They seldom went into the fields on their inspection tours. Thus, the working officers directly handling the inmates paid a great deal of attention to the plots at the head of a strip of land. The fields were much flatter there, ridges more evenly built, more fertilizer applied, and the crop on them looked more luxuriant.

I allocated these plots to my men also according to much the same principle. Though I held Pan Rong in contempt, I assigned him the four plots next to mine. He was a hard worker and too fearful to neglect his duty. The eight plots handled by him and me would satisfy any inspection officer. I placed Black Head at the northern end of the fields to guard the rear – to keep watch on anyone who might want to make a break for it across the main drainage ditch that separated the Chadian Farmland from that of the villagers. He wouldn't let me down. But I knew he wouldn't take very good care of his rice either. That was secondary as far as my personal interests were concerned.

Life was much easier now. As the leader in charge of an inmate squad tending rice fields, I was given the privilege of leaving the Big Compound earlier, and returning later on my own most of the weekdays, and on Sundays, too. I liked to be out, not only to enjoy the privilege, but because I really loved the fields. They refreshed the obscured memories of my childhood life in my native village.

As did everyone else, I left my spade and sickle under a bush at the sluice gate near my plots, sparing myself the trouble of taking them back and forth. During work hours, I would often take my tools and walk around the plots. I usually looked for some inconspicuous spot where I could daydream, since there was not much work to do in the fields.

All the sluice gates had been reinforced and had passed Master Chao's inspection. The others didn't bother to make the ridges in their plots straighter or to cut weeds that were growing fast in the ditches. But I did, because I wanted to keep physically fit in case I was later assigned to hard jobs, and because I didn't want either Director Feng or Officer Niu to catch me neglecting my work. My top priority was to win a cut in the term of my sentence.

I took great pains to be sure I was always visible in my plots working. My ditches were cleaned of grass, my ridges looked strong and neat. Instructor Feng came to check on me a couple of times, and told Officer Niu that I was very conscientious in correcting my former counter-revolutionary attitudes through honest labor.

"He's dogmatic, and he possesses a paltry amount of theory," Officer Niu once told me in speaking about Instructor Feng.

In another week, the fields would be flooded for transplanting seedlings. My men had been doing fine with their preparation work. Master Chao and Master Huan were now present more often to make sure that everything would be able to withstand the first test of flooding.

"Through the winter," Master Chao told me, "the

earth became loose and filled with many mice holes. The sluice gates and ridges can be very easily washed away by the first flooding. But if they are secure after that, they will be OK all through the summer."

When the day came, the two pumps at the pumping station were turned on. The loud whirling sound vibrated the air and ground. The red-brick superstructure perching over a huge pool seemed to swagger as arrogantly as the five electricians working in it. We all gathered on bank of the irrigation canal to wait for the water to come. When it did, it threw up a sheet of dust and pushed dead grass bits and rubbish ahead of the flow.

We followed the watershed to each of our sluice gates and opened them. As I drew the wooden board from mine to let water rush into my plots, I had an exalted sensation of human dignity rush through my being. Now I had something more under *my* control, and *myself* under less control.

"Hey!" Han Jen called out across the irrigation ditch. "How are things over on your side? If there is no breach in the ridges, we will have nothing to do but enjoy a day or two of rest."

He walked down the bank of his side to the water edge, thrust his spade in the middle of the ditch, and heaved his body over the four yards of water in a vault to my side. "Let's go down to the fields and see if we can pick up some fish."

The dry earth absorbed the water thirstily, and here and there small fish were struggling in the mud. We looked for a while and found none that were worth eating. "Damn!" Han Jen swore. "Last year we could pick up two or three pounds a day during the flooding time. The sons-of-bitches at the pumping station must have erected a net at the mouth into the irrigation canal to stop them from entering the irrigation canal. The greedy bastards. There are enough big fish in the pool under the station for them to catch. Still, they want the smaller ones that are sucked up in the pipes – the ones that usually come over to the irrigation canal." He lost interest in the search for fish and we climbed up to the dry bank.

Looking north, I saw the rest of our men sauntering in the mud, busy collecting the tiny fish. Small sea birds were also busy catching them and catching the insects which had been driven out from underground by the water.

"Teacher Sun was transferred to my squad," Han Jen said. "He's over there."

I looked at the man in a plot north next to Han Jen's. There must have been a breach in the ridge, because Teacher Sun was standing in the drainage ditch with his trouser legs submerged in the water. He was laboriously scooping up earth from the bottom of the drainage ditch with his spade to pile on the field edge. His hands were too low on the spade handle to gain much leverage. His white shirt was soaked with muddy water.

"Can he manage the breach alone?" I asked, indicating we should go and help.

"He's all right," Han Jen said and sat down on the irrigation ditch bank to smoke.

"He was born into a wealthy family," Han Jen continued after drawing on the cigarette deeply several times.

I looked at the glowing tip and smelled the pleasant aroma. I hoped Han Jen might offer me one. He didn't. I sat down by him.

"Both his parents taught at universities, and he's their only child. Though he never did manual work before he came here, he's a hard worker and has learned fast. He finishes all the work he's given. Of course, he has to use more energy than others. He talks very little. After supper he sits alone most of the time, lost in his own thoughts. I've told the boys not to bother him. He has a picture of his wife and daughter in his pocket all the time and often looks at it. His wife and daughter came to visit him during the Spring Festival. His wife is very attractive: slender, fair-skinned and tall. His daughter is pretty too, with large, bright eyes. I just can't understand why he wanted to sleep with another woman when his wife is so beautiful. He doesn't seem that bad to me. But who knows, one just can't judge others by appearances. Right?"

I nodded my head in agreement.

10

The Stolen Fish Feast

In early June, the morning still felt chilly in the open fields. Most of the water in the rice paddies had been absorbed by the dry earth. Thousands of small fish gulped painfully for air in the many muddy potholes. Mouse trudged around from one pool to another, picking them up. His short legs looked like two dead willow tree twigs, and his tattered trousers were smeared with mud splashes. He crawled up the irrigation ditch to show me his harvest in a plastic bag. "These are gonna make for some good eating," he said happily.

"Let me see 'em," Tiger ordered.

Mouse grasped the bag tightly with both hands. "I found them," he said, his beady eyes darting in panic.

"Let me have a look at them, you turtle egg!" Tiger stretched out a hand.

Mouse looked at me, begging me to interfere, his eyes blinking. I said nothing. He needed someone like Tiger or Black Head to hold him in check. Sometimes, he was too strange to be tolerable.

As the saying goes, people with mental or physical defects often do irritating things. It is perhaps because they are suspicious of people with normal minds and physiques. Though they deserve sympathy, they are most often ridiculed. I had been sympathetic to Mouse ever since they assigned him to my squad in March. He had been bullied at home and, after he ran away from home, the ridiculing had continued out in the Beijing streets. His tiny, dried-up body called for pity. I told the boys not to bother him, but from time to time I would get impatient with him, especially with his filthy habits.

He hadn't washed his body once in the three months since he arrived, except to take the monthly baths required at the general headquarters. The first time we were taken to the general headquarters bathhouse, he hid in the room, and Officer Wang was careless enough to miss him during the head count. The next time, I had to drag him the whole way.

Every morning he would just splash a handful of water from the tap over his eyes and cheeks and then dry his face with the lap of his jacket. His neck was as dirty as any cart ax in the Small Compound. He didn't wash his bowls or chopsticks after mealtime, either. Instead, he licked them clean like the Tibetans do. But I doubted he had learned the way from them.

He was bearable in cold weather, but when the days became warmer, he began to smell. One Sunday afternoon, the boys in my squad stripped him and doused him with a bucket of cold water. He shivered and sneezed like a dog. I quickly mopped him up with a dry towel, and stuffed him into his filthy quilt. Then I set a rule for him: he was to wash his entire face and neck in the morning, and his feet before bed.

The next night he tried to slip under his quilt without washing his feet. I pulled him out of bed stark naked, dragged him out to the tap, and pushed him under the gushing torrent of water. "You're killing me!" he whimpered. I slapped him in the face, although I felt sorry for this poor wretch. However, as I dragged him back into the room, he laughed and told others that I had too little strength to hit people. "The slapping only made my head itch," he related to anyone who would listen.

Now I wanted to see him suffer a bit.

Seeing that I wouldn't lend him my support, Mouse turned to Tiger and pleaded with him, "I'll give you some of my fish after I cook them."

"Who wants to eat your filthy slop," Tiger said, snatching the plastic bag from Mouse's clasped hands and tip-ping it so that the contents slipped slowly into the irrigation ditch.

Mouse whined with the utmost helplessness as he watched his fish being washed down the stream. At last he plucked up enough courage to protest. "Those are my fish!" he cried out, and rushed toward Tiger to retrieve his bag.

Tiger then emptied out the last of the bag's contents. Mouse grabbed Tiger's arm fiercely, but Tiger thrust it high to put it out of reach of Mouse's mouth. When cornered, Mouse fought back like a mad dog. However, since he didn't possess much strength in his limbs, his most useful weapon was his teeth. He sharpened his teeth and kept them strong by chewing on the bones of eels and fish.

I realized the situation was getting serious, and so I said sternly, "All right, Mouse! Stop it! Your fish were too small to eat. You can pick some larger ones later. Now both of you go to your plots and see if any of your ridges needs to be strengthened."

Mouse hung onto Tiger's arm for one more second and then released it. He walked away, crying.

"Take your bag along so you can use it to hold fish," I called after him, feeling somewhat guilty for having made him miserable.

"Tiger!" I called. "Give him the bag!" I was angered at Tiger for making me feel guilty.

Two tractors from the general headquarters were soon coming to smooth the flooded plots. So Master Chao instructed us to let more water into the fields.

"Why should we let more water in?" Pan Rong asked Master Chao.

"The water is just lubrication so that the tractor drivers can fuck the eels."

The Farm's tractor drivers were the guards' sons. They performed all the skilled jobs within the Compound. Though they were innocuous for the most part, they were still related to the guards, and so we didn't like them very much.

"When the land is dry," Master Chao explained, "the tractors can only make ruts in the fields. The water dissolves the earth so that the tractors can spread it evenly. The tractors cause water to roll. You'd better check again to see if the ridges can stand up to the water rushing in. If there's a break, all the water in the plot will rush through it. That will wash away a great amount of earth. Your officer will keep you there repairing the breach no matter how long it takes. There's never enough earth from the drainage ditch near the breach so you will have to carry earth from dry fields hundreds of yards away. By then you will want to kill yourself for not having built the ridges strong enough. Get the picture?"

I sent the men immediately away to work on their plots.

"Your ridges are straight and reinforced well," Master Chao commented on my work, as he followed me into my plots, "but they are not strong enough. You'd better add another layer of earth to the ridges before the tractors come in. Don't worry about how they look. After all, you're not doing professional landscaping." He laughed good-naturedly.

I had thought of showing my elaborate job to the officers because my ridges were perfectly smooth and straight, and their edges were at exact right angles. Now they seemed too delicate. I shoveled another layer of mud onto them, making the ridges look swollen and ugly.

Tiger came over. His legs and arms were dripping with mud. "I can't find any fish," he yelled angrily. "I'm going over behind the pumping house to tear down that damned net. To hell with those son-of-a-bitch electricians!"

"No, you can't do that," I said. "If Officer Niu finds out, there will be hell to pay. And he won't let you off easily. Probably switch you to another squad..."

At the same time, however, I wished he would do it. A pot of fresh fish was extremely enticing. Yesterday the boys caught some of the sea birds that were hunting insects in the flooded fields. They cooked the birds in their lunch boxes. I had thought they would be delicious, but the birds tasted too fishy. Though we finished eating them, we craved the taste of real fish.

Under the pumping house there was a deep pit. The water from the Chaobai River couldn't come in fast enough to feed the two powerful pumps. Every hour or so one of the pumps had to be turned off to wait for more water to accumulate. Twice or three times a day, the electricians would run both the pumps ten minutes longer to drain the pit. Then they would climb down into the pit with scoop nets to catch the fish stranded at the bottom. The electricians turned part of the catch over to the officer's kitchen, but they kept the rest of the catch for themselves. The electricians' families had so much that the other officers were jealous.

The pumps sucked many fish up the pipes and spit them out into the irrigation canal. Larger ones were either knocked out by the force of the water or cut some into irregular halves by the turbine blades. The wounded ones floated down along the canal.

We had expected to enjoy the booty, especially those in Squad One. Han Jen had boosted his men's expectations high by touting the new job's many advantages, including regular fish feasts.

The next morning, as the water rushed into the irrigation ditch, I opened my sluice gate to replenish the water in my plots, keeping the soil well saturated. Master Chao said that doing this would make the land easier for harrowing with the added benefit that the tractor drivers would be more patient with their job, and wouldn't deliberately break the plot ridges.

Around eleven o'clock Tiger and Black Head ran over to my sluice gate where I was watching the leisurely flow of water into my plots. They were jubilant.

"See what we've got!" Tiger said. He spread out a bundle made from his wet shirt. In it were three carp, each almost a foot long, and a dozen white stripes. Some of the fish were mutilated, but all of them were fresh.

"Black Head pretended to catch some fish in the pit

in front of the pump house," Tiger explained, "so as to get the bastards inside to chase after him. As he did this, I slipped down into the canal behind the pump house, slashed the net apart with a sickle, and picked out these fish from the net."

"Those assholes at the station think they can scare me," Black Head said, pointing with the thumb of his left hand over his shoulder toward the pumping station. "They grabbed my arms and said they were going to take me over to the discipline officer. But how could I let them? With a twitch, like this," he turned his left arm outward and pulled his right arm sharply downward in a wrestling position designed to throw an opponent sideways, "and bang, one guy was on the ground. Then I told them if they ever wanted to go to Beijing in the future, they'd better be careful not to make trouble for me here, or I'd find them there. So they let me go."

"Hold on, now," I said with irritation in my voice, "we've only been on this job for a week, and already you're forgetting where you are. Don't go near that pumping station again, and that's an order. I'm serious. I don't want trouble with those guards' sons. They can be worse than their fathers. If you want to stay here for an extra year, that's fine. But I don't. I don't mind if you perform your antics in the fields, but quarreling with the guards' children is absolutely out, understand me?"

"All right," Black Head said, immediately subdued by the rebuke, but still triumphant for having threatened the electricians. "Don't worry. We won't let you down. We'll work hard and say nice things to Officer Niu about you so you can get out of this damn place six months early. How's that? Now, let's go back to get our pigs-won't-bother-with-it lunch. Tiger, remember to bring the salt and chili peppers."

We hid the fish under a bush near my sluice gate and returned to the Big Compound. I made it known that Tiger, Black Head, and I had to check the ridges after lunch.

They stole salt from the stable for the horses and

"picked up" dried chili peppers, garlic, scallions, and other small things near the officer's kitchen when they were sent to transport coal for it. We left the Big Compound carrying our steamed corn buns from lunch, but gave away the boiled vegetable.

After walking over the perilous single plank bridge across the irrigation canal and down into the ditch bank, Black Head and Tiger hooted and cheered. We picked up the fish near my sluice gate, walked along the irrigation ditch further north, and in fifteen minutes arrived at Black Head's sluice gate, the last one at the northern end of irrigation ditch Fifteen. The main drainage ditch that separated the labor farm and the land of a peasant village was a hundred yards away, beyond a stretch of wasteland.

The spot chosen for the feast by Black Head and Tiger was in the leeway corner of Black Head's sluice gate. The short elbow of the embankment of the sluice gate prevented the northwesterly wind from blowing in directly and trapped the warmth from the sun. A willow tree shaded this spot to give it cool shade when the sun got too high. The two boys had built a fire hole at the base of the bank. There they could roast every living thing they caught.

"We have such good fish," Black Head said. "It would be a pity to eat them without a drink."

I didn't comment, knowing that he was thinking of making a trip to the village store.

Before my squad was assigned to the rice fields, Tiger and Black Head had twice waded over the ditch and sneaked into the village to buy hard liquor and tidbits. We inmates were not allowed to keep cash on our persons, though many had hidden funds they acquired from their relatives who visited the Farm. The villagers were supposed to report to the labor farm authorities about any inmate who crossed the drainage ditch. But Tiger and Black Head had had no trouble. Perhaps they had pretended to be a couple of the guards' children. It was more likely that the peasants just didn't care who they were.

Officer Niu knew about these secret visits, and also about some of the mischief the other boys had gotten into, but he didn't interfere. This showed he was wiser than the other officers. He handled the discipline of the inmates much as a coal feeder handles a boiler: too much pressure might cause an explosion.

Officer Niu treated the inmates with neither indulgent leniency nor overdosed punishment. By giving the most aggressive inmates a chance to relax once in a while, he reduced the threat of their fighting or escaping. While the other officers kept a constant watch on their charges, stretching their blanket of authority to the breaking point, Officer Niu relied on the squad leaders to maintain order. He knew that the wildest boys would pay more respect to their squad leaders than they would to their officers, and that most of the squad leaders understood how to take advantage of brotherhood loyalty.

Every time they planned to wade over the main drainage ditch, Black Head and Tiger would whisper in my ear: "We'll be back in forty minutes," and then they tilted their heads toward the village. I wouldn't ask them where they were going. It was important that I didn't give such an obvious consent. I never shook or nodded my head. Instead, I smiled and walked away.

After we were assigned to the rice fields, whenever Tiger and Black Head returned from such excursions, they would invite me to "booze" with them in a quiet corner against the bank of an irrigation ditch. The colorless, fiery liquor they bought in the village was sixty-five percent alcohol and made primarily from the local sorghum. It was raw and caustic.

I never drank hard alcohol at home, though my father was a champion drinker in his younger years. Even one beer would make my head swim. At the Farm, with my stomach and downtrodden spirits, the hard alcohol had an immediate effect. After two swallows I would forget all my troubles. Within ten minutes, I would find myself telling old stories that I would be ashamed to utter at other times. The feeling of inebriation was magnificent.

Now that we were mostly on our own, and the rice paddies of Black Head and Tiger were at the northern end of the field, it was quite convenient for them to cross the main drainage ditch and go to the village store. I set a condition on them, however, to do this no more than once every two weeks.

"I'll wash the fish," I said, and took the catch down to the drainage ditch. Meanwhile, the two boys began building the fire.

The water in the drainage ditch was dark green from the reflection of the tall grass growing at its side, and it looked much cleaner than the water in the irrigation ditch. I scaled and gutted the fish. When water at one spot became red with fish blood, I moved several feet away.

Tiger knelt in front of the fire blowing air on the dry grass to kindle it. A wisp of smoke rose along the trunk of the willow tree, spread into its dense leaves, and dissipated into the air. No one from the southern end of the fields could see the smoke.

The red dot in the dry grass enlarged to affect dry tree twigs around it. The fire rose timidly. Tiger was less careful in putting more twigs onto the fire now that the fire was going. Black Head washed an aluminum lunch box in the drainage ditch, filled it half full with drainage water, and placed it gingerly on the clay abutment around the fire. He rummaged through the pockets of his jacket, took a small package of old newspapers from one of them, and emptied the salt and dried chili pepper crumbs into the lunch box. Then he walked over to a bush and drew from behind it a sickle with which he chopped the larger fish into chunks small enough to fit into the lunch box. In five minutes the water began to simmer.

"Water's ready," Tiger raised his head to announce, his eyes watering from the smoke and heat. Black Head dropped the fish chunks one by one into the boiling water. The pink meat began immediately to turn white, oozing blood in thin threads. We broke sturdy grass stalks to serve as chopsticks and watched the fish pieces as they cooked.

Black Head picked out one chunk and turned it over to look at it. After a moment, he pronounced, "Time to eat." He plunged his improvised chopsticks into the box, and picked up the largest piece of fish. He shoved the fish into his mouth, and screamed out as the hot meat burnt his tongue and lips. After the burn had subsided, he grinned, "Mmmm...delicious." He slipped down the bank to a bush near a drainage ditch edge, still munching on the morsel, and withdrew a bottle of whiskey from behind the bush. There wasn't much left in it.

We ate the fish and took turns swigging from the bottle. From time to time Black Head would replenish the lunch box with more pieces of fish, while Tiger fed the fire. The two boys had broken some willow twigs for fuel and spread them in sunny spots to dry. But they were not dry enough. Tiger placed the damp twigs around the fire. When they were sufficiently dry, he pushed them on top of the flames and arranged more wet twigs around the fire, thus keeping the fire going for some time.

"Huang Longsen," Black Head said, his face flushing from alcohol and satisfaction with the fish. "How come they put you here? And why for three years! Your case must be serious. You're not one of us."

I didn't want to talk about why I was given three years of hard labor. I asked instead, "Not one of you, huh? And exactly who are you?"

"We," he guffawed, "are the hooligans, and thugs, and ruffians, and rapists, and pickpockets – 'social scum' as the guards call us. You don't steal, you don't play with girls, you don't fight in the street...so why did they send you here to eat pig feed, and work like a draft animal?"

"Because I said something my superiors didn't like," I confessed, feeling an oppressive cloud lifting for the first time since I arrived.

"I don't get it. What kind of things could you have said that would be that bad?" he persisted.

"You're too young to understand," I said.

"Don't play big brother," he retorted.

"I'm not playing big brother," I said seriously. "For one thing, I am not supposed to talk to you about my crimes. Besides, it would be dangerous for you to know about it." He looked at me as if to say, "give me a break." So I restated my plight in the words used by my superiors at the Bureau. "I'm here to be remolded through hard labor for my counter-revolutionary ideas." He still didn't seem to understand. "You know, against socialism and the Communist Party, and against the dictatorship of the proletariat," I added. "They accused me of making plans to overthrow the present government, and take control of the country." I was done explaining myself.

"You? Hah, hah, hah..." Both Black Head and Tiger burst out laughing, blowing bits of corn bun all over my face.

"Goodness gracious, dear grandmother!" Black Head exclaimed. "That's serious! Do you really want to take over the country?"

"Can I?" I asked.

"I don't know," Black Head said. "You seem to be able to. You're a natural leader. Even Officer Niu and Han Jen have taken to you."

"Nonsense!" Tiger grunted. "How could Huang Longsen take over the country? He has no army."

"He could rally up an army if the time was right," Black Head argued. "When the heavy famine comes, people will rise up against the rich. Then it'll be easy to raise an army. Many people in history have become emperors during times when the country was hit by famine."

"That would be wonderful, Huang Longsen," Tiger said. "You would be the emperor and we would be your generals. Then we would eat big chunks of pork, and drink all the best liquor in huge flower vases. I can see it now."

"Cut it out," I shouted. "Eat your fish, and drink your horse shit!"

The two boys looked at me, wondering what was wrong.

"I'm sorry," I said, calming myself. "but I can't stand this kind of talk. I was not playing big brother when I said you were too young to understand many things. I am thirteen years older than you are, and know this world better. I tell you the truth, I was brought here because I liked to make jokes just like you. Once, I said that some of the government officials were impotent, and that if I ever had power I would kill all the corrupt officials. I never thought anyone would report me, or accuse me of harboring hatred toward the government."

"The most hateful people are traitors," Tiger commented.

"I have a big mouth," I said. "and got rewarded for my use of it. Actually I've never dared to think of overthrowing anyone, even my department chief. I've never hurt anybody in my life. I still feel guilty for tricks I played on people in primary school."

I was suddenly feeling very bitter about my fate, and my eyes began to fill with tears. "Let's have more food and drink," I said as I gulped down a large shot from the bottle.

Black Head took it from me and gulped down an equal amount. "Huang Longsen, you're a good man," he said. "You mean well when you try to warn us about stuff. You're not like Chan Wen, or those others who always try to find fault with us young guys just so they can report it to the guards."

I grew tired of such heavy talk, and said, "All right. Let's forget all the bad shit for now. We've still got good fish and drink to enjoy. So tell me, you two cuisine experts, which restaurant in Beijing has the best fish dish."

By switching to this subject, I unintentionally ignited a heated argument between the two boys. It was amusing to watch these two try and outdo each other. One said it was Fengzeyuan because even Chairman Mao Zedong ate there. The other said Sichuan's Spicy Fish was the best because Deng Xiaoping and his close friends ate there almost every weekend.

"Sichuan people don't know how to eat fish," I told them. "I was with a bunch of Sichuanese in the army for six years. Some of them had never seen fish before they joined the army. They were afraid of eating fish because they didn't know how to pick out the bones. I don't blame them for being ignorant. Sichuan province is made up mostly of mountains." I wagged my finger at Tiger, "You should have learned your geography better at school."

He went on, however, to say that I had never put my foot inside a decent restaurant, and so I was completely and utterly ignorant about food. He then reminded me that the longest river, the Yangtze, passed through Sichuan province. "How can there be no fish in Sichuan?" He demanded.

I had no answer for that. He was right, and I was embarrassed.

A snake slithered passed us through the grass, and down into the drainage water. It was two and half feet long, as thick as a dough roller, dark green, and ugly. It moved lazily, having not recovered its vitality from winter hibernation. Perhaps it was driven out early from its underground nest by all the flooding. The two boys were a bit lethargic from the fish feast, and so they didn't bother to get up to run after it. At any other time that snake would have been skewed and roasting over a small fire in no time flat.

Watching the snake swim into the field, Black Head commented, "Huang Longsen, I'm not trying to run you down or anything, but you haven't really seen much of the world, have you? One's life is short, and we should make as much as we can out of it. Why should we be hard on ourselves? In Beijing, when we picked several dozen yuan from a rich man, we went to eat at the best restaurant. We had girls after us. Money, girls, what else does a man need? Yes, the guards may pick us up, from time to time. But, in the past five years, this is the first time I have really served a long term. Usually they keep us at a detention center for a couple of weeks, and then let us go. Most of the time the cops don't bother us. They are afraid of us, you know. If they can't find a way to put us away in a reform farm or prison, we make their lives miserable in the neighborhood.

"Remember Chi Fei, the guy who stayed behind at the Liangxiang Detention Center? He was a big player in the Qianmen area. He can give the appearance of being a harmless college student, but cross him and he can be your worst enemy. His handsome face deceives many people. Everybody says he's a good guy. Of course, the police know how good he is. He is the most famous pickpocket in the Qianmen area. When he saw a plainclothes guard in a crowded bus, he would walk over and put the tip of a knife against the man's side and say, 'Brother, you'd better get off at the next stop.' The guard would get off. He had half a dozen girls running after him all the time. But he's a decent guy – only one girl at a time for him.

"Anyway, the bottom line is that I've enjoyed five great years of crime to serve my two years here. You, on the other hand, haven't enjoyed anything, but got three years. See what I mean?"

"Are you trying to tell me that in order to get the most out of life, I should be stealing from others? Do you ever think about the people you steal from? I'm sure they wouldn't appreciate you benefiting from their losses." I said.

"Don't get me wrong," Black Head said. "I have a conscience. I never steal from poor people. It's just that, as I see it, some people have too much money to burn. So why shouldn't others, poor saps like myself, take some from them? It's not as if they're going to miss a couple of bucks here and there."

"That is the old outlaw's principle," I said, "to rob the rich to give to the poor, but this is a different time."

"See that's exactly what I'm talking about with you." Black Head said. "They put you in this damn place for living a decent life, and still, you stick to your hypocritical principles."

"But this is a peculiar period," I insisted. "Right now, the authorities are too busy dealing with political enemies. When the situation clears up and settles down, the police will have plenty of time to deal with criminal offenders. Don't waste your life when you have a chance to make it good."

"Hah! You sound like my eldest brother," Black Head sneered, and he took out a crumpled sheet of paper from his trouser pocket, and tossed it at me. "Read this, it's a letter from my brother."

His eldest brother was four years older, and used to be a playboy himself. After several years of cavorting, he had settled down and married one of his former girl friends.

"He now accuses me of leading a wasteful life," Black Head exploded, his young, handsome face glowing in the bright, afternoon sunshine. "He has enjoyed the best things he could get out of life. He used to collect a grand a month without lifting a finger, and he used to have half a dozen girls around him all the time. Now, since *he's* changed, he wants to tell me that *my* life is no good? Fuck that..."

Half a dozen girls, all gorgeously sexy and willing, and a grand every month! My wife's and my own salaries combined only came to nine hundred yuan a year!

"That fish hit the spot..." I said.

There was no more fish cooking in the lunch box. The soup had become milky white and thick. The crumbs of chili pepper were a lovely shade of red. Tiger removed the box from the fire, balancing it dangerously on his straw chopsticks. "Take a sip of the soup," he urged me.

I took the lunch box from him and sucked in some soup slowly. It was even tastier than the fish.

Although I had spent my childhood by a pond and my grandfather was a spare-time fisherman, no fish meal I had ever eaten, either at my native village or in Beijing, ever tasted better than the fish had we just feasted on in the wild fields, cooked in drainage ditch water, and with only salt and chili pepper as spices.

Black Head was probably right. In all my thirty-two years, I had never known a day as free as theirs. Bragging aside, many boys in the Big Compound had eaten at famous restaurants that I would never dare to go in, always painfully aware of my financial situation.

At the beginning of my school years, my father pressed me hard for good grades. Later I urged myself to learn, hoping one day to find gainful employment. Now I was in Chadian, at the bottom of society, with those who had been at the bottom of the society both outside and inside the labor farm. As I've heard lamented by others in my situation, I was now "eating food from the same filthy cauldron" as the lowlife which surrounded me. Tiger was right when he said he had enjoyed five years to serve a mere two years of hard labor, while I had not enjoyed anything, but somehow managed to get three years.

But, did this mean that I should want to be more like them than I already was?

The snake came back over the drainage ditch, perhaps having found nothing in the flooded rice paddies. All the mice and rats had already been driven from their holes.

Black Head stood up, raised his spade, and struck the snake as it neared his feet. Stupid snake, I thought. It must be its destiny to end up in Black Head's hand. The wounded snake writhed painfully on the ground. Black Head picked it up by the tail, swung it savagely around in the air and knocked its head against a dry lump of earth.

"Hold the head," he said to Tiger, who grabbed the creature's tiny head tightly so it wouldn't be able to bite if it revived. Black Head then took out a pocket knife and began to make a round incision around the snake's neck. His movements were unhesitating, precise, and quick, like those of a surgeon. I wondered if he had ever cut a human being with such impassiveness. A regular threat made by him and Tiger to other inmates was: "I'll put a white knife in you and draw it out red."

Having completed the incision, Black Head gripped the broken edge of the snake skin with the forefinger and thumb of both hands and pulled downward with a sudden force. The skin slipped down the body of the snake, inside out, and peeled smoothly off at the tail. The snake's pinkish flesh seemed to quiver. Black Head threw the skin into the drainage ditch.

Snakes must have many lives as some people say. Without its head and skinned, the snake still writhed. I found myself wondering again: what might a human being be like if his head was suddenly cut off?

Black Head laid the snake on a spot free of grass, cut its belly open, and pulled the guts out. Examining the tangle of organs, he raised them and pointed at a tiny, dark green ball with his index finger tip for me to see. "This is the gall bladder," he said. "Guangdong people eat it whole. They say it can strengthen eyesight. We northerners don't even eat snake meat. It's really a pity."

"Do you eat snake gall bladders?" Tiger said, more as a challenge than a question.

Black Head said nothing, but separated the bladder meticulously with his fingers from the tiny liver leaves, snapped the dark green ball off, held it up over his head, and dropped it into his waiting mouth. He then picked up the bottle and took a swallow to wash down the gall bladder. I winced and felt a movement of upheaval starting in my stomach.

"If we had not had such wonderful fish meal, we could have a snake stew," Black Head said. I turned my eyes away from the bloody spot where the snake's heart throbbed and its gutted body twisted slowly.

Seeing my expression, he said, "Snake meat is a delicacy in Guangdong, you know. They have great dishes such as Two Dragons Playing with a Pearl, Dragon Jelly, Dragon and Phoenix Paying Respect to the Sun, and Battle Between Dragon and Tiger, Dragon referring to the snake, Phoenix to the chicken and Tiger to the cat. Guangdong people are notorious for eating just about anything. The only thing on the ground with four legs that they won't eat is a table; the only thing flying that they won't eat is an airplane. They eat rats, maggots, rice worms, live monkeys' brains, and anything else you could imagine. They let pork rot in order to breed maggots. And not just those gray, filthy maggots in the Big Compound latrine. I'm talking about big, shiny white ones by the millions.

"Chairman Mao once invited the Soviet president, what's his name? Aw, forget it. Who cares what his name is...all foreigners have such strange, long names. Anyway, the two leaders had the dish Battle Between Dragon and Tiger. The Soviet president wouldn't go near the snake. It was whole, you know, with head and tail coiling in the center of a big platter. Chairman Mao ate a mouthful to show the Soviet there was no harm. So the Soviet had a small bite. That evening he complained to Chairman Mao that he had a stomach ache. Chairman Mao told him the tiger and dragon were fighting in his tummy."

I had never eaten a snake dish and didn't know what it would be like, but I was sure it wouldn't look very appetizing with the whole snake on the table, no matter how well the Guangdong people prepared it.

11

An Errand to General Headquarters

Odd assignments, such as helping transport coal, raw building materials and fertilizer from the railway station, or repairing houses and roads in the Officer's Village and general headquarters, were in high demand among the inmates. Only at those times could we feel a connection to the outside world, see faces other than those of the officers and each other, and see some of the local women. If we were lucky, we might even have a bite of a cake, given to us by sympathetic farm workers. Some of the more courageous might purchase something to eat with cash they had secretly obtained from visiting relatives.

In late May, the rice shoots had grown a foot tall and had shed their tender green color. The warehouse needed to be restocked with fertilizer. Master Chao was going to the general headquarters to fetch it, and he needed two inmates to help with the loading and unloading. Officer Niu asked me to go along, and take someone with me. That he let me choose a companion was a huge display of trust. Officers always reserved inmate selection for themselves.

I could have just gone back to the row house, and picked out someone from my squad, but I wanted to let Officer Niu know that I still remembered my place at all times, and that I would pay the required respect to all the officers. So I suggested to him, "How about Sun Pu?"

"Sure, he's all right, I suppose. Go ahead and take him," he said.

I went over to Han Jen's squad room, and told him I was being sent to the general headquarters to transport fertilizer and would like to borrow Teacher Sun to go with me. I told him Officer Niu had agreed. He smiled, knowingly, and said, "Whoever you want from my squad." He must have been thinking the same thing that I was. Namely, that this would be a perfect opportunity to explore why the teacher had slept with another woman, when he had such a beautiful wife.

Teacher Sun and I checked out at the gate of the Big Compound, walked fifty yards to the northeastern corner of the high wall, and followed a short driveway south to enter the Small Compound.

The wall of the Small Compound was lower than that of the Big Compound and had no barbed wire or red electric bulbs above it. The driveway was deeply rutted with rubber and wooden wheel grooves, and cattle hooves. Two row houses in the northern part of the Small Compound were identical to those inside the Big Compound. One of them consisted of sleeping rooms for the three farm workers and their kitchen. The other was a warehouse, which held farm tools, fertilizer, seeds, ropes, spare machine parts, and an enormous assortment of odds and ends. The southern half of the compound contained stables and a cow shed.

Tiger and Black Head took every opportunity they could to sneak into the southern part and scavenge there. Besides the salt that they used for cooking living things that they caught in the fields, they made away with handfuls of corn and black beans, which they roasted over small grass fires.

We followed the lead of the Big Compound veterans, calling the three workers of the Small Compound our "Masters." They served as instructors in farm work, warehouse keepers, farm tool maintenance men, teamsters and herdsmen over the five milk cows. The other inmates didn't think much of them. They were, after all, only ex-inmates. I, however, liked talking to them. I felt that we had much in common.

Every day one of the three workers – Master Chao, more often than the others – came to the rice fields to check our work. They had learned over the past fourteen years to keep a safe distance from any discussion which centered around dangerous political subjects, and to camouflage their bitter grievances in seemingly light-hearted jokes. They avoided engaging in long conversations with inmates. If they ever heard an inmate shouting curses at the farm authorities, they would simply walk away.

At first these three workers treated me with caution, but I was always straightforward with them. I knew I would win their sympathy if I was honest and told them that it was wrong for me to have been put into a labor reform farm and that the various political campaigns had wronged too many people. I had little fear of the consequences of such statements, for I knew none of them would report on me.

They soon came to understand my bitterness, sarcasm, and cynicism. After several conversations with them, I learned about their backgrounds too. Without their having to say it, I knew what they were driving at. Thus we developed a safe way of communication – we talked by innuendo.

Master Chao was the most open among the three. He and I talked quite often. He had just turned twenty-one when the murderous campaign against Rightists began in the spring of 1957. He, a senior of Chinese literature at Beijing University, was an intern at a literary magazine. At the time, the Communist Party called on the whole country to criticize and expose the mistakes and shortcomings of its leadership and members. Some of his classmates wrote criticisms against the school authorities with ink brushes on huge pieces of paper. They pasted these on the walls of the university. The campus was filled with such criticism posters.

Since Chao was considered an easy-going guy, he wasn't concerned with these political affairs. "They are too complex for my simple head," he would say when questioned by his colleagues about his opinions of the posters. He never worried about anything, even the fact that he had no girlfriend.

He also had no misgivings about stating his opinion of the Communists' misdeeds when his classmates talked. But as for writing them down, there was not a chance. "It's a waste of one's time and energy to write political criticisms," he said to his classmates. "Political tides rise and fall. Only universal themes last. I'd rather write a love letter to a girlfriend than compose a criticism poster. In fact, if any one of you is willing to be my girlfriend, I'll guarantee hundreds of long letters from me. I'd promise to send you two every day. Any takers?"

The girls hooted at him.

But his more politically intense classmates didn't find his words so charming. "We're helping the Communist Party improve its workings so that it can lead us to build a strong and prosperous China," they would impart. "You're the king of letters in our class. You must write some posters to demonstrate your talent."

It seemed as if everyone was busy writing these giant-sized posters. Chao began to feel like the most idle person in Beijing. It made him feel uncomfortable that his classmates, after writing or reading the giant-sized criticism posters, would steal out to the ruins of the Old Summer Palace – just a short walk from the university – without inviting him.

Although it was forbidden for students to engage in courtship during the four school years, all his classmates had been able to find future life partners among the other students. He did not try to do so because he didn't want to break the rules. Of course, the other students had to keep their prospects for marriage secret from the Party branch secretary who was in charge of ideological work in the department.

One night Chao was sitting alone in the dormitory, extremely bored. He was thinking about how he needed a girlfriend. Many classes had been disbanded to leave more time for the teachers and students to raise their political criticisms. Because Chao was not interested in such things, he had little to do. It was too lonely to sit and read in the library.

People said it would be difficult to find an ideal spouse after leaving the school. By then, the young men and women who had remained single throughout the school days would be taking jobs that would scatter all over the country. He began to think about the girls in his class and realized that all fourteen of them had boyfriends now. There were twenty-five boys in his class.

Then he thought about the girls in the junior classes, and realized he wouldn't be able to find one among them either. He just didn't know how to approach any of them. Though many of the girls on the campus liked to hang out and joke with him, none took him seriously, because *he* didn't take them seriously. He found the notion of approaching a girl and asking her to be his girlfriend absolutely ridiculous.

So he was alone, lonely and bored.

There was a stack of paper in various colors on the desk in his dormitory room, as well as ink and brushes. His three roommates had brought them back from the classroom. He decided to write a criticism poster expressing his opinion, and in two hours finished a long political essay advising the Communist cadres on how to run the school properly.

His essay began, "The decisions made by Communist Party officials in our school are arbitrary." The style was straightforward, a type often characterized by the saying, "as soon as the gate is opened, one sees the mountains."

He continued, "They are like patriarchs running the house during the Middle Ages. They tell us when to eat, when to piss, when to go to bed, when to get up, what we should say and not say, and what we should think and not think. Their comprehensive instructions fall just short of spoonfeeding. In sum, we are made to follow their orders in every physical and mental movement. They treat us as if we were toddlers in kindergarten. Of course, they mean well – they are afraid we may fall and break our teeth, or learn bad manners. But this is a university in the 20th century, and the world is talking about sending men into outer space. Please, beloved Communist leaders, don't always look over your shoulders. And please leave the scholars and specialists alone to run the school."

He then went on to cite concrete examples of how arbitrary the Communist cadres were, examples such as the way they blew a whistle and went into every room to rouse the students for morning drill, and how they cut off electric power to the dormitory to get the students in bed, and so on and so forth.

In one separate line he wrote with a bold brush: "Stop giving orders!" He left a large space at the end of the poster to write in still larger characters the ever-shouted slogan: "Long live the glorious, correct, and great Communist Party!"

When his classmates returned and read his work, they cheered him and endorsed his poster as a masterpiece of political thought. Chao felt very heroic. He was soon composing larger posters.

In May, the Chinese Communist Party Central Committee mounted a counterattack against the nationwide criticisms, which came mainly from professional people of higher learning. The criticisms were becoming more and more ardent and vehement. Then suddenly, they became a threat to Communist rule.

People's Daily, the mouthpiece of the Communist Party, ran an editorial which denounced the social critics for "fishing in troubled waters." Many famous scholars and social activists were openly attacked as anti-Communist Party elements. Beijing University president Ma Yinchu, a world-renowned scholar in demography, was severely criticized for his advocacy of a government program to control the population growth rate. The Party propagandists called him a Malthusian thinker. It was said that Chairman Mao Zedong himself refuted Ma Yinchu by stating that "the largest wealth of China is its people."

The time was no longer healthy for criticism. Most

people stopped writing these criticism posters, and took care to avoid controversial topics in their conversation.

The Communist Party coined a new label to describe those whose criticism posters most offended them. They called these people "new born counter-revolutionaries" and "Rightists" – labels which encompassed all persons who "attacked the Communists with evil notions." A dozen of Chao's schoolmates were labeled as such.

Chao stopped composing criticism posters and, as a matter of fact, seldom stayed on campus. As soon as a class ended, he would ride his bike into town, and while away his time at home. His parents, both middle school teachers, became worried about his restlessness and short temper. They warned him to lay low to let the storm pass.

By the end of the year, Chao was summoned to the office of the Party secretary of his department. The summons verified the apprehension that had haunted him for several months.

"Chao," the Party secretary greeted him with a very solemn expression on his face. "Sit down." Chao sat down on the edge of a chair near the door, three yards from the Party secretary's desk.

"I sent for you to tell you something," the Party secretary said. "Our Party branch went over the criticisms you wrote and found all of them to be groundless, and a great many to be slanderous. Some of the remarks you've made have been anti-socialist and anti-Communist Party."

Chao began to feel a cold wave sweep inward from his extremities. He shivered inwardly. Anti-socialism and anti-Communism? Good heavens! These were the most grave accusations that could be made against a Chinese citizen.

He was too scared to protest.

"But we think you are still young and might have said some of these things without thinking them over very carefully," he heard the Party secretary drone on from somewhere far away. "So we decided not to classify you as a Rightist. Instead, we have asked the Beijing

Security Bureau to put you in a labor reform farm to remold your thinking."

The Party secretary stood up, poured some water from a thermos bottle into a porcelain cup and placed it on the window sill near Chao, who was beginning to sweat along his spine and forehead.

The Party secretary, a veteran Communist of thirty years, feared Chao might fall off the chair, and so he steadied the young man by placing his hand on his back. "Chao," the Party secretary said, "behave well and work hard at the labor reform farm. After you are reformed through hard labor, you can put your intelligence to better use in serving our socialist country. Is there anything you want to say?"

Chao didn't know what to say. His mind was whirling frantically. Dazed, he walked out of the Party secretary's office. Many years later, he recalled the vague expression of pity on the Party official's face.

In the middle of 1958, Chao and several hundred other citizens who had been labeled "Rightists" were packed onto a train, and sent to Chadian. Still more were sent to the wilderness in the far Northeast. At the outset, there was no definite time frame specifying what terms these labor reform elements would serve. Some months later, the Beijing Public Security Bureau set the term, the longest being three years. All the Rightists at Chadian served full terms.

During the fourteen years since that time, only a few who had strong contacts had been able to find their way back to jobs in Beijing. The majority were assigned jobs on the farm, now mostly working at the farm factories. Master Chao, Master Huan, and Master Fang had been assigned to help the officers at Farm 583 look after the fields. They had never made any trouble, and were regarded as trustworthy.

Comparatively, they had much more freedom than those working in the workshops. They could move around freely without being under an officer's surveillance, and could work or rest pretty much as they pleased.

Over the past decade, they had learned all the skills a farm hand needs. They knew how to plow; how to sow; how to care for the corn, sorghum, and rice fields; how to repair tools; how to milk the cows; how to handle minor machine problems; when and what kind of fertilizer to apply; when and how much water to retain in the rice paddies; and many other things. They knew more about farming than any officer at Farm 583, and so they were indispensable. Master Fang also treated the inmates when they became ill since he was a medical intern at the time he was branded as a "Rightist."

Among the three Small Compound workers only Master Fang, the oldest, had a family. He was married before 1957, and his wife didn't divorce him as many other wives of Rightists did. She raised their daughter and a son single-handedly on her own salary of only fifty yuan a month.

Master Chao was short and solid. His muscular arms and legs moved fast, like the pistons of a truck engine, when he walked from one plot to another checking the water level in the rice fields. In all the years he had been confined to the farm, he had roughened not only his muscles but also his manner and language. Unlike the other two, who had retained some of their scholastic manners, Master Chao could be mistaken, at times, for one of the older ruffians.

Master Huan and Master Fang kept a peaceful distance from the young inmates, while Master Chao liked to mix it up with them. He, himself, exuded a youthful cheerfulness, and he had managed to extract a certain degree of respect from the boys by knocking one of them out. "I've seen many tougher guys than you," he had said coolly to the young man who refused to follow his instructions in the field, and was threatening him with a spade. "You'd better be prepared to use that thing. Well, don't just stand there like a tree! Come on, let's see what you've got!"

The young man looked around for help from his "brothers." But no one wanted to declare a clear stand against Master Chao. They diverted their eyes to some-thing in the drainage ditch. The young man loosened his grip on the spade and began digging. One would never have believed that fourteen years earlier, this short, middle-aged Master Chao had been a top student at the prestigious Beijing University, majoring in Chinese lit-erature.

Presently, he was harnessing two horses onto the cart as Teacher Sun and I walked into the yard of the Small Compound. He said he was glad I would be assisting him, and not someone else.

Although he was rough on other jobs, Master Chao was tender with the horses. "That fool eats plain buns but feeds the horses eggs," Black Head once said. "You know why he is so nice to the animals? He fucks them at night."

Master Chao did keep eggs for the stock horse in a safe place, and would be angry if the horses' fodder was stolen, though he didn't seem to mind the occasional loss of salt which he had stored specifically for the animals.

Soon the three of us were off. Turning around onto the road along the irrigation canal, Master Chao cracked his long whip in midair and the horses raised their heads high and started into a lively trot.

My squad was crossing the canal at the time. Every-one turned their heads to watch, so I kept talking with Master Chao to avoid looking at them. Black Head and Tiger wouldn't be happy if they learned that Officer Niu had let me choose a partner for the wonderful job, and that I didn't choose either of them.

The drainage ditch on the south side of the road was filled with water that came from the rice paddies, bring-ing along the alkali in the soil. Reeds were shooting out of its edge in lush green. As we went past the Officer's Village, I remembered a question I had long wanted to ask Master Chao: "You are already thirty-eight," I said. "Why aren't you married?"

"Me, married?" Master Chao laughed heartily. "How could I hope to support a family on thirty-five yuan a month? Anyway, no woman would marry a counter-revolutionary like me. Besides, even if a woman were willing to marry me, I wouldn't marry her. To be alone is wonderful. After you have had a full meal, you don't have to worry if the world is starving.

"Sure Master Fang has a family, but is he happy with his wife and two kids? Good God, I don't know how they've survived. He only goes home to Beijing once or twice a year. I know I wouldn't go back more often. Why *should* he? Just to see his kids in rags, eating plain cabbage? 'Out of sight, out of mind.' That's his philosophy of life.

"My philosophy is 'When there's wine, enjoy it. Don't worry about whether it will be there tomorrow.' With a record like mine, I wouldn't be any happier outside of Chadian. Here I have the horses, and I can fish when I want to. We have a little garden behind the Small Compound where we grow vegetables enough for the three of us. Sometimes I think my life here is easier than any government minister's life in Beijing. I don't have to worry about losing anything because I don't have anything to lose. They leave me alone because I am already at the bottom of the society. You see there *is* an advantage to being disadvantaged."

I nodded my head, but doubted if he really thought this. If there were a chance for him to get an office job in Beijing, even just to copy manuscripts for others, he would probably jump at it. Doing manual work was a waste of his extensive learning. And he had to live in submission. For a learned and proud man, such a life was a constant humiliation. The only way for him to be able to live was to disguise his bitterness in a cynical and sarcastic philosophy.

Master Chao straightened his back a little to make himself more comfortable against the cart fender. His short legs were dangling beneath the cart shaft, and his Big Cannon was hissing as he drew the pungent smoke deeply into his lungs.

"In the beginning of the world," he continued, "what a man needed was to find enough food for his stomach.

When the climate got cold, he skinned an animal and wrapped its hide around his body to keep himself warm. Only later, when man got more food than he needed did he begin to think of other things. Now people work themselves to death for wealth, power, fame – things they don't really need at all. 'When a person is too warm or too full, he becomes greedy and evil.' That's what our ancestors taught us thousands of years ago. We all know it's true, but few have internalized the warning. I think I have now. I have no desires, and enjoy the few things I do have."

He puffed on his Big Cannon to bring it alive. Tiny sparks jumped out of the lit tip, and dropped on his lap. He brushed the ashes and unburned tobacco bits onto the road, and spit nicotine-diluted saliva into the drainage ditch. His trousers and shirt had many small burnholes caused by smoldering tobacco.

Master Chao's philosophical talk reminded me of what Pockmark often said to the younger men in my squad, only Pockmark did it in much coarser language.

The warehouse took up two-thirds of the southern side of the yard at the general headquarters. We stopped in the shade of a locust tree in front of it. Master Chao propped a sturdy stick under the shaft on the driver's side to lift the weight of the cart off the horses.

The warehouse gate was locked. Its keeper was nowhere to be found.

"I'm going to look for him," Master Chao said. "You two can have a look around. Don't worry about the horses. They won't move a step from where they are until I give the order." He patted both horses on their necks, affectionately. "Oh, and if you want to buy something, I can lend you some money," he added.

I said, "Thanks, but I don't think we want to buy anything."

Of course, I actually wanted desperately to buy a cake or two, some candies, or anything edible from the store. It was on the north side of the yard opposite the warehouse, a mere fifty feet away. Master Chao offered to lend

me money only to make me feel at ease. He couldn't expect me to repay him because I wouldn't have any cash
until I was released in two years. How could I possibly
accept money from him when he was paid only thirty-
five yuan a month? That was barely enough for three
meals a day. And his position was only little better than
that of an inmate in the eyes of the police. He might receive a dressing down for giving me money to buy things
from the police store.

"All right," Master Chao said. "Wait for me here then."

Teacher Sun and I sat on the steps of the warehouse
in the shade of its eaves. We didn't walk around because
we didn't want to cause unnecessary embarrassment to
ourselves. Our appearance was too conspicuous as it was.
I didn't doubt that some policemen, especially their sons,
might become combative.

The yard was quiet, unlike when we first arrived from
the railway station. Then it was lunch time and officers
and their families had been coming in and out of the
kitchen. Now, there were only the buildings and the three
of us.

The red brick row house on the northern side of the
yard contained the kitchen, the store, and several offices.
The west side housed the auditorium, where free films
were shown on weekends to the farm community, and to
which we had been taken twice attending punish-reward
meetings. It was said, in the late 1950s, a large number
of actors and actresses were rounded up in Beijing because of their rotten life styles, and sent to Chadian. Some
were quite famous. The farm authorities often entreated
them to perform in this auditorium.

The ugly structure of red brick and tile, however, had
long outlived those glorious years. Missing glass in the
windows had been replaced by plywood; the cement pave-
ment around its base was cracked, and its wooden doors
were tied with thick steel wires.

The boiler room and bathhouse were situated behind
the auditorium. This was where the inmates were allowed bath once a month during the cold season. More

office rooms and multi-purpose rooms comprised the row houses to the north of the auditorium, behind the store and kitchen.

A tiny stream flowing from north to south in front of the entrance to the general headquarters was the earliest irrigation canal here. It was built by the Japanese four decades earlier, and was now out of use. An abandoned turbine waterwheel, driven by steam, and a rusted boiler to the west on the stream were all that remained from the years of Japanese occupation. Young reeds sprouted abundantly in the thick layer of garbage and debris that lay along the banks of the stream.

The inside of the store was dark. I strained my eyes to see if I could make out what was on the shelves. But from my place on the south side of the yard, it was impossible. I gave up looking, and started to imagine that I had become invisible and was walking into the store to pick up links of sausage, pieces of cake, and a bottle of sweetened grape wine.

"I hear you got three years for political reasons," Teacher Sun said suddenly. "Right?"

I looked at him, finding an honest curiosity and nodded my head.

"It is feudal and stupid to punish people for airing their political opinions," the teacher said vehemently. I was surprised, wondering if he was trying to ingratiate himself with me.

"Yes. Stupid," he emphasized. "That's why China won't make progress very quickly. Since 1949, when the Communist Party took over the mainland, there have been numerous political campaigns. In each of these, many were wrongly condemned. They are like a draw net pulled through a narrow river: Only the most cunning fish could escape.

"The three workers of the Small Compound didn't steal, didn't do any harm to society. But they have been here for many years, like petty criminals. They had college educations, but these were wasted. For what? A few remarks the powers that be didn't like. The anti-Rightist campaign in 1957 killed far too many highly educated people. These people were the pillars of our Chinese nation. Since 1957, no one with a right mind dares to say what he really thinks.

"How old are you? Must be too young to understand what happened in 1957. For good or bad, I am ten years older, and I remember. Several of the best teachers in my college were labeled Rightists. They did nothing, but were arrested for writing a couple of poems and prose pieces. At that time, the central authorities set quotas for each unit, quotas to ferret out Rightists, like the designation of witches in Europe during the Middle Ages. The teachers in my college had worse luck than the three workers of the Small Compound. They were sent to a wilderness in the far Northeast. You see, the authorities strangled the most learned people by attaching political tags to their necks, like dog licenses."

His words showed me he was a good school teacher, knowledgeable, and eloquent.

"Don't you feel bitter?" He asked.

"I did in the beginning," I said, "but now I'm indifferent. I understand China better. The Communists are no different from any other rulers in Chinese history. They came from peasant families to start a revolt, using well-worded slogans, designed to win people's support. They might have actually believed in what they were advocating in the early war years. But after they came into power, they became just another batch of court officials and local magistrates, building personal privileges and accumulating wealth. Now, anyone who dares to challenge their power is crushed. Chinese history is filled with these kinds of power struggles. Of course, you know more than I do in this respect."

Teacher Sun smiled modestly.

"China is too poor," I said, hearing no comment from him, "and the populace is too poorly educated. It's just not possible for a few enlightened people to change it in such a short time. Reformists have never succeeded in changing it, including Sun Yat-sen and those among the

Communists. I learned that too late. Like the three workers of the Small Compound, I was a fool for a while and now I'm paying for it. It's nobody's fault, but my own. I'm not bitter any more. I've been making plans to live the rest of my life in my own way, for myself."

Two young policewomen came out of the store, laughing about something. The same baggy uniform all the police wore looked smart on them. Their gait was erect and proud, quite different from most of the local officers. I decided they must have come from Beijing.

The policewomen looked briefly in our direction, and resumed their conversation. I didn't think they had noticed us. We, the labor reform elements, were invisible when we didn't cause trouble. My desire to look at them turned sour.

"See how arrogant they are," I commented, "nothing but guards," and immediately I felt incoherent and silly. Teacher Sun looked at the policewomen and lowered his eyes to his trousers. The patches on the knees were of two different colors with uneven stitches.

Our conversation had been intimate, and I felt good for having someone trustworthy to talk with so freely. Teacher Sun was older than me and better educated.

"Teacher Sun," I said tentatively.

"Eh?" he looked up, inquiringly.

"May I ask you a question?"

"Shoot."

"Those who saw your wife on her visit told me she was very beautiful. Why did you, eh, well... have an affair with someone else?"

I thought he would be reluctant to talk about it, or be annoyed at my having asked. But his face didn't change color, which to me meant he was neither ashamed nor angry at my probing.

"Human feelings are strange things," he said thoughtfully. "I knew then, and still know now that my wife was much more beautiful than the girl I was with. Every time I slept with that girl, I would feel guilty and regret my decision. I tried telling myself never to sleep with her again." He paused, and chuckled a bit. "When she was naked, I compared her body with that of my wife. Her waist was much thicker, her shoulders wider, and her stomach was like an overripe watermelon. But when she asked me to go to her room, I went, like a piece of iron attracted to a magnet. I just couldn't help it. Sleeping with that girl was much more enjoyable than any sex I'd ever had with my wife." He picked a weed from the ground and twirled it between his thumb and forefinger. "The saying is true that wild flowers smell sweeter than the flowers at home. Maybe it was her youthful vitality and frankness about sex that drew me to her. Ah hell, it was probably just a mid-life crisis."

Teacher Sun sounded quite rational.

"How's your wife?" he switched the subject abruptly. "I mean how does she treat you?"

"She looks after me well," I said. "But she can be overbearing at times."

"That's exactly what I mean," Teacher Sun said. "I realized later why I went to bed with another woman. My wife cared too much for me. She would examine me to see if I had buttoned up my shirt, tied my shoe strings and combed my hair properly. When we walked on the street, she would constantly remind me to straighten up, not to put my hands in my pockets, not to spit, not to do this and not to do that. I would become very irritated, and would end up brushing her off like the imaginary lint she thought she was picking. Sometimes, I would shout, 'I am not a kindergarten boy!' in public to embarrass her into ending her grooming."

"But she loved you," I reminded him.

"That's true. She still loves me. Any other woman might have divorced me, but she sticks by me."

"Do you feel like you've let her down?"

"Yes, I do. She always meant well when she picked at me. I should have let her know that I didn't like such picking when we were first married. She might not have become like that. Take my advice, Huang Longsen, let your wife know if you want more independence. Don't wait until it's too late."

I looked up. The two policewomen had come back around the northern row of the houses, swaggering in their usual manner.

"I can't complain about my wife," I said. "I won't ever be able to repay her for all of her kindness in all my life. Many of my friends who have been incarcerated and labeled 'counter-revolutionaries' have been abandoned by their wives. My wife has never complained despite all the disgrace, inconveniences and vicious chiding my situation has brought on her. How could I ever complain about her being overbearing? I simply won't, no matter how trifling she may be."

Teacher Sun then said, his tone unchanged, "Don't misunderstand me, Huang Longsen. I only meant that if you and your wife can understand each other better, life will be easier for both of you. I no longer have any right to complain. I am only grateful to my wife for staying by me. After I am released, I will do whatever I can to please her."

"Tell me something," I said, no longer worried about causing embarrassment or hard feelings in Teacher Sun. "Many people have had affairs with women, but didn't end up in here. Why did you?"

"Ever heard the saying that 'if the common people don't report you, then the magistrate won't bother you'?" Teacher Sun asked flatly, as if he was talking about another man's problem. "The girl was a fellow teacher. She was twenty-four. Twenty-four is considered old for a woman to have no boyfriend, but she didn't seem to mind. In fact, I doubt if she wanted to marry at all. I often felt she was using me to fill her boredom." He chuckled as he released the weed from between his fingers. "Our affair only lasted for two months before the principal discovered us. He had an eye on the girl too. I'm damned sure of that. She wasn't exactly pretty, but she was attractive in her own way. The principal was jealous of me, so he reported us to the education board. He made the girl accuse me of seducing her, but that wasn't enough. He pushed for having me do three years in labor reform. The education board, in their infinite wisdom, decided two years was enough, and neglected to take away my teacher's certificate."

"You must hate that bastard for putting you here."

"As a matter of fact, I don't hate or blame the principal anymore, only myself. A man over forty should learn to control himself. I couldn't. So I take the blame and the punishment with no hatred toward any of them.

"Everyone has desires. The question is how to prevent them from expanding too much. You may not believe it, Huang Longsen, but I'm not much interested in women. I don't know why I started this affair in the first place. Only way I can explain it is to say that human feelings are strange..." He stopped talking and looked up at the locust tree. Several sparrows chirped noisily in it. The two horses neighed. Master Chao had not come back.

"Fate," Teacher Sun concluded. "Everything is predestined. 'All is set by fate. It is useless to toil against it.'"

"You don't sound much like a teacher," I observed good-naturedly. "Did you teach predestination to your students?"

"No, of course not," Teacher Sun laughed dryly. "I never considered it at that time, but I believe in it more and more these days."

Master Chao came back. "That motherfucker!" he cursed. "That bastard warehouse keeper must be drinking horse piss this early in the morning. You know what he said when I asked him to come over? He said, 'Go fuck your horses.' I wanted to smash in his pig face, and tell him that I had already fucked his mother..."

Master Chao slumped down to the steps next to me. I could feel the burning anger inside him so I tried to calm him down, "Don't bother with that ignorant bastard. We'll just wait here until he comes out." Seeing his outward frustration, I actually felt my own anger toward them subside. "The morning's still early," I said cheerily.

"All my thirteen years here , I've tried not to be bothered by such things," Master Chao said bitterly. "But every once in a while, I feel like I can't take it any more. On this farm a pig is given more respect than I am. Everyone has the right, and almost the duty to swear at you and intimidate you. And, if you dare fight back, they find a new way to torment."

I looked at him with concern. He had always seemed to be the most carefree among the three workers of the Small Compound. His motto of life was well known, and had been copied by many: "When my stomach is full, I don't care if the whole world is starving." He could always make light-hearted jokes when an officer picked on him. "I don't have a wife," he would say, "so I don't know how it would feel to be slapped in the face by my son." Now his outburst of anger showed that his self-esteem was not yet fully eroded.

"What are they?" Master Chao demanded. "Ignorant peasants wrapped in guard uniforms! What do they know? Their shoes, when they're not in bed, and the wives' asses when they're in bed! I would vomit if they offered their women to me for a fuck. Those motherfuckers..."

I found myself enjoying his string of curses, feeling somehow assuaged and vindicated by them. I wanted to swear, and to curse all of them with the foulest words I had learned in my childhood: "Your mother is so smelly, I wouldn't screw even if you paid me," one of the curses went, "but I would make her happy with a dough roller greased in sesame oil."

Teacher Sun stood up, looking around uneasily.

I said to Master Chao, "If you haven't changed your mind, I would like to borrow one yuan to buy a few cakes."

Master Chao turned his face to me, blinked his small eyes, and rubbed his chin with his left hand. "See what a fool I was," he said, relaxing the muscles of his jaw and cheeks rapidly. "Why in the hell did I work myself up so much, wasting my energy, on a stupid, drunkard cop. You wait here, and I'll go and buy something for the two of you to eat. These bastards at the store may not sell things to you, but may instead report on you for keeping cash."

He stood up and walked across the yard. His bow-legged gait was even more pronounced as the sun shone between his legs. "I was on the soccer team at Beijing University," he would brag when he was teased about his bow legs. "Like riding a horse, playing soccer makes you bow-legged after a while."

Soon, he was swallowed by the dark door frame of the small store. Within five minutes, he walked out, a package wrapped in an old newspaper in his hand. He spread the package on the steps. The six cakes looked to be at least a week old, dry and cracking. "Eat them up," Master Chao invited.

"I'm not hungry," Teacher Sun said, standing there and looking away.

"This is not the time for false modesty," I said, and pulled him down. So each of us had two cakes, which eased the ache in my stomach, and reminded me of the saying: "When one is hungry, anything will taste as sweet as honey."

Master Chao folded the old newspaper wrapper, gathered the cake crumbs in the bottom of the fold, and tipped the paper to slide them onto his hand. Then he licked up all the greasy crumbs that lay in his palm.

By the time we loaded our cart with bags of fertilizer, some rope and spade handles, the sun was approaching noon. "You'll miss your lunch," Master Chao said. "On second thought, don't even worry about it. If they didn't save any for you, I'll see if I can get you something from the officer's kitchen."

The three Small Compound workers were entitled to eat with the officers. They never did, but instead cooked for themselves on an outdoor stove that burned dry crop stalks and tree branches.

"I'm sure Officer Niu will tell the kitchen to stay open for us," I said. I didn't want to put Master Chao in an uncomfortable situation by forcing him to consort with the officers in order to get our lunch.

It had gotten quite warm. The asphalt surface on the

road was uncomfortably soft against the tires. The horses' hooves seemed to trudge on rubber cement sheeting. But the two horses still held their heads high. After we passed the wooden bridge which marked the beginning of Farm 583, our cart began to skip over the dried-out ruts in the road. Master Chao told me later that he hitched the horses in such a way that their heads were always held high. Master Chao's mood now became as merry as that of the horses. He played with his whip expertly, cracking it sharply in midair. The report was musical. But he fell silent and impassive whenever an officer came into sight.

A group of children had finished morning classes at the general headquarters and were returning to the Officer's Village for lunch. The boys ran after the cart, wanting to hang on to the tail gate.

"Old chap Chao," one called out, "give us a ride!"

Without looking over his shoulder, Master Chao swung his whip backward. I turned to see the braided tip sweep menacingly just an inch over the boys' heads. They released their grip on the railing, cursing, "Old chap Chao, you rotten Rightist. You will die childless!"

"Have your mothers told you where you came from?" he shouted to the boys. "Because I fucked all of them!" He laughed uproariously, his eyes lost in the folds of the thick lids.

The boys swore and threw lumps of dirt at Master Chao. He cracked his long whip three more times, and the horses picked up speed, leaving the children behind.

We reached the entrance to the Officer's Village, marked by two wooden poles on either side of the road, with one balanced on them overhead. Master Chao fell silent, and the horses slowed down to match his mood. Smoke rose from earthen stoves in every courtyard. The aroma of scallions fried in lard was tempting.

A rooster dashed out of the alley between two columns of row houses, squawking, its wings flapping wildly. Running after it was Officer Wang and behind him his wife, Chulan. Fascinated, Master Chao reined in the horses and let the rooster run across the dirt road over to the bank of the drainage ditch.

"Get off and stop it!" Officer Wang shouted at us.

Teacher Sun and I jumped down and joined the chase.

"The weasel!" Officer Wang shouted again.

The rooster seemed to be trying to jump into the water. It hesitated and then swerved to run along the water's edge. Getting closer, I noticed that a yellow weasel was riding on the rooster's back.

There were many weasels around the farm, and I had heard all sorts of stories about the many ways they used for stealing chickens. A weasel of little more than a pound in weight could make away with a chicken weighing six or seven pounds. One way a weasel was able to get a chicken was to jump on the chicken's back, bite into its neck, and claw into its flesh. In pain, the chicken would begin to run wildly. Then the weasel, by knocking the chicken's rump with its bushy tail and striking the chicken's head with its fore paws, would pilot the chicken in any direction the weasel chose. When the weasel had driven the chicken to a spot safe away from its owner, the weasel would bite deep into the chicken's neck, suck out its blood, and then eat it. Most of the time, the weasel would only eat the internal organs, leaving the carcass to rot in the wheat fields. During the early summer, when baby weasels were born and began to demand food, many owners lost their hens. They would usually run across the gutted bodies in the ripening wheat fields.

Now a weasel was playing this trick on Officer Wang's precious rooster. The officer was outraged, having lost two hens since spring, and he was bloodthirsty for revenge. At other times, he might just pick up a lump of dirt and throw it at the weasel to scare it away from the bird. This time Officer Wang was set on killing the damned thing.

He ran along the bank of the irrigation canal, parallel to the bare-back riding weasel. It tried several times to drive the rooster into the water, slapping mercilessly on the rooster's head with its fore paws. The weasel had probably made a vast mistake in grabbing a rooster, instead of a hen. It might have succeeded in driving a hen into the water, but the rooster was determined not to spoil its beautiful plumage in the dirty water of the drainage ditch. It began to climb up the bank in sheer defiance of its tormentor's cruel beating.

The weasel clutched the rooster tightly, despite our shouting. Only when the rooster finally made it to the flat road above the bank did the weasel give up. It loosened its claws and was about to jump off, but the rooster jumped first, flying four feet high in the air, and throwing the weasel off its back onto the ground.

The weasel righted itself too late. Both Officer Wang and I landed on it with our heels, and Officer Wang ground its small head under his shoe. I heard the crushing sound of its thin skull as it caved in. The weasel kicked desperately, its tail flailing and beating the ground, its body twisting. Officer Wang stamped on the skull several times more than necessary, mindless of the whitish brain and blood that were splattering on his shoes and trouser legs.

I carried the rooster back to Officer Wang's backyard. Chulan examined its bloody neck, where the weasel's claws had dug into the flesh. The rooster crouched forward in the hands of Chulan, impatiently waiting to be released so it could go to the hens. I watched Chulan sheepishly for a long minute until Teacher Sun called out, "Huang Longsen, time to go. We may still be in time for lunch."

12

Political Instructor Feng and a Food Riot

It would be unfair to say Political Instructor Feng was a bad man. He was the most conscientious policeman at Farm 583, in an orthodox way, or, as Pockmark put it, "serious as shit." He was the only officer who dressed properly – in both uniform and civilian clothes, alike – he rode an old bicycle on the rough path all the way to the northern end of the field to check on the inmates to make sure they were working. He would actually go so far as to take off his shoes, and get in the paddies to see if the land had been leveled according to the standard, so that the young rice seedlings wouldn't dry up on high spots or drown in deep spots.

Early June was still quite cold. We worked in the paddies in knee-high rubber boots while Instructor Feng walked in the paddies barefoot. "He wants to show to us how much hardship *he* can take," Pockmark would comment. "He wants to coax us into working harder. He's only ever in the paddies for ten minutes. Of course, he can go barefoot. Let him soak in this damned mud for eight hours, and see how he feels!"

"Yeah, he's full of shit!" the other boys agreed.

Other officers usually walked away from where Instructor Feng was standing. While they swore, kicked at and beat the inmates from time to time, quarreled among themselves in front of us when they were in bad mood and played with us when they were in a good mood – all against the police code – Instructor Feng never used dirty language when speaking to us. I didn't like him, nevertheless. In fact, nobody at the Farm liked him.

He kept a straight face all the time, and I have never been able to see anyone who constantly has a serious expression on their faces, because I get the feeling that they are hiding their true feelings. When Instructor Feng stood on top of irrigation ditch Number Fifteen, near my sluice gate, my heart would automatically palpitate with premonitions. I would immediately take up my spade and find something to do, even when there was nothing to do. I would jump into the drainage ditch around my plots and scoop mud from the ditch bottom to rub another layer of plaster onto the plot ridges, splashing mud drops onto my shirt as I did this.

I had no reason to be afraid of him, I always told myself. Still the fear wouldn't go away. Instructor Feng was always critical if I asked to be released early. Officer Niu could argue on my behalf at the meetings, but it was Instructor Feng who had the final say.

Still, I could almost feel sympathy for Instructor Feng. Chadian was no place for an intellectual-type policeman like him. The coarse local officers were a much better match to the thugs from the Beijing side streets.

Needless to say, he hadn't gotten what he'd bargained for. The two dozen officers under him at Farm 583, all but three or four, were older than he. The harsh winds from the sea, the alkali-saturated drinking water, and the coarse food turned all of their hair gray before they reached forty-five. Furthermore, it made their skin wrinkled and rough, so they all looked older than they actually were. As a group, they had received him coolly and politely. They had remained so throughout the two months after he arrived. During this time, he had tried to make friends, but was unsuccessful. He was quickly singled out to be overlooked in all the socializing among officers, such as playing cards, or visiting another officer's home.

He could have brought his wife here. She might have been able to help by making friends among officers' wives. But, he denied himself the comfort. It was a sacrifice, but his wife had a nice job at a middle school in Beijing, and might be promoted to be deputy principal in another year. Their daughter couldn't leave Beijing, either. She needed to attend a good school. The one primary school and one middle school at the Chadian general headquarters were not up to Beijing standards. The schools were, after all, for country kids.

He simply couldn't ask his wife and daughter to come to Chadian. That would be too selfish of him. Also, how could he let his family live in a damp, gloomy house at the Officer's Village, and sleep on brick beds or cook on a brick stove by burning crop stalks? He would rather live at Chadian alone, and in exile.

Political Commissar Guan had told him that he had been assigned to Chadian so that he would gain field experience. He would probably be transferred back to Beijing in two or three years so that he could take on a more important job.

So Political Instructor Feng traveled back and forth on weekends and holidays. He would take Sunday duty for three weeks at a stretch so that he could save his rest days and spend them with his family in Beijing. As a result, his mind was as unsettled at Chadian as was his life.

One problem after another had arisen among the 300 or so inmates in the Big Compound since he came, and his fellow officers had not been cooperative. Now, one issue was pending that had to be dealt with – the strong protest from the inmates about the food. The corn flour buns were always undercooked, the dirty vegetables were prepared badly and cooked with hardly any oil, and there was too little meat to account for the rationed amount of two pounds a month.

To make matters worse, Officer Wang, who was in charge of the kitchen, swore at the complainers instead of putting pressure on the cooks to improve the fare. "Don't like the food here?" the young officer would say. "Then don't eat it. I have a dozen pigs to feed. You know what? If you eat less for two or three years, you'll have a bigger appetite when you go back to Beijing so you can better enjoy the fancy restaurants you brag about."

That kind of response aroused more of an outrage among the inmates. Their anger swelled like a balloon. The inmates were threatening to stage a protest when the political commissar from the general headquarters came to Farm 583 on his inspection tour.

Instructor Feng couldn't let that happen. He might lose face in front of the commissar, who had recommended his promotion.

On the other hand, rice transplanting had begun. If the inmates decided to sabotage the process, say by inserting rice seedlings too deep or too shallow or going slow on the work, the crop would suffer immense losses at harvest time. And that would be his responsibility.

The general headquarters sent two hundred workers from the paper mill to help in the rice transplanting at Farm 583. The inmates, including those of Squad One and Squad Two, were kept in the fields from early morning to dusk. These city boys had never experienced such hardship before. Driven by the officers, they bent double to plant young rice shoots in the earth, two inches under the water. They were able to stretch their backs and arms only when they reached the other end of each row. They became smeared with mud from head to toe. Their hands and feet bloated from long days of soaking in the muddy water and they all bore cuts incurred by sharp objects that entered the fields along with the store compost. At the end of each day, the inmates dragged their bodies over the dangerous single plank bridge, exhausted and hungry, only to find two corn flour buns, and a bowl of boiled turnip waiting for them in the kitchen. They were so exhausted they had no energy left to play cards or to retell their favorite stories.

As the days wore on, the officers became more flexible in administering the regulations. Evening study sessions on political doctrines were cut unannounced. As soon as the inmates returned from the fields and after supper, they were allowed to lie down on the platform bed and go to sleep.

The Big Compound was shrouded in a weird silence, except for sudden bursts of cursing or yelling from one of the squad rooms. Fatigue and hunger had shortened each inmates' temper. Fights took place more often and turned savagely brutal. Master Fang had to be sent for twice in one week to patch up cuts on various inmates heads. Many wanted to be put in solitary for a day or two to rest, so they broke every regulation they could think of. One inmate pushed a wheel-cart, loaded with rice seedlings, into the drainage ditch, and another followed suit by smashing another wheel-cart into a tree. Before long, they had wasted many of the young rice shoots.

The officers, however, decided not to put these "discipline-breakers" in solitary. Instead, they kept an even closer watch on them. They tied two culprits up with the "penalty rope," and afterwards made them finish their daily quota. When the other thugs witnessed this, they quickly abandoned their strategy of trying to steal a day of rest through "foul play."

Each hand was needed in the fields. Even officers' wives and middle-school students had to pitch in during the rice transplanting season at the various sub-farms.

I was spared the ordeal when Officer Niu assigned me to deliver drinking water to the fields. It was the easiest job on the whole farm in that season, even easier than the tasks of the officers. The weather was cool, and people worked close to the water in the paddy fields. They breathed in enough moisture to quench their thirst. I would have been more welcome if I had brought wine in my two buckets.

Not having much to do, I wanted to avoid giving others the impression that I was enjoying myself. That would arouse jealousy and resentment even from the officers. So I busied myself by carrying my buckets back and forth along the irrigation ditch and down the ridges into the fields so that the workers and inmates didn't have to climb up the bank whenever they wanted a drink.

I also spent some time transplanting the rice. I had learned the job in the army where it was required that soldiers help with field work during the sowing and harvesting season. It was done to show their close relationship with civilians. My unit was stationed in the south for two years. There, rice is the main crop, and so I learned how to do the work in the rice paddies. Even Instructor Feng registered a fleeting smile when he saw how quickly and neatly I could set the rice shoots into the mud.

During one break I talked with the paper mill workers, all ex-inmates. They were a pathetic lot, dressed in rags, dull in expression, and pale from malnutrition. They came and went in groups with a policeman in escort. Comparatively, the three ex-inmates of the Small Compound were much better off. At least, they were free within the boundary of the Chadian Farm.

The heavy field work sapped everyone's energy. No one but Pan Rong had saved the little food that his relatives had brought on their May First (International Labor Day) visits. The cooks didn't do any better than usual, despite Instructor Feng's admonition that they improve the fare. With Officer Wang's unreserved backing, the cooks didn't feel the need to pay attention to this up-and-coming political instructor. The corn flour buns were still undercooked, and the vegetables were still boiled in plain water and salt.

At every meal, the inmates at the front of the line would beat in protest on the wooden boards guarding the two small windows in the back wall of the kitchen. The boards had to be repaired and reinforced every couple of days.

"The cruelest land owner in olden times would feed farm hands better in the busy season," Pockmark said. "If he didn't, they would take it out on his crops."

The next day more bundles of rice seedlings became loose and the young shoots flew down the irrigation ditch or scattered in the fields in piles, going to waste. Officers yelled at the inmates who splashed in the paddies carelessly, plowing out behind them a mess of foot prints in irregular patterns and depths, making the transplanting process difficult.

One boy from Squad Eight threw a rice seedling bundle at Officer Wang, missing his head but causing muddy water to splash onto the officer's white shirt. Officer Wang yelled at the boy and had him tied up with the "penalty rope." All the other inmates straightened their backs and looked at the officer impassively.

"Go on, get back to work!" Officer Wang shouted.

No one moved. In a minute, the offending boy began to perspire profusely. Sweat sliced the mud on his face into thick stripes.

Officer Wang gave the boy a vicious kick, sending him toppling down backward into the muddy field. "I'll take care of you later!" he threatened, and then stalked back to the Officers Compound.

After supper, however, Officer Wang hurried to grab a place at a quartet game of cards in the duty office, and forgot to punish the culprit.

The next day, the growing resentment between Officer Wang and the inmates finally exploded into a confrontation. The inmates came back from the fields at noon, unwashed and swearing. They lined up in front of the tiny windows to the kitchen. A man from Team Four took two steamed corn flour buns, smelled them, and threw them into the face of a cook. "You motherfuckers!" he yelled at all the cooks. "You sons of bitches have no conscience. The buns are undercooked again."

At this point the whole dining hall erupted. Those who had already received their meals started throwing their buns at the windows, and over the wall where they fell in front of the duty office. Those who had not received their food yet threw broken bricks, yelling obscenities at the cooks.

"You sons of bitches," they shouted. "Come out here! Kill them!"

The cooks immediately shut the windows. Several officers from the duty office ran over to see what was happening.

"What's going on here?" Officer Wang shouted angrily.

A dozen voices shouted back: "Just have a look at

what the cooks are feeding us!"

Officer Wang kicked at a bun near his feet. "What's wrong with it? Is it made of horse dung?" He picked one up, and sniffed it. "Hmmm, smells all right to me. You know what I think? I think that lot of you have been fed too much. If I closed the kitchen for three days, you wouldn't complain about the food. Now, you go back to your rooms!"

No one moved. They just stood there, and glared at him. Officer Wang looked around, and shouted again, "All of you go inside!" His voice did not sound so sure now.

"Bullshit!" Pan Rong yelled in suppressed loudness and bent his knees to hide among the crowd.

"Bullshit!" all responded.

"Bullshit!" Another hoot rose higher.

Officer Wang was bewildered by such a demonstration of rebellion. His stature seemed to shrink.

Instructor Feng came over from the Officers Compound and stood beside Officer Wang. He said with calculated calmness, "Well, what's your complaint?"

One of the inmates pushed the vegetable out of his bowl onto the ground and showed the instructor the thick layer of dirt at the bottom of the bowl. "The cooks stew our food with dirt instead of oil," he said.

Chan Wen went up to the instructor and reported: "The buns are undercooked. The cooks should give more heat to the steamer. Or perhaps there's something wrong with the stove."

We all knew it was Officer Wang's fault for the poor food. But Chan Wen put the blame on the cooks and the stove. He was smart. In this way, he made himself a spokesman for all of us, and at the same time didn't offend Officer Wang.

I didn't much like that fact that it was Chan Wen who acted on our behalf. I was a squad leader too, and was looked up to by many Big Compound inmates. But I didn't have the guts to protest to Instructor Feng about the food.

Instructor Feng took a bun from Chan Wen's stretched hand, broke it in half and smelled it. His brows knitted in disgust. "Well," he said, wanting to cough – a habit of all government officials – but checked himself. "This bun is only half done. The cooks should be blamed for it. You go inside, and clean up. The cooks will reheat the buns. You will have a well done lunch in half an hour."

"Bullshit! The cooks must be replaced!" Pan Rong yelled again behind a cluster of people. Others followed: "We want different cooks!"

"Your demand will be discussed," Instructor Feng said, beginning to show his impatience. "Now go back to your rooms and take a rest. You need it. The work is heavy these days."

I looked at Han Jen and, without saying anything, motioned to him that we should compromise for the time being. He understood, and turned to go back to his squad room. As others followed, Officer Wang shouted: "Don't move! There will be no more lunch today! You either eat those buns you threw on the ground, or starve!"

We turned back and looked at Instructor Feng, who was staring at Officer Wang in disbelief.

"We are not a summer camp!" Officer Wang shouted. Although he was facing us and not Instructor Feng, Officer Wang's target was clearly him.

He now turned to Instructor Feng and said, "We are a labor reform farm. These people are here because they did bad things in Beijing. They don't have the right to complain."

Instructor Feng's anger began to show. Officer Wang had driven him into a dead corner where he had to show his authority. Otherwise he would eventually be forced to ask for a transfer from Farm 583.

"Making them suffer is not the goal of the government's labor reform program," he retorted coldly. "Our goal is to correct their bad habits, and transform them into useful people for the society. Giving them undercooked meals won't help."

"Then why don't we feed them meat and rice every day?" Officer Wang retorted sarcastically. "And let them enjoy their stay here? Don't forget, Instructor, they are here because back in Beijing they ate too well at the expense of good people. They should be made to remember that, while they are here, they must pay for what they did."

"You're absolutely right," Instructor Feng said, conscious of our presence, and making an effort to be calm. "It's our job to remind them of their former misdeeds. But physical punishment alone can only do the opposite. Recently Chairman Mao Zedong said that all prisoners must be treated as human beings."

"That's right!" several voices rose noisily among the inmates, amid laughter. "We are human beings!"

Instructor Feng looked over to where the jeering came from with an annoyed frown.

"Yeah right...human beings!" Officer Wang sneered loudly. "You're social scum!" He walked to the back window of the kitchen and shouted to the cooks who were watching from within, "Go to the vegetable garden and collect vegetable for supper! There will be no second lunch for you, hear me!"

That was too much for Instructor Feng. His face flushed. Suppressing the urge to raise his voice, he commanded, "Officer Wang, you're no longer in charge of the kitchen. I'll report the matter to the general headquarters this afternoon. For now, I will take over the charge!"

Though I didn't like Instructor Feng, I hoped the other officers would take his side. I felt embarrassed for the political instructor, the highest officer at Farm 583. Officer Wang wouldn't be bothered losing face in front of us. But, as scholarly as he was, Instructor Feng would. I looked in the direction of Officer Niu, hoping he would say something. He stood silently, smoking a Big Cannon.

Officer Wang stampeded out of the courtyard, yelling, "That's fine by me. I quit!"

Instructor Feng restrained from turning to look at Officer Wang. Instead, he addressed us in a calm, mild tone: "Life here is hard. This is what a labor reform farm is supposed to be. But, you must establish a correct attitude toward the life here. Most of you are in your twenties. Many people do bad things when they are young. The question is how to correct them. The labor reform program is designed to help you to learn from your past mistakes.

"You should take the initiative in reforming yourselves. As you grow older, society will become less tolerant of your wrong doings. The government means well by sending you here for a period of time. Remember, our country is still poor. The government can't raise your food allowance. Besides, you eat much better than many people in the countryside. You must have seen what the villagers near the farm eat. Their food is considerably worse than yours, and many don't have enough of it.

"Think of it. You steal from them in Beijing. Let's not talk about your obligation to the country. Let's talk about your conscience. You should make greater efforts to correct yourselves so that you can embark on a new road when you return home."

Instructor Feng waved his right arm over the crowd, his eyes sparkling as if with tears. He must have been expecting his words to move our hearts.

The inmates stood there, untouched and getting impatient with the instructor's preaching. I felt pity for him. He didn't fit in with the local officers, much less the inmates. Comparatively, the inmates seemed more like the local officers in their dress, talk and mannerisms. Instructor Feng was too refined for either group.

In half an hour Officer Jian, who was on duty, blew the whistle. We lined up in front of the tiny windows of the kitchen again to receive our second lunch that day. The buns were thoroughly reheated. The cooks had quick-fried another cauldron of vegetable. Molecules of peanut oil floated on top of the mixture of spinach and turnip.

Officer Wang didn't come to the Big Compound the following day, or the day after. Later we learned he had been transferred to Farm 588. For some strange reason, we actually missed his presence. Although he was mean sometimes, he was also the most negligent among the officers, often forgetting to end work breaks, or going to "attend private matters" and leaving us to play around in the fields. When he was in a good mood, he could forget that he was a policeman guarding petty criminals. At these times, the inmates were happy.

At the same time, it was a relief that Officer Wang had left Farm 583. Now his wife Chulan would have fewer pretexts to summon Han Jen to her home for a tryst. But as the days got warmer, Chulan seemed to grow more eager for Han Jen, and Han Jen and I became much more apprehensive.

Officer Guan came to replace Officer Wang as Officer Niu's partner, and took over the administration of the kitchen. The cooks were not changed, though the food was much better. On the Saturday after the food riot, the cooks slaughtered a hog, and served each of us a bowl of soup with slices of various pig organs for supper. The lunch on Sunday was a real feast: two steamed wheat buns and a bowl of pork stew. Officer Guan announced that from then on through the rice transplanting season to summer harvest, a hog would be slaughtered every two weeks. "You'll have a bowl of pork stew every Sunday," he told us. We praised him loudly for his "conscientiousness in observing the government policy as pertaining to labor reform elements."

There were two dozen pigs in the pigsty, meant for Big Compound inmates. They were big and fat, thanks to Officer Wang's generosity with our food rations. Much of our food ration must have gone into the pigs' bellies. During the nearly four months after I first came, Officer Wang had killed only two of them for us.

"His wife won't screw him," Black Head said, "so he screws the pigs. He's so thin and small he could probably climb into the pig's ass. Man, that must be satisfying."

We liked the new policeman. Short and beer-bellied, Officer Guan had the kindhearted face of old country folk. His shiny, smooth chin and puffy cheeks reminded me of pictures I had seen of an imperial court eunuch. His eyes, buried in heavy eyelids, were always smiling. Officer Guan had been demobilized from active service three years before. He then went back to his native village in Henan province. Only recently had he been recalled and given back his uniform.

One night Officer Guan walked into our room. I gave up my squad leader position at the western end of the platform bed and moved to a stool. He sat down in my place, took off his shoes, and reclined against the wall. He had come to our evening study sessions several times before, and we now could recite his several favorite sentences intended to teach us how to behave.

"You're young," he would say, "and have more years at school. You still have a bright future. Work hard and reform your bad habits." He must have said these words over and over again for many years because he had it down pat.

After giving this formal speech and at the prompting of some of the boys, he would tell us stories about some of the worst convicts he had guarded since 1951. That was the year he was transferred from the army to the police force. The boys were fascinated by the heroic deeds of gangsters and arch-enemies of the Communist government from the old regime.

"Why did you leave the police for those three years?" I asked, to get him to say more and to make the study session pass by more quickly.

"Beijing wanted to trim the police force at Chadian," he said. "They cut me off. I was only forty-three. Many of the older ones stayed, the ones who knew how to manipulate the authorities. I don't know how to play tricks. When others play tricks on me I usually don't know it. You see, one just can't be too honest."

"You should have fought back," Tiger said, putting on a false tone of sympathy. "Kill those bastards who cut you off!"

"Kill!" Officer Guan scolded Tiger like an aging father. "You seem to understand nothing but kill! That's why you're here! Never say that again!"

Pan Rong made a Big Cannon and handed it to Officer Guan, who examined the two ends and then stuck it into his mouth. Black Head clicked his lighter and placed the flame a bit too close to Officer Guan's chin. Officer Guan leaned back to align the handmade cigar to the light. He puffed several times to get it going, then took the lighter from Black Head's hand. It shone under the light from the bare bulb hanging from the ceiling. "Nice lighter," Officer Guan said admiringly.

"Of course it's nice," Black Head said. "It is gold plated."

"Really?" Officer Guan raised the lighter to examine it more closely. "Nice lighter," he said once again in his heavy, nasal Henan accent.

"You like it?" Black Head squeezed his eyes mischievously. "Then it's yours."

"No, no," Officer Guan said, and gave the lighter back to the boy. "Such a valuable thing? No."

"Don't believe him," I said. It was obvious the boys were making a fool of Officer Guan. "That lighter's made of copper. It's not worth a thing."

Officer Guan seemed to understand and said slowly, "I was wondering how you guys could keep such a valuable thing on the farm. It's against regulations."

"Still it works," Black Head said, happy with his trick on the officer. "You have it. I'll ask my brother to bring me another one on his next visit."

"No," Officer Guan responded hastily. "It's against the rules."

"This is nothing," Pan Rong said, flattering. "Just take it as a box of matches."

"You have it," Tiger also urged him. "No one will tell."

Black Head put the lighter in Officer Guan's shirt pocket and brushed off the officer's protesting hands.

"Then thanks," Officer Guan said happily, without feeling embarrassed, as if accepting a small gift from an acquaintance instead of a labor farm inmate.

I found myself wondering if his three years of absence from the police job had obliterated his sense of being a policeman. Or had he been discharged because he had never had any common sense?

13

Chen Min Makes a Break

Rice transplanting went on for ten days, including two Sundays. We worked at it for at least ten hours each day. Both the officers and the inmates were exhausted. When the job was finished, the inmates could relax for two weeks until weeding time – all except for Han Jen's squad and mine. It was a critical time for us to be tending the paddies.

The newly transplanted rice shoots needed most intensive care. The water had to be kept at an exact depth. If it was too shallow or too deep it would kill the young plants. Almost all the ridges in the fields had to be repaired because they had been so badly trodden during the days of the transplanting. They now had numerous breaches in them. We also had to replant many spots where rice shoots had either drowned or been dried out.

Because the paper mill workers were ex-inmates, they had many grievances against the Farm and were glad to have a chance to make it lose some of its crop. We found that after we refilled the plots with water, patches of rice shoots either floated up or went under, depending on what tricks the ex-inmates had played. We replanted some of these "blank spots" ourselves, and reported the others to the officers because the need for replanting was too formidable for us to manage on our own.

The kitchen was ordered to give us night snacks. We were pleased to have such a privilege. Every day we would stay late in the fields, having intentionally left something we could have finished during the day so that we might work "overtime." The kitchen would give each of us a quarter of a pancake with half an egg spread on it. Instructor Feng praised us highly for our strong sense of responsibility.

Despite the delicious night snacks, all of us lost at least a dozen pounds within one week from the additional work in the fields.

Soon the young rice shoots settled, their leaves growing hardier. They began to rise above the water surface like a bed of nails. After the first application of chemical fertilizer, the leaves turned a luxurious green and grew twice as fast.

Instructor Feng came to the rice field every day to inspect our work. Fortunately for me, each time he arrived at my plots I was working in the fields, either repairing bridges or replanting rice. I cut all the weeds along the plot edges, and padded the banks of the ditches solid with my spade. My four plots looked nice even up close. Although Instructor Feng must have had a good impression of me, he caught several less responsible rice tenders catnapping.

June 24th was my birthday. To celebrate, Tiger waded across the main drainage ditch to buy a bottle of liquor, some seasoned bean curd, and roasted peanuts to share with me and Black Head. At first I thought we should ask Han Jen to join us, but I changed my mind. Tiger and Black Head were members of a rival street gang, and though they had a kind of truce with him, they were certainly not friends. I didn't want to know what they had against each other because I didn't want to get caught up in their gangland games. Officer Niu had warned me from the beginning not to get myself mixed up with such things.

By now we had put Instructor Feng at ease with our "sincerity in repentance." The chance was slight that he would suspect we were stealing several hours from field work to enjoy ourselves. As Officer Niu had commented over and over, "Instructor Feng has very little real knowledge about farm work. I bet he can't even tell the rice plants from weeds. How could he possibly know how much labor and time is needed for any job in the fields?"

Under the auspices of "Squad Leader Inspection" duties, I liked to walk along the irrigation ditch to the northern end of the Chadian Farm land. The water in the drainage ditches shimmered gloriously reflecting the afternoon sun. Beyond the drainage ditches lay the villagers' sorghum and corn fields. Their plants were much smaller and thinner than those on the Farm because they lacked fertilizer. About half a mile further to the north, the villagers' adobe houses sprawled out behind a shroud of fine dust.

Rural villages in the north plains are all very similar in their layout, being composed of several dozen to a hundred households, and dotted sparsely with trees. Northern villages are drab and bare, but large in size, while those south of the Yangtze River are much smaller and surrounded by trees or bamboo groves and streams or ponds. The villages around Chadian Farm were poor. The one nearest Farm 583 was one of the poorest.

The walls of the houses in the village were made of packed earth. The roofs were made of mud, smoothed on top of rafters. They were directly anchored atop adobe walls without pillars because wood was too expensive for the villagers to use in building houses. Ironically, most of them saved a lifetime to buy the several planks they would need for their own coffins.

The windows were nothing but tiny square holes in the adobe wall covered with paper. Some houses had courtyard walls woven out of sorghum stalks; most were exposed to the threshing grounds and dirt roads.

Villagers, adults and children, moved sluggishly in the dust, like shadows. Their clothes were of no distinctive colors, and there were no colors in the street bright enough to catch one's eye. I could imagine how sparsely furnished the inside of those houses were by the observation that the people didn't have enough money to dress decently for outdoor appearance.

"Every time I go to the village," Tiger said, "the children swear at me. They must think I'm the son of one of the guards. They say we have eaten up all the good things and they have only bitter sorghum flour left."

I know how sorghum flour tastes. During the famine years of the early 1960s, a time in which people were starving and dying by the millions, I had to eat it for a week. Fortunately, I was in the army then, and the Soviets were threatening from the north. The government was afraid that we soldiers might not have enough strength to fight them if we were given too poor fare.

I remember the children in a poor village near the barracks in Cangxian county, three hundred miles south of Beijing, where our unit was stationed for a year. They would shout curses at us every time our trucks passed their village. "You've eaten up all the wheat flour and meat," they would yell at us, as they threw clumps of dirt at our trucks.

That village was so poor that when one crop failed, the whole village went out begging. It seemed so ironic that the bitterest complaints against life I ever heard all came from the poorest villagers, yet the Communist Party was meant to serve the poor.

If people in the cities, especially those with a college education, dared utter such complaints, they would be in as much trouble as the Rightists were. After all, they had complained in the mildest ways in 1957. I was in Chadian only because I had complained that some Party leaders had made the life of the common people difficult, and hurt too many innocent people...

I got drunk for the first time in my thirty-two years that noon on my birthday. I slept under a bush for nearly two hours. Black Head and Tiger were great drinkers, as young as they were. They finished the bottle while I slept soundly. They sang merry and sad songs, one after another, mostly about women. "Good flowers don't last long; good times don't last forever," were some of the lyrics. Fortunately, neither Instructor Feng nor Officer Niu came to inspect that afternoon.

My fatigue grew as the field work slackened. Over

several nights I had had the same dream. It consumed some of the energy that I wanted to preserve. In that dream, I was climbing up a steep slope, sticky mud sucking at my feet, drawing me toward the core of the earth. My legs were sore, and my brain felt clogged. Half of my mind seemed to be awake. I knew the mud-dragging effect came from the constant walking in paddies and applying fertilizer during the day. The fatigue I felt in the dream was even more tormenting than the fatigue I felt when I was awake. I wanted badly to stop the dream, and I made every effort to open my eyes to stare at the bare bulb overhead.

Whenever I awoke, the room would be deadly quiet. The inmates' snoring only enhanced my perception of how quiet it really was at night. During the rice transplanting season, the power station kept the power on all through the night, so the bulb remained lit. In the reddish light, I sometimes imagined I saw the face of my wife and hoped she would remain in my mind after I closed my eyes. But as soon as I did, the scene of climbing in mud would reappear.

One night I dreamt that all around there was nothing but water. The water was placid, no filthy debris like that in Beijing streets when it rained. There was no sound. There were no people, no cats, no rats, no living things whatsoever. There was only myself, alone, thinking nothing, doing nothing, feeling nothing. Then I would come to a spot where the land dropped abruptly thousands of feet below. Jet fighters, like those I maintained in the army, were dashing around like flies with their heads cut off, up and down, and shooting at each other. Several fell and exploded into flames.

Houses like those in the narrow alley of my home in Beijing were crumbling soundlessly, killing those in them. Qianmen's city tower crashed. Underground water rose to inundate the grand buildings around Tiananmen Square. The world was coming to an end, just like it was described in those novels about nuclear war. I felt strangely relieved that all my troubles, sufferings, worries, and concerns had become unnecessary. I wouldn't have to hate anyone any more.

I sank to the muddy ground and took a rest waiting for things to vanish on the earth. Suddenly, a plane flew overhead, its guns spitting bullets toward me. I tried not to care, since all would be over in a few seconds. But I couldn't suppress the fear that was rising within me. I wanted to stand up and run, but the mud, the same kind as in the rice paddies, anchored my feet and calves staunchly to the earth.

I could see the plot now, the face of Director Hong of the political department of the Beijing Foreign Trade Bureau, the one who had announced my verdict several months before. His grin was menacing. I grabbed a broken brick, and threw it at the cockpit. The face was obscured by the shattering glass, but the plane was almost on top of me. The opening at the tip of the plane's nose took in visible air currents and emitted an earsplitting, whistling sound. The two black guns welded to the plane's fuselage spit out two fire balls that exploded in my face. I screamed and woke up, sweat-drenched.

Whistles shrieked and several voices were shouting in the compound: "Get up, come on, everyone outside! Now! That means all of you!"

I rolled off the platform bed, shouted to the sleeping figures: "Get up! Something's happened!" and ran out into the courtyard.

"Count your squad," Officer Niu ordered as I walked toward him in the dark. He swept a flashlight over the inmates running out of the row houses. Other officers were checking their charges too. Jets of light and shadows flew helter-skelter across the yard. I wanted to ask Officer Niu what had happened, but refrained from doing so. His tone was that of a stern policeman, which reminded me once again where I was. I called the men of my squad together and waited for further instructions. Two policemen in uniform, whom I had never seen before, were strolling in the compound, pistols out of holster.

"What's the matter?" Black Head asked me. For possibly the first time in this daredevil's life, he seemed extremely uneasy. The other boys cowered in small clusters. I smiled inwardly. I was convinced that those street thugs could only be brave when they were dealing with helpless women and old people.

"Someone must have made a break," I said to Black Head. "You guys had better be careful. The guards are going to be pissed off, if that's what happened..."

Officer Niu pointed his flashlight at me and told me to come over. "Tell your men to stay inside. Warn them to behave. You're coming with us to find Chen Min. He's escaped."

Chen Min was a quiet boy of seventeen who had never caused any trouble at the Farm. He was in Squad Three. Officer Niu had taken a liking to him, and had told me he would transfer him to my squad when he had the chance.

"He will surely learn bad things without proper guidance," Officer Niu had said. "He's a good boy and got mixed up with bad company. Lou Hong is not a good role model for him, so I'd appreciate it if you'd keep an eye on him."

Lou Hong was the leader of Squad Three. Everybody hated him. He was made a squad leader because he was older, thirty-eight, and he had been the deputy chief of a police station.

He was interred in Chadian for abusing his official position. A man was arrested. His wife came to Lou Hong for help because they lived in the same neighborhood. Lou Hong promised to help on one condition, which he got across to the woman in a roundabout way. During the two months while the man was under investigation, Lou Hong went to the man's home and slept with his wife. The husband was sentenced to four years in prison. The woman reported the rape to the police, and consequently, Lou Hong was stripped of his uniform and was sent to Chadian.

I had waited for someone in my squad to be released to make a place for Chen Min. I hoped to get rid of Pockmark, and could do so easily because Officer Niu had suggested that Pockmark be moved out of my squad. But I didn't do so because other squad leaders would blame me for dropping a rotten egg in their lap. Then they would say I couldn't handle a real hardened reform element.

Now Chen Min had made a grave mistake by breaking away. When caught, it would likely mean several months extra on the reform farm for him. Even if he succeeded in getting to Beijing, he would likely be found by the neighborhood committee, who would dutifully report his presence to the police. He was not of the street-gang type – someone who could "float" on the outside for as long as half a year before being caught again. If he had been, it might have been worth his while to escape. In that time, they would usually have hooked up with their girlfriends, satisfied their stomachs and gotten their fair share of freedom.

Chen Min, however, got entangled with the law by accident, not because he was a member of a gang. He had gone with friends who were members of a gang to "move house," as they called it, and was caught. The police interrogator coaxed Chen Min into admitting he had taken a TV set, the most valuable among the things stolen from a house. Chen Min apparently had wanted to impress his friends with how brave and loyal he could be and took the main charge. He got one year in Chadian, while his friends were released after a week of custody at the police station.

Now he had escaped, and soon would be caught and sent back since he had no place to go but his own home.

Instructor Feng was determined to catch him before he made it to Beijing. He reported to the general headquarters, which mobilized one-third of the police force and civilian employees (excluding ex-inmates), four hundred in all, for the search. Trucks and jeeps delivered some of these people to areas Instructor Feng designated as the possible territory Chen Min might have covered within an hour.

Officers and a dozen trusted inmates from Farm 583

were sent to comb the fields immediately surrounding the Big Compound. Sorghum and corn stalks had by now grown waist high, higher than the winter wheat. We spread out, each of us covering a dozen rows. In minutes we were soaked to the bone and shivering. The crop leaves were as sharp as knife blades. They cut through our shirts and skin, leaving tiny lacerations on our arms and other exposed parts. Some of the officers walked out of the field and climbed up the irrigation ditch bank to catch their breath.

"Why don't we spread out, and set up watch right along here?" Discipline Officer Tian suggested. "If he is still in our area, we can hear him moving. If he has gotten out of our area, then we're wasting our time and energy, searching through these miserable fields."

All the other officers agreed with that suggestion, and splashed through the dense crop plants and out of the fields. Officer Niu brought the four squad leaders in his Team One together to sit on the edge of the dirt path between two strips of the field. The night was dark. Insects chirped here and there. Frogs croaked, rising and falling in their undulations. "In another month there will be hordes of frogs," Master Huan said. "Then you'll have difficulty getting a good night's sleep."

No one else replied. The officers began to doze off, reclining against the ditch bank. We inmates were eager to show our sincerity in helping the police, and dared not flick an eye. Black clouds were gathering in the east over the Bohai Sea and coming landward slowly.

"Looks like rain," Officer Niu said quietly to no one in particular. "That's going to be the first real rain of the year."

It had drizzled several times since I had arrived, but I had a feeling that it would not compare to the water being carried by those portentous clouds on the eastern horizon.

"What are those at the general headquarters going to do with Chen Min?" I asked Officer Niu.

Officer Niu didn't answer. He rested his head on his

knees against his chest, trying to sleep. He must have felt bad. He had previously assured me that no one under him would ever escape, but Chen Min had done it. I gathered my knees in my arms and bent my head on them, unconsciously imitating Officer Niu's posture. I longed to go back to the row house, even if it meant that I had to resume my dreadful dream. The night air was chilly and discomforting, and I was water-logged.

"I'll talk to the Political Commissar," Officer Niu raised his chin from his knees a little. "Chen Min's too young to be here for a longer time. The longer he stays, the worse he will become. Sometimes I wonder if this kind of reform is any good for the younger offenders. Many of them will commit even more serious crimes, thanks to the experience they gain here. After they are released to Beijing, some of them will be sent back here for another three years, and some will go to prison. Here, it's like shop talk. The inmates swap their methods for breaking the law and cheating their fellow man. Pickpocket turns into burglars, and highway robbers. A street brawler turns into a killer. We should really be dividing them up according to the kind of crimes they committed and according to their ages."

Officer Niu stopped abruptly, perhaps realizing he was talking to a labor-reform inmate instead of a fellow officer. But, I wondered, who among his fellow officers would understand him?

I didn't make any comment, afraid that I would remind him of the inappropriate setting for such talk. After a while, he said, "I'll see that Chen Min isn't given extra time."

When the eastern sky became tinged with a crimson glow, we were called back from our vigil in the fields. Chen Min had been caught near the railway station, and was now in custody at the general headquarters. He had been waiting by the tracks for a train, and planned to jump onto a freight car as it pulled out of the station. Officer Niu hurried over on his bicycle to find out why Chen Min had tried to escape.

"I only wanted to see my mother," the boy told Officer Niu. "She is in the hospital with cancer, and does not have many days to live. I wouldn't do anything bad in Beijing, and would have returned to the Farm as soon as I saw mother."

Officer Niu cursed him: "You damned fool!"

By breakfast all the inmates in the Big Compound had learned the news. "What an idiot!" Black Head said, sounding as if he were an old hand at jail breaks. "Everyone knows the railway station is guarded. Chen Min should have gone directly to the west, and thumbed down a truck on the highway. The truck drivers don't know what we are."

Pockmark said thoughtfully, "How come the duty officer set off the alarm an hour after Chen Min broke out?"

His remark stirred up a series of ardent speculations. Such an escape couldn't be kept a secret by only one person. Usually it was known to several: his friends and the two sleeping on either side of him on the platform bed. It would be unusual for friends or the two persons next to him on the bed to report on him. They would naturally pretend ignorance.

"It must have been Lou Hong," Black Head snarled. "That son of a bitch takes every opportunity to lick the cops' boots because he thinks it will get him a shorter sentence."

"Well," Pockmark said, in a pacifying and fair tone, "don't jump to conclusions so quickly. Even if he did, he wasn't in the wrong. He was helping the police and Chen Min as well. That young man must be reformed."

"Don't give me that kind of bullshit!" Black Head sneered. I disliked Pockmark's double talk. This old bastard was inciting the younger men against Lou Hong, but he didn't want to commit himself at the same time. On the other hand, I would have liked to see Lou Hong get taught a lesson so he would remember that making the police happy at the expense of a fellow inmate was intolerable and immoral.

By the time the whistle blew to announce that the

kitchen was ready to serve breakfast, the boys had come to the conclusion that Lou Hong was the informer and pledged to teach the traitor a lesson.

"If he didn't want to involve himself because he was the squad leader," Pockmark said in order to fan the anger, "he should have talked Chen Min out of trying to escape, or he should have just pretended he knew nothing. He must have known all along of Chen Min's attempt, but he waited until he could have evidence to report. For this, he might gain a reduced term. Instructor Feng likes him, you know." A torrent of obscenities ensued among the younger men.

On the way out to the fields I said to Black Head, "You'd better not touch Lou Hong. Instructor Feng hasn't forgotten the way you beat up Hu Shen yet. Officer Niu got in trouble with Instructor Feng because he got you out of solitary early. You'd better not make trouble, at least for Officer Niu's sake. Chen Min's break is already too much of a headache for him."

"You're not suggesting that Lou Hong should get off easily, are you?" Black Head said impatiently.

"I'm just saying that you don't have to do it yourself, get it?" I said.

Black Head looked at me for a second before he smiled his comprehension. "You're a smart devil, Huang Longsen," he said. "That's how you keep the guards wrapped around your finger."

Just be careful, not to let Instructor Feng suspect anything."

"Don't worry, I won't. I'm learning how to be smart from you."

The rain swept Chadian for twenty minutes that day, and then it was over. The heavy clouds, however, remained in the sky. Officer Niu argued with the general headquarters, persuading them not to extend Chen Min's term. After two days in solitary, Chen Min returned to Squad Three.

The real rain arrived from the sea three days later, pouring down in buckets. Sheets of water poured down like curtains falling from the sky, obliterating everything in the fields. We, of Squad One and Squad Two, stayed in the rice paddies the whole day during the torrent to guard the ridges and let extra water flow out of the paddies. By dusk, the rain slackened a little bit. The ridges had stood the test. We returned to the row house to change into dry clothes.

The rest of the day, everyone was confined to their squad rooms. They bragged and played cards, or dreamed of making love with their girlfriends. The weather was uncomfortable, though many liked it because no work could be done in the fields. The officers didn't come to inspect the row houses, leaving the inmates to make as much noise as they wished.

Someone left an old shirt on the clothes line in front of our row house. The two fragile willow trees that supported the line swung madly in the strong gusts of wind. The shirt, originally white in color, was now a dull yellow, the color of the earth at Chadian. It flapped and slapped crazily against the slender trunk of one tree.

A swash of rain water cascaded down from the roof of each row house. Rivulets rushed into the grooves cut in the earth, taking debris of a hundred varieties toward the latrine at the northern end of the compound. The open pits in the latrine overflowed with the added rain water. A thick layer of white and gray maggots floated in each of the latrines. The insects wriggled on top of one another, struggling up the crevices in the brick wall.

I hated to use the latrine at such times, but couldn't bring myself up to urinate as many others did – by pissing over the threshold. Shortly after I relieved myself and waded back to my squad room, I heard a cry. Through the sheets of rain I could see Lou Hong running out of the latrine, covering the back of his head with one hand and holding his trousers up with the other. He was yelling, "Someone hit me from behind!"

Heads popped out of doorways to watch as Lou Hong dashed over to his squad room, right next to ours. Blood dripped through his fingers. The men in Squad Three stepped back from the doorway to let him in.

"Someone hit me in the back of the head!" Lou Hong told them. He began to examine his head with his fingers.

"Oh, I forgot my umbrella in the latrine!" he said. "Would one of you get it for me?"

"No one wants your broken umbrella," one of the inmates said. "You can get it when the rain slackens."

"I'll go over and have a look," Pockmark said, twitching his mouth into an ugly smile. He picked up a wash basin, placed it upside down on his head to block the waterfall from the eaves, and dashed out the door. Water hit the bottom of the washing basin and ricocheted a spray of drops in the doorway. I moved further inside and continued to stare at the mist that rose from the roof of the row house in front of ours.

It was evident Pockmark had been a part of the conspiracy against Lou Hong. I looked over my shoulder. Black Head and Tiger were on the platform bed, both leafing through children's picture books, mindless of the sudden turmoil outside the door. They were extraordinarily cool that day.

The rain slackened for a moment. So, on impulse, I stepped quickly over to the Squad Three room.

"What's happened?" Pockmark asked Lou Hong solicitously. "Someone hit you with a brick from behind when you stood pissing? What a weasel! An honest guy would fight in the open. Why hit people from behind? Are you going to report it to the duty officer?"

A crowd had by now gathered in Squad Three. They joked and teased each other loudly, deliberately ignoring Lou Hong.

"Right. Go and report it to the guards. I'm sure they'll cut your sentence after this indignity," someone said, echoing Pockmark.

Pockmark took a towel from Lou Hong's wash basin and dabbed away the blood on Lou Hong's head. "It's nothing serious," he said. "Just a small cut."

"It hurts," Lou Hong winced as Pockmark dried his hair around the wound.

"Well, you don't know who did it, do you?" Pockmark asked. "Liu Bin was hit from behind, when he was pissing in the latrine at night. Remember? The officers haven't found who did it. You'd better wait until you're sure who did it. Otherwise he may hit you again for reporting it to the officers. You may not be as lucky next time – only a small cut in the head. What do you think? Well, now you must go and ask the duty officer to take you to patch the cut. Tell him you fell and hit your head."

Lou Hong changed into a dry shirt. "There's no need to go to Master Fang for a treatment," he said. "A small tincture of iodine will do."

"Let me rub some on the cut for you," Pockmark offered.

The smart old bastard! He must have known who hit Lou Hong. Now he had coaxed him into not reporting it to the police. Perhaps Lou Hong himself didn't want the officers to know about it. Officer Niu had been very cold toward him since the night he reported Chen Min's escape. Lou Hong could do nothing but swallow the humiliation and pain in silence.

I felt relieved when I learned that the boy who hit Lou Hong was not from my squad. He was in Team Three, and a sworn brother of Black Head. Despite the intensive work in the rice paddies, Black Head, Tiger, and Pan Rong had carried out an investigation, and had soon collected enough evidence to prove Lou Hong "guilty."

"He had known all along that Chen Min planned to make the break," Pan Rong reported to me. "Lou Hong watched Chen Min closely for several days, followed him out of the room that night, watched him dig a hole in the wall to crawl out, and waited for an hour before he went to report the matter to the duty officer."

"Why did he wait for an hour to report?" I asked.

"That's easy to explain," Pockmark said. "If Chen Min was caught close to the Big Compound, the punishment wouldn't be severe, and the award wouldn't be so big. Understand?"

"Old bastard!" I cursed under breath.

After two days, the excitement caused by Lou Hong being hit was forgotten. The boys had to look for, or cause, another event to make life at Chadian less wearisome. Like the nicotine in the Big Cannons they smoked, any kind of excitement would stir a glimmer of liveliness into the stagnation of the Big Compound.

14

Summer Days and Nights

Those of us tending the rice paddies would now had an easy time of it for about two weeks. The ridges in the plots had all been consolidated; inlets and outlets had been readjusted so well that water could flow into the plots automatically and stay there at the required level for a couple of days; and the young rice shoots were growing strong and healthy.

The only annoying problem was the eels. They would drill holes in the ridges at night, and the next morning we would find one of the plots low in water, sometimes totally dry. We knew there must be a hole somewhere. We would then go around the four sides of the plot looking for that hole, usually four or five inches in diameter. Though narrow, the smooth-walled tunnel could let a ton of water out in several hours. Pan Rong got so mad at the eels, he tried to dig down along the hole in one plot to get at one of them.

"You're not digging for a nest of field mice," Han Jen observed coolly. "Even if you dig up the whole plot, you won't find it. Eels are like earthworms. They don't stay in one place."

Pan Rong continued to dig, found the hole branching in several directions and gave up in frustration. It took him half a day to repair the damaged corner of his plot and to replant the ruined rice shoots.

At first we thought we could catch many eels since there were so many burrowing holes in the rice paddies. We saw them moving along the bottom of the drainage ditches like slim submarines, but no one could catch any. Now out of hibernation, they were as crafty as they were slippery.

Since there was little to do in the fields, the boys got together in threes and fours to have "spiritual feasts" – talking or bragging about restaurants they frequented or the women they knew. Han Jen and I would chat for a while, and then he would go to join his men. At these times, I would go to find a quiet place to read, or daydream.

Then came July, the busiest month of the year. Wheat had to be on the threshing ground, corn and sorghum plants needed to be hoed, and the rice had to be weeded at least twice.

We didn't know if we preferred hoeing in the dry fields, or weeding in the wet paddies. The corn and sorghum had grown two feet over our heads. The dense leaves shut out any moving air. Hoeing among the plants was like being inside a steamer. The razor-like leaves left tiny cuts on our arms and faces, hurting and prickling at the same time. But when we were sent to weed the rice, we soon missed the corn and sorghum fields.

"At least we can stand on solid earth there," Pockmark would groan. "These mother fucking rice paddies always make me queasy. You never know what you're going to step on. They throw everything in here: condoms, tampons, and the hair they rub off their dicks and asses when they fuck. You name it. You could probably find the aborted remains of a baby produced by some officer's wife who screwed an inmate in the corn fields. Ha, ha, ha..." He laughed loudly, amusing no one as much as he amused himself.

We were all lined up to weed the paddies, five rows for each person.

The sun became fierce, beating down relentlessly on our backs, scorching our skin. The mud felt sickening around our feet and calves. Sometimes we would step on glass or a pottery shard that would cut us.

Even the officers were wary about the weeding time, as they had been the transplanting time. The responsibility was heavy. They had to be very watchful. Some treacherous boys might deliberately pull out rice seedlings and leave the weeds behind, or put the pulled-out weeds back into the earth with roots down so they would grow again.

We were required to pull the weeds completely out, make a knot of the leaves, and stick them upside down in the mud to let them decompose. The officers got into the paddies from time to time to check our work.

I was always present when others came to weed my plots. I would make friendly gestures to the assigned inmates so that they wouldn't do such tricks in my area.

Five combines from the general headquarters came to cut the wheat. We inmates were once again kept in the fields for long hours, this time on day and night shifts. Han Jen's squad and mine were allowed to attend the paddies only in the afternoon. We had to join the others in the wheat fields in the morning and at night.

Wheat harvest is the time of rain in northern China, and the threshing must be done quickly. A downpour would soak the wheat on the threshing ground, and the wet ground couldn't be used for sunning the grain for a day or two. If the rain lasted longer, the grain would get moldy.

Officer Niu was put in charge of the threshing ground, a critical assignment. In two days, his eyes became dark and withdrawn from constant worrying and lack of sleep. His relationship with Instructor Feng became even more tense. Afraid the instructor would find fault with him, he would pay particular attention to his duties. I volunteered to take several night shifts, and suggested that during that time he catch up on some sleep. The first night, around ten o'clock, he came to see if everything was all right. He didn't show up on the second and third nights of my shift. The two squads under me all worked diligently, doing much more than they would have under an officer.

For a spell of three days the rain poured. Fortunately, most of the wheat grain had already been dried and put in makeshift bins on the threshing ground. The remainder was under proper cover, too. Officer Niu went to the threshing ground several times a day, checking for leakage. He was worried. If the rain went on much longer, the grain would still be dampened. The other officers were happy about the rain. Now they could stay inside, indifferent to the crops. Large sections of the corn and sorghum fields were flooded.

"The drainage ditches should be dredged," Officer Niu said to me. "Instructor Feng knows nothing about farming." Officer Niu could have told Instructor Feng to take action, but didn't. Why should he give such a suggestion and send fellow officers out into the rain?

We inmates were kept inside to read political doctrines and discuss how we could repent. But most of the time the inmates played cards, some for small stakes such as cigarettes or candies saved from family visits, and a few for bigger stakes such as one yuan a game. The debts thus incurred would be settled either in kind or cash after the next family visit. Either way, the officer on duty was usually glad to keep an eye shut. As long as there were no serious fights, these days inside proved easier for the officer than the days when he had to take the inmates out into the fields to work.

When Officer Guan was on duty, he would make an inspection tour of the row houses, from time to time, and order all card games to cease. But more often than not, he could be coaxed into sitting down on the platform bed, and joining in a game. He would soon be chewing on a candy bar, or smoking a Big Cannon that an inmate offered to him. Then, before he knew it, he would find that he had stayed there for an hour. "Damn it," he would groan. "Time to resume your studies. You can't play all day. How will you ever make a new start in your wretched lives if you play your time away? Now read this article!"

He would then move from door to door yelling into each room, "Stop playing! I'll take your cards, and throw them into the latrine pits!"

Several voices would respond cheerfully, "We're studying, Officer Guan. Would you come in, and tell us how to make quicker progress?"

"Next time," he would yell back solemnly, and return to the duty office to read the newspaper. Then, bored, he would go over to the Officers Compound to join a card game there.

The kitchen always served the same vegetable for a week at a time. One week we would have turnips, then spinach, then celery, then tomatoes and then cucumbers. I had never known vegetables to taste so bad. During the week of rain, the whole compound smelled of decaying onions. For this week we had onions, stir-fried without much oil, boiled, and floating in soup. Finally, as we had with other vegetables, we asked the kitchen to give us raw instead of cooked onions. We ate them with plain salt.

The open pits in the latrine overflowed with rain water and feces. Fat maggots crawled and rolled in tangles on the ground and up the wall. Onions, decomposed through the human system, were aggressively pungent and the inside of the row houses smelled dank with wet rubber shoes and unwashed underwear piling on the soggy dirt-packed floor.

The dirty jokes and talk of women in the most minute graphic manner drove me crazy. I preferred to spend most of the day in the field, returning to the compound only for lunch. I had no choice after dark, but compromised by joining the "carnal dinner" discussions to make the time more tolerable.

I built a shelter near my sluice gate with willow branches and plastic sheets made out of chemical fertilizer bags. Alone in the shelter, I read in English. Material in foreign languages was forbidden on the farm. But Officer Niu had told me that he would ask the general headquarters for an exception in my case. This was refused, but with his approval I wrote to Shalin asking her to tear sheets from English magazines to wrap the food packages she mailed to me. I wanted to carry on my study of English during the three years, or at least not forget too much. Without a dictionary, I had to guess at the meaning of many of the words.

It was difficult for me to concentrate on the text. So much of the time, I stared out beyond the Chaobai River dike to the west, and absent-mindedly watched the wisps of mist and rain, whirling and twisting through the fields. Perhaps because of the lack of nutrition, my brain was much less active than when I was at home. I even found it an exertion to think of my wife.

The slanting rain that obliterated the landscape beyond a hundred yards gave me a peculiar sensation that quickened the circulation of my blood, especially on the surface of my skin. It felt as if it was suddenly exposed to the chilly air at dawn. I liked the sensation.

Sometimes I wanted to shout, to cry, or to laugh at the top of my voice into the rain, to prove I had the world alone, and to release the depression that weighed on me constantly. I knew I would die either of a stroke because of this heavy depression, or of liver cancer caused by my long suppressed anger.

In autumn, when the water got low, there would be fish trapped in the holes at the bottom of the drainage ditches, Master Chao told me. There was a large, deep spot in the drainage ditch near my sluice gate. The water in it was darker. A huge eel dominated the deep water hole. Other living creatures avoided going near it. The lone eel would rise from the depth of water very slowly, its head up, and then hang there motionless. At first I mistook it for a piece of dead wood, but then I noticed the huge head. Its mouth was wide open. There were small, white air bubbles floating from it up to the water surface. I would sit in my tiny rain shelter, as motionless as the eel, watching it, enlarged by the depth of water, hanging there, spitting air bubbles. I thought it must be as long as three feet. It would have made a wonderful feast for the boys. I didn't tell anyone there was an eel there, however, afraid they would try to catch it or scare it away. Besides, I was lonely, and the eel was a good companion.

After a stretch of five days, the rain broke at last. Now the sun burned down, releasing a wrath which could no longer be suppressed by dark clouds. Steam rose from the paddies. The mud on the road leading to the general headquarters dried and cracked. The horses drawing Master Chao's cart selected their steps tentatively to avoid the ruts. The two rubber tires bumped up and down, slid right and left. Whenever a wheel dropped into a hole where water had not yet evaporated, the cart would tilt to one side.

Master Chao would yell at the horses, and swing the long handle of his whip to make clear, sharp reports over the ears of the horses. He would never lay his whip on the animals, but enjoyed immensely the musical sound that the whip produced in the air. When a wheel got really stuck, he would have to jump down and shovel away the mud in front of the wheel, and push the cart from behind. It seemed the horses understood their master, and would always give a powerful pull at the right moment.

Summer was a time of more breaks. It was also easier for the breaking inmates to "float outside." With food easy to obtain, and the warm weather convenient for sleeping in the open, the times were marginally better. Officer Niu had warned me to keep a close watch on the boys, but I was not worried at all. The boys in my squad were content with their job, and Black Head and Tiger had struck fear among them with their threat: "I'll put a knife in anyone who plans a break."

After five days of rest, the inmates had partially recovered from the exhausting work on the threshing ground and hoeing in the corn and sorghum fields. The Big Compound, which had become dangerously restless, seemed to settle down once again – at least for the time being.

Han Jen had not been summoned to the Officer's Village since Officer Wang transferred to Farm 588. He had stopped mentioning Chulan to me. I assumed that Chulan must have decided to break it off with him, so the sight of her one morning in our rice paddies was a shock. I was seized by a sudden fear.

Chulan was walking along the drainage ditch instead of on top of the irrigation ditch, so she couldn't be seen from the road. I realized she must be looking for Han Jen. I followed her from a distance. It was too dangerous for Han Jen to be caught having a tryst so near the Big Compound. Chulan had no business here, now that her husband was no longer working at Farm 583. Her presence would undoubtedly arouse suspicion. I sat down near my sluice gate to listen to her conversation with Han Jen.

"You haven't come to me for more than a month,"

Chulan grumbled. "Don't you miss me?"

At first there was no answer from Han Jen, but then I heard his voice in panicked tone, "No, we can't do it here."

"No one is around, and no one followed or even noticed me. I was very careful." Chulan said with an urgency.

Silence again.

The silence was so long, it became unbearable. I stealthily crawled up the bank from my side, and looked beyond the five-foot irrigation ditch. It was impossible to see the couple, who must have been sitting very low in a corner of Han Jen's sluice gate.

There was little water at the bottom of the irrigation ditch. I slipped down from my side into it, stepped across the wet bottom on my toes and climbed up the other side on hands and feet. Hidden in the reeds, I craned my neck to look down. I almost cried out.

They were doing it from behind. Han Jen's face twisted grotesquely, like an ape king mating his female subjects. Chulan crouched forward, her head buried in a cluster of reeds, her skirts up around her waist to bare her creamy buttocks as they stuck into Han Jen's belly. I stood there in silent amazement for what seemed like fifteen minutes before slipping down to the bottom of the irrigation ditch and, bending low, running silently northward away from the spot. I felt ashamed of myself and for Han Jen and Chulan.

I returned to my sluice gate an hour later to find Han Jen sitting on my side of the irrigation ditch. I sat down beside him.

The water in the drainage ditch was warm around my feet and calves. "Hot, isn't it," I said.

"Damned hot," Han Jen said, puffing at a cigarette. He never smoked Big Cannons. In fact, he wasn't even a real smoker.

The weeds had grown fast during the past four days. The paddies were in need of weeding.

"The boys will be pissed off," I said, "because they're going to have to go out in this weather and do the weeding."

"They may actually feel better for a change," he said. "The hoeing in the corn and sorghum fields is no better. At least they can breathe more easily in the paddies."

I searched for a way to warn Han Hen not to meet Chulan again. But the scene of Chulan's buttocks sticking into his loins crammed my whole vision.

I shifted my own buttocks. Where I sat had become quite warm. Something was on my left calf, so I drew my leg up. A leech had driven one third of its body into my flesh, its belly swelling. "Fucking shit!" I cursed, and slapped fiercely at my calf where the leech was.

I had learned the way to get a leech out of flesh from farmers south of the Yangtze River. There they had water everywhere, and the water was inhabited by millions of leeches. The southern farmers would pick out leeches from their arms and legs as if they were brushing away flies. You can't pull leeches out of flesh with force, they told me. The more you pull, the deeper a leech will drag its body. You must slap it hard repeatedly, and it will then contract its body and gradually come out by itself.

I slapped and slapped, as I watched my leg turn red and the leech's dark brown body twist itself out of my flesh and roll down my leg. It left a red dot on my skin. I shoved the leech onto a hard spot on the ground, and sawed it in half with a piece of broken tile. The leeches skin was elastic and tenacious. I finally succeeded in cutting it open. My blood spilled from its belly, and darkened a small spot on the ground.

All the while Han Jen watched, unconcerned. In the end, I didn't give him my advice about his dangerous affair with an officer's wife. Why bother? I told myself. Han Jen's philosophy of life was more practical than mine. "When one has the dough, one should enjoy it. Why worry about tomorrow?" Or, as many put it, "When fucking, hold out as long as you can and enjoy every moment."

I felt a heavy burden because I worried too much about moral values and their consequences. I worried about Han Jen and what it would be like if he was found out. He would be handcuffed and dragged onto a platform in the auditorium at the general headquarters to be used as an example during a punishment meeting. I knew that if such a thing happened to me, I would want to kill myself. Being a counter-revolutionary was one thing, but to be accused of having rotten morals was another. For me, saving face was far more valuable than saving my life.

Night time in late July and early August at Chadian was much worse than daytime. After it cooled down to a bearable temperature around 10 o'clock in the evening, the duty officer would blow his whistle, and herd us inside the row houses. The heat trapped during the day in the poorly ventilated rooms was not yet dispersed, and the tarred roof was beginning to release whatever heat it had absorbed during the same period. The steamy air inside was suffocating.

Mosquitoes rushed, charged, and bit savagely at any parts of one's body that touched the mosquito nets. When flesh quivered from irritation, the biting insects would buzz in protest for a second and then land again on the nets, their bellies swelling from the blood they had sucked in through the tiny needles of their mouths. The nets couldn't be fully spread out because the strip of space allocated for each inmate on the platform bed was too narrow. The bed was exactly twenty-five feet long, a little more than two feet wide for each of the twelve members of a squad.

The reddish light of the bare bulb intensified the heat and attracted hordes of mosquitoes, bugs, moths, grasshoppers, toads, and tiny "ghost-faced" crabs that infested the filthy ponds around the Big Compound. At night, thousands of frogs croaked, the noise rising and falling in unison. Then, suddenly, the croaking would stop to plunge the night into a surreal quietude.

As at the Liangxiang Detention Center, one end of each platform bed – the end near the door – was reserved for the squad leader. I was privileged to have this spot that provided more coolness from the open door. But the bulb hanging directly over my head irritated my eyes. I wished the power station would cut the supply more often than it did, at least during the nighttime.

We had to lie straight, and somewhat stiffly to avoid sticking our knees into the backs or stomachs of the persons sleeping next to us. My sinuses troubled me all year around, even during the hottest summer nights. I first lay on one side, then, when the upper nostril declogged due to reduced blood pressure, I would turn to lie on the other side so the swelling in the other nostril would disperse. It would usually take about twenty minutes before both nostrils gained enough free passage for me to go to sleep. By then, all the others had fallen into deep slumber.

That night my brain was filled with the scene of Han Jen and Chulan in the fields. It kept me awake for an hour longer than usual. I looked through the open door into the night outside. If only I could lie on a cot in the courtyard! Shalin and our son must be outside the door of our tiny room in Beijing now, our son sleeping on a reed mat with Shalin sitting beside him. Was she watching the same stars as I was?

I turned my body half over to seek a drier spot on the sheet, and failed to find any. Half awake, I pulled the sodden sheet from under me, rolled it up, and tossed it to my feet. The bare reed mat, though also rough and wet, didn't cling to my skin. I lay flat on my back and stripped off the only piece of cloth around my loins, knowing that everyone else on the bed was the same: stark naked and breathing like dogs. Millstone was snoring thunderously. Others were tossing, flapping, and twisting in their dreams.

We had to remain in bed because it was forbidden to be out at night.

Suddenly Tiger poked me through the mosquito net. He curled the thumb and forefinger of his right hand to form an O and thrust the forefinger of his left hand in and out of it. "He's at it, again," Tiger mouthed.

I shook my head in disgust, and closed my eyes. Pockmark must be masturbating again. Tiger poked me harder, and gestured for me to get off the bed quietly. Several other heads raised a little. The signal had apparently been passed to me in relay.

Tiger and I slipped out of the nets and down to the floor. We walked barefoot over to the other end of the room and peeped into the net. Pockmark's immense body, stark naked, was sprawling face down, heaving spasmodically like a water buffalo. Tiny Mouse was invisible under him, except for his arms, like those of a baby, stretching out under the armpits of the big man. Pockmark was having difficulty breathing. Tiger jerked the mosquito net aside and yelled, "What are you doing?"

Startled, Pockmark looked up, his face covered with a thin, filmy membrane of sweat, shimmering waxily in tiny rings around blackish dents. We watched his features constrict and twist strangely. Suddenly the man shook violently and crashed down, his limbs going limp. I heard small whimpers of pain coming from under Pockmark.

All in the room jumped down to the ground and swarmed over to see what was happening. Several voices yelled, "What the fucking hell is going on here?" Then they laughed and cursed and gawked at the scene.

"Get up!" I hissed at Pockmark. "You shameless old bastard!"

Weakly, Pockmark rolled over to one side to reveal the pitiful Mouse, cowering toward the inner end of the bed and wiping the liquid on his thighs with a piece of dirty rag.

Tiger grabbed Pockmark by the hair, and dragged him onto the ground. Black Head kicked him on the calves. Pockmark's waxy face flushed with anger, ready to fight back.

"Let him go!" I intervened, hastily. A fight would arouse the whole compound and alarm the duty officer. I didn't want this event to be known to the authorities. Pockmark had only three months left of his two years. He might be given another year because of this incident. Though he probably wouldn't care if he stayed on the farm one year more, I would feel guilty to be involved in such an outcome. Also, I wanted Pockmark out of my squad and out of the Big Compound as soon as possible – and permanently.

"Everybody go back to sleep, and nobody talk about this," I commanded. Pockmark looked at me and said nothing.

"You go to sleep, too," I said to Pockmark. "We'll talk about it tomorrow. Now get under your net."

The next morning, after we arrived in the fields, Pockmark mumbled to me, "Huang Longsen, I didn't do it for real. I only held Mouse and rubbed. I didn't put it in."

"How many times have you done that to Mouse?" I asked.

"Three times, oh, four times. But I never put it in. You ask Mouse if you don't believe me. You know my weakness. I just can't help it."

I knew how Pockmark got his two years. The mothers of two boys reported him to the police. He was telling the truth, however, that he never put it in them. Otherwise, he would now be serving a jail sentence instead of time on a labor-reform farm. I had thought of moving Mouse to another sleeping spot, but knew no one would agree. Despite the narrow space on the platform bed, there was a strip of twenty inches separating Pockmark and Mouse from the rest. They were the two "untouchables" in the Big Compound.

"You're not to touch Mouse anymore," I said to Pockmark in a mild tone. "If I catch you again, I will make the rest of your days here as uncomfortable as they can be."

Pockmark got the message. "I won't do that again," he said humbly. He must have been fuming inside. He had never been humble to any officer, not even to Officer Niu. But with me, he had no choice. If I told him I would make his days uncomfortable, he knew I meant it. I was friends with all the toughest guys in the Big Compound. They could play vicious tricks on him. He might find a scorpion inside his bed cover at night, or his shoes soaked with urine in the morning, or a cut on the back of his head as he was relieving himself at the latrine after dark. And he wouldn't dare to retaliate, or report to the police.

The officers would be more than glad to see him suffer.

"I won't do that again. I promise," Pockmark repeated.

I talked to Mouse, too. "You let him do it only because he can buy you some cigarettes?" I said savagely.

"He also said I could look him up after I am out," Mouse murmured. "He said I could stay with him. I don't want to go back to my home."

I didn't know what to say. I could give Mouse old clothes and some food sent by Shalin, but I couldn't help him with his future. Mouse's mother was dead. His stepfather wouldn't accept him. He never treated the boy well. "All right," I said, feeling helpless. "I've told Pockmark not to bother you again."

Mouse's name was Shuangxi, or Double Happiness. The nickname "Mouse" was given to him by Black Head. Almost nineteen, he had the stature of a twelve year old. His features were like those of a newborn baby. His eyes, mouth, and ears converged on the flat nose bridge, causing wrinkles on his forehead around his nose and between his invisible brows. Inmates teased him because of his looks, but seldom bullied him seriously. Black Head and Tiger sometimes gave him a slap on the back of his head, or kicked his butt when he refused to steal for them from the officer's kitchen, or the warehouse.

Despite his tiny form, he ate a great deal. After the holidays, many inmates ate from packages their families had brought, and would give all their kitchen leftovers to Mouse. They also gave him old shirts, pants and socks. He also collected all the things left behind by those who had been released and put them in a small storage area he created at the foot of his spot on the platform bed. He was only five feet tall so he could spare a space at the foot of the bed.

Above all else, Mouse was extremely frugal. He kept all the shirts and pants he collected in comparatively good condition, putting them on only on holidays. In fact, I don't remember his wearing anything on the regular days other than the jacket and trousers he came with. The black jacket, a gift from police at the Beijing railway station, served as pajamas and underwear on cold days. It bore at least fifty patches of various colors and materials, as did his pair of black trousers, also a gift from the police in Beijing.

On Sundays, he would sew up tears in his "suit" with a big needle and thick thread, which others gave him or which he obtained by undoing an old sock. Mouse was quite self-reliant, never begging from others, at least while he was "inside."

Officers tolerated his "wealth" accumulation. But after the weather turned warm and wet, his rag riches began to smell of mildew. From time to time others would force him to sort his things out, and discard some of the useless stuff. If he was reluctant to do so, one of the boys would scoop up the whole bundle, and throw it into the yard.

Mouse would plead, "All right, I'll throw away some." Then he would spread the contents on the platform bed, examine each article carefully, smooth out wrinkles and folds, put one item aside, put it back in the pile, and put it aside again, hesitating to throw anything away.

Many boys from other squads enjoyed such occasions when Mouse was sorting out his things. Someone would grab a shirt, and say, "This is mine."

Mouse would respond urgently, "You gave it to me last Sunday!"

"I want it back," the former owner would tease him.

"You can't have it!" Mouse would protest, placing his tiny hands tightly on the shirt.

Others would tease him until tears welled up in his beady eyes from the anxiety of losing one of his possessions. The former owners would then say, "Who would want anything back from you, you filthy rug rat? I would have to burn the shirt after you used it."

My squad, however, benefited from having Mouse with us. He was frequently forgotten when an officer assigned work quotas to us, and actually, he could do as much work as anyone. The food he ate didn't go to waste. Back from the fields, Mouse always volunteered to do the "household chores," such as sweeping the floor, or fetching a bucket of water from the tap.

Mouse came to Chadian in March. His lined jacket

and trousers were infected with lice. I made him take his clothes off and boil them in a cauldron for cooking pig feed. Since he had nothing else underneath, Mouse lay under a quilt while his clothes dried.

"We can't get rid of the lice by boiling his clothes," Tiger had said. "The eggs are probably hiding in his navel and ass. And I bet they'll hatch any day now. We'd better boil him, too."

I assigned Mouse at the far end of the bed, next to Pockmark. Nobody wanted to be next to him, and Pockmark didn't care.

Mouse was sentenced to only six months. The police didn't give country boys long terms. Perhaps this was because Beijing didn't issue grain allowances to the Farm for those from the country villages, as they did for those from the city. Or, perhaps it was because country boys didn't consider serving on a labor-reform farm as punishment. Many of them liked the farm life better than life back in their poor villages. The food from the inmates' kitchen was horrible according to the city boys, but Chadian meant a secure, almost luxurious life for the country people. At least they were allowed to have more food than they did in their villages.

For Mouse, there was a place to sleep at night and the police didn't beat him, as they often did in the Beijing streets. Within two months, Mouse's term would be over, and he was worried. He was afraid to go back to his stepfather in the mountain village north of Beijing. He also didn't want to go back to the Beijing streets. In warm weather it was all right. But in winter...

When he was three, Mouse's mother married a drunkard in Liubao Village in Changping County. His stepfather was a villain, a local terror. No one in the village dared to cross him. He had sex with his wife during the daytime while the boy huddled in one corner of the room.

Mouse never had enough to eat. The villagers were poor and harvests in summer and autumn couldn't carry them through the whole year. His stepfather drank up everything in the house, and then "begged" by the side of the highway. The county police put him in jail a couple of times for begging, and finally left him alone.

"Ah, good food there," the father would tell the villagers on his release. "The only thing wrong with the police station is that they don't serve liquor."

Back home, drunk, he would strip his wife and rape her. After that, he would kick the boy around for not collecting enough firewood.

The village was located just two miles beyond Badaling, where Chinese and foreigners flocked to see a section of the ancient Great Wall. Mouse had been to the wall twice. He found that the people in his village and the sightseers at the Great Wall lived in two different worlds. The sightseers seemed to have everything, and the villagers had nothing. At the foot of the Great Wall the city people ate snow-white bread and sausage, drank beer and soda water, and smoked cigarettes.

A primitive urge propelled Mouse to walk up to a middle-aged couple and stretch out his hands. The man looked at him and then tossed to him a piece of bread wrapped in wax paper. Emboldened, Mouse begged from others. By the time only a few sightseers were left, he had filled his stomach with meat and bread, and had quenched his thirst on soda water and beer from opened bottles abandoned by the wayside. The ground was littered with cigarette butts. He picked some of them up and smoked.

Mouse didn't dare to go back home. His stepfather would surely give him a good beating for not doing anything the whole day. He slept that night on the mountain side, under the Great Wall. Next day he had no difficulty filling his stomach again. When the weather got cold, he followed the road from Badaling to the city, where he began a new life.

His small physical stature provided the greatest advantage for begging. The police rarely noticed him as he curled up under the benches in the railway station for the night. His mother and stepfather never looked for him. At least if they did, he never knew about it. One day in Beijing he came across a man from his village.

The man told him his mother had died. That cut the last connection between him and the village.

After four months at the Farm, Mouse's strangled conscience began to be aroused. He developed a vague sense of shame. "A man lives for his face; a tree lives for its bark," an older inmate had told him, quoting the ancient sages. Begging was shameful. Mouse wasn't looking forward to roaming the Beijing streets again. He could cope with the hard work on the farm, he told Officer Niu, and asked if he could stay.

"We can't keep you here," Officer Niu told him. "If you were an urban resident, we might assign you a job in one of the farm's factories. But you come from a village. We can't get a permit to change your rural status into that of a city resident. You have no choice. You have to go back to your village."

Mouse blinked his small eyes, unable to comprehend the theory. The city boys looked forward to their release so much that they constantly counted their days left on their fingers. Even the tough ones like Black Head and Tiger were scared to death when Officer Niu threatened to retain them on the Farm if they didn't behave. But the police didn't want Mouse, even though he volunteered.

"You don't have to pay me," Mouse begged Officer Niu. "Just give me three meals a day and six yuan of pocket money a month, like you do now."

"I can't make the decision," Officer Niu said kindly, and patted Mouse on the head. "It is a regulation set by the Beijing Security Bureau. No one can change it."

Mouse looked up, his features twisting pitifully. Everything on the boy's body was underdeveloped, like a turnip growing on a pile of rocks, dry and small, but with a tough texture. "I'm not going back to the village," Mouse announced stubbornly. "I'll run away, and the police in Beijing will catch me and send me back here!"

"All right," Officer Niu said patiently. "I'll talk to the general headquarters, and see if they can make an exception in your case."

I knew he wouldn't.

15

Mid-Autumn Festival

In late August, after one hundred days of intense care –
harrowing, weeding, applying fertilizer, and maintaining the water at a meticulous level – the rice began to
ripen. The depth of water in the paddies was no longer
critical to the crop's survival. I watched the rice leaves
turn from dark green to light green, then a yellowish
green, and finally golden yellow. The sluice gate at the
bridge to the east of the Big Compound was lowered to
cut the flow of water from the Chaobai River into the
deep pit under the pump house. The two powerful pumps
whirred for a couple of minutes to drain the remaining
water in the pit.

The younger officers and electricians climbed down
into the pit, each with a scoop net to clear the pit of fish,
which, mostly carp, flopped desperately on the muddy
floor. Older officers and their families gathered around
the pit to make sure each got their fair share of the booty.
The little water in the irrigation canal had long since
dried up. Grass was growing fast and fat in it. Soon the
grass would die as the earth became too dry and the alkali surfaced once again.

The sunning period for the rice now began. The paddies were left to dry so the rice grains would harden.
Our two squads were allowed to keep working out in the
fields, this work having been reduced to scaring away
sparrows. The rest of the inmates picked corn and cut
sorghum stalks. Officer Niu sent our two squads to help
with the corn harvest for four afternoons a week so that

we had a relatively easy time of it – a reward for our diligent work, and for not having any serious accidents or escapes during the summer.

"They have to guard the rice from sparrows and peasants," he told Instructor Feng.

The sparrows didn't do much harm, though the peasants from nearby villages often came over the main drainage ditch, pretending to cut grass in order to make off with bundles of rice. Officer Niu told me in private, "Tell your men not to fight with the peasants. Just yell and scare them away." I passed down the message.

Earlier in the year, when the young reeds in the drainage ditches had grown two feet high, villagers came to cut them for fodder. The inmates of the labor-reform farm threatened the men and teased the young women. Soon thereafter, the young men from the village returned in force with the intention of beating the crap out of these elements. This wasn't the only occasion for such confrontations.

The officers hated the villagers because they often stole the farm's and the officers' personal belongings. The officers reported this to the general headquarters, and the authorities sent for the village chief, ordering him to restrain his men. The young villagers, however, continued their thievery. Farm property continued to turn up missing, including sections of power cables and poles.

We guarded the rice during the day and the officers and the three workers of the Small Compound took shifts during the night. I told the men in my squad not to go near the villagers when they came into our fields; if they came to cut grass, just to let them, and if they tried to steal any rice, then to yell and wave their spades.

"No fighting," I told Black Head and Tiger. "It's not worth it for us to shed blood for the farm. If you hurt a villager, you'll be punished for it. If you're hurt by the villagers, you won't be rewarded for it."

I told Han Jen the same thing. He replied, "It's not my business whether the rice is stolen or not. I'll pretend I don't see them if the villagers steal rice from my

plots. All the rice we grow is being sent to Beijing, anyway. When it's all harvested and ripe for eating, we'll be
still gnawing on corn buns. Why not let the poor villagers have some?"

In autumn, the fish swim downstream to seek deeper
water for the coming winter. They usually make their
migration at night. After we stopped watering the rice,
the water in the drainage ditches began to flow more
rapidly into the main drainage ditch. Han Jen taught us
how to build dams in the drainage ditches so we could
catch fish. We built three or four of these along each of
the north-south drainage ditches. The dams blocked some
of the flow of water and raised it two feet higher. We put
a shallow gap at the top of each dam, a gap like the inlets
we made to let water into our rice paddies. The width of
the gap was determined by the discharge volume of the
drainage ditch. The larger the volume, the wider the gap.
Thus the water could flow through the gap and provide a
constant depth of about two to three inches. At the base
of each dam we placed sieves made out of willow twigs
and bamboo strips. Whenever fish swam over our dams,
they became trapped in the sieves.

We built the dams in places where the willow bushes
were dense, and we camouflaged them with tree branches.
To make sure that the officers and their families didn't
steal our catch, we went to the fields every day as soon
as it was light and made our rounds of the sieves. Some
had invariably caught fish, while others had not, but we
never came away empty-handed.

We seldom saw any large fish in the drainage ditches,
and decided this was because all the big fish must have
been killed by the chemical fertilizers, or the sea birds.
Every time we applied fertilizer to the fields, there would
be a layer of tiny fish floating on top of the water in the
paddies, killed by chemical fertilizer. We were thus surprised to catch a few one-footers each morning. They must
have hidden in holes in the drainage ditches.

After we completed our rounds, we would hide our
booty under a bush, return to the Big Compound to have

breakfast, and then go out to cook the fish at the far end of Irrigation Ditch Fifteen where we would not be seen. If we found we had caught too many, we would bring some back into the Big Compound and give them to friends in other squads.

"During the sixties," Master Chao said, watching me clean one of the fish from the drainage ditch, "no one would eat fish this small. When the pumps were shut down, fish could be picked up anywhere in the fields.

"Crabs were the worst curse to crops at that time. We didn't have chemical fertilizers. We used compost instead. The crabs cut off rice ears with their scissor-like pincers. They could climb up sorghum stalks to cut down ears of sorghum. In the morning, we would find large patches of ruined grain on the ground. One task of the inmates was to catch a bag of crabs every day. The farm sold these in the Beijing market. Crabs are fattest when the sorghum ears have ripened. There were so many of them, we ate only the roe. Many inmates got stomach aches from eating too many, so the doctor finally set a limit as to how many we could eat. Now you can't find any real crabs even in the Chaobai River. The chemical fertilizer has killed them all, killed the fish and the crabs."

It was a joy to see fish trapped in the sieves under our dams. Still, I felt sad at seeing so many fish trapped in the footprint-shaped puddles of water that remained in the drying rice paddies. The stranded fish were usually half in water and half exposed to the mercy of the swirling flies and insects. Still alive, their mouths opened and closed laboriously as if they were trying to speak, but could not find the words. On one fish, maggots had eaten the eyeball that was exposed to the air. They would bore deep into the fish through that socket. When I found it in such a state, I was reminded somehow of my own plight. I hacked at it with the blade of my spade to give it a quick death.

For about a week we had a rich supply of fish from our traps. As the water in the drainage ditches dwindled, we cut the gaps in the dams lower and lower to maintain a certain flow over them. Finally, we could no longer catch any fish in the sieves. But the number of shrimp we caught increased. So we cooked shrimp.

In another week, we found nothing in our sieves and so we decided to drain the ditches section by section to get at any remaining fish. Building dams and scooping water out from the dammed section of each ditch was tiring, dirty work, and the fish we caught this way always tasted muddy. But by doing this we had fish to eat for one more week.

Mouse had been sent back to his stepfather. He had wept and pleaded with almost all the officers at Farm 583 for them to let him stay. But he was sent anyway, escorted by a policeman from Chadian to Beijing, and then handed over to another policeman from Changping County who took him back to his village in a jeep. They made sure that Mouse wouldn't "hightail it" before he was put into the custody of the village security personnel.

Mouse took his rag riches with him in a big bundle. For a moment, I wished he'd stayed longer. He would have been overjoyed to have so many fish trapped in our sieves, just waiting to be eaten. And those left in footprint puddles wouldn't have gone rotten. Mouse would have searched the fields high and low to collect them all. I felt a little guilt for having slapped him on several occasions and for not intervening when others intimidated him, but now he was gone, and all but forgotten. His place on the platform bed was not filled since there had been no newcomers.

Pockmark now had two persons' space to sleep in on the platform bed. It was only two weeks before his term would end. But the factory where Pockmark originally worked wouldn't take him back. The Beijing police argued at length with the factory security department. They stubbornly refused to accept him.

Pockmark's relatives didn't care for his interests, and he had no friends to go to. Chadian had no choice but to place him at Farm 586 to look after the graveyard. His original factory promised the Beijing Public Security Bureau that, as long as the police didn't send Pockmark back to the factory, they would pay his monthly salary of sixty-five yuan till the end of his life no matter where the police kept him. Of course, there wouldn't be any raises for him in the future.

Farm 586 was only ten minutes on foot from Farm 583. So, I went over one afternoon to see Pockmark. He lived alone in an adjoining house, set in a courtyard like the Small Compound. Here there were no cows, horses, or farm tools. The three row houses were falling down for lack of care. The courtyard was littered with debris of every description. Pockmark told me the place had seen its golden days when Chadian was filled with Rightists.

He took me to the graveyard, a short distance from his living quarters. "Now I'm in charge of the dead," he chuckled. "They haven't buried women inmates since I came. I wonder if there are any women underground. I don't have a wife above the earth. I may find one to accompany in the netherworld here."

"Do you remember what you told me five months ago?" I asked. "In late April, just before our squad was assigned to the rice fields? You said that you wouldn't mind if you were buried in the graveyard at Farm 586. You were very farsighted then."

"Fate," he laughed. "Everything is predestined. Now here I am. I'll dig a nice pit for myself. It will be spacious, and it'll have steps. When I don't feel like moving around anymore, I'll walk down into it, lie down and wait for the time to come. I bet you a bowl of Sunday pork stew, no one will notice my death until they want a new pit dug."

His face was puffy. I doubted it was because he had better food now. His factory was kind enough to pay him his original salary. Sixty-five yuan a month was big money among the ex-inmate workers at Chadian. Master Chao was paid for only thirty-five.

"You see, the mounds have become tattered," he said. "Who cares about dead inmates? Their relatives are only too glad they are dead. You see over there? Those buried there died during the hard years in the early 1960s, most of them were Rightists. They starved to death. Their names were written on bricks or pieces of wood. There aren't any marks left now. If relatives suddenly wanted to collect the remains of one of them, they wouldn't be able to find the right one.

"I doubt if there are any remains under the mounds, anyway. They were wrapped in reed mats, or in their own quilts without a coffin. Wild dogs may have eaten their flesh and scattered the bones. Some of them, you know, were once the 'pillars of the nation.' See, this is where their great learning got them. I'll be buried here, one of these days, among those great men. What a glorious death for me! Well, when you think of it, isn't it stupid to worry about what will happen to you after you die?"

Pockmark had been carefree inside the Big Compound. Now, outside and comparatively free, he seemed dejected and downtrodden. Inside, at least he and the other inmates were equals. Now he was rejected by both officers and the other workers.

"I've got to get back now," I said.

"Can't you stay longer?" Pockmark said pleadingly. "I know you guys despise me, but I'm not such a bad guy, believe me. I was not this bad looking when I was young. The pockmarks didn't show then because my skin was not this dark. I used to be a good mechanic, the best in my factory, and I read books. Several girls were wild about me, and of course I married the prettiest one. We got along well until we had a child, a daughter. My wife changed suddenly, became a hawk. I did everything to please her: washing diapers, cooking all the meals, washing her feet, you name it. I stopped smoking and drinking inside my own house. I ate what she liked. Still, she kept complaining, and she to top it all off wouldn't let me sleep with her. 'You wait on a woman in birth confinement because you can screw her when she's clean,' as they say."

"Never heard that before," I interrupted, to show that I was listening.

"Anyway," Pockmark waved his puffy hand weakly. "I couldn't touch her for weeks. Why would a man want a wife if she didn't let you fuck her? Her pestering drove me crazy. I forced her one night. The next day she reported me to the factory authorities and they held a meeting in my workshop, accusing me of rape. Ever heard of a woman accusing her husband of rape? I was mad, so I gave her a good beating that night. So she left me, and I became a laughing stock in the factory."

The sun was going down near the Chaobai River dike. Its soft light gave a golden touch to the sparse patches of wild grass among the graves. Would I care if I were to be buried here? I asked myself, and knew I would.

"I could've asked to be transferred to another factory," Pockmark said, apparently determined to pour his soul out to me. He must have kept all this in for too many years. "I could have gotten another wife. I could have if I had wanted. I was just over thirty, and made good money then, and I had no one to support, but I didn't want to. One marriage was already too many for me. Women are a troublesome lot. After they catch you, they begin to boss you around. What have they got to entice me with, anyway? I'm no longer interested in that sort of thing, so I decided to do without them. Don't think I'm cheap. It's much easier doing it my way. This way, I don't hurt anybody."

"I have to go now," I said. "It's not good for me to be away for so long. I am still on the inside, you know."

"Come next Monday," he said to me in the tone of a great friend. "I'll buy you wine and meat."

"I don't think I can come again," I said. "We are going to start work on the threshing ground next week."

Walking back to Farm 583, I thought of the conversation with Pockmark. I found his attitude toward life much more practical than mine. The majority of people are bound by conventional norms. Many complain about how those norms destroy their pleasure, but when a person frees himself from such restraints, others around rise in unison to condemn him.

Though I didn't want to see Pockmark again, I hoped that he would live out the rest of his days in satisfaction, and die in peace. His end didn't seem that far away.

At the end of summer, we were all assigned to cut rice. For this busy season, the kitchen served more wheat flour buns and two pork dishes each week. As in the transplanting time, sabotage meant great losses of grain, so the officers watched us closely.

Middle school students from the general headquarters and paper mill workers came to help. I was once again assigned to bring drinking water to them. With children in bright colored clothes, the fields seemed much livelier. Several students were always kept isolated from the others. I figured they must be the children of ex-inmate workers, and that the children of senior officers were showing their superiority by not associating with them. I was reminded of the children living around the army barracks. They treated each other in a manner according to the ranking order of their fathers.

After the rice had all been harvested, the fields were desolate. Rice-stalk stumps stood unevenly. The paddy plots were thoroughly dry, cracked, and littered with numerous foot prints. Soon, the general headquarters would send tractors to plow some of the strips for sowing the winter wheat. The inmates were kept at the threshing ground, south of the Big Compound, to knock the grains of rice from the stalks. The job was dirty and uncomfortable.

The threshing machine was composed of wooden tubes, anchored to which were small, steel-wire loops. The tubes were turned horizontally by an electric motor.

We lined up at one end of the thresher, each of us with a bundle of rice to place against the tubes. We then walked the length of the thresher. By the time we reached the other end of the thresher, all the grains of rice had been knocked off onto the spinning wire loops. The dust, smashed leaves, and particularly needles and shells of the rice got in every part of our bodies and hair.

The work pace was leisurely, however. There was no rain in autumn to worry about and there wouldn't be much work to do in the fields until next spring. The autumn sun was comfortably warm, and the breaks were unusually long.

During these breaks we lay or sat against the crop stacks, smoking and joking. Some demonstrated their pickpocketing skills.

"I can take this slip of paper out of your pocket in five minutes," Tiger said to me, and put the paper in my jacket pocket. I didn't think much of Tiger's trick and kept my ear to the talking about favored dishes we would order after we got back to Beijing. "Huang Longsen," Tiger called out, showing the slip of paper in his hand. "How's my skill?"

I felt my pocket, suspecting him of having used a substitute, but the slip of paper in my pocket was gone.

"You guys should teach me how to guard against you when I get back to Beijing," I joked. "On the other hand, you'd better keep the secret. Otherwise you'll lose your livelihood."

"On the subject of protecting yourself against pickpockets," Black Head said, "let me show you something." He pulled me up to stand next to him. "Many people think the breast pockets are safer than the lower pockets," he said. "Actually it is easiest to steal from a breast pocket. In a crowded bus, I would pretend to hold on to a bar in the bus." He turned to face me at a casual angle and raised one arm up to my eye level. Then he began to demonstrate. "See, as my left arm blocks your downward vision, my right hand reaches into your breast pocket." He flipped the forefinger and middle finger of his right hand to unbutton my breast pocket, and then used the same fingers to quickly extract a letter from my wife. It happened so fast and smoothly that I hardly knew he had touched my shirt.

"See," Black Head said, as if lecturing a class of primary school pupils. "But it is difficult to get a wallet out of the lower pocket," he continued, "because people usually keep their hands there. To keep money in your hip pocket is foolish. Many pickpockets carry a small razor blade to slash the bottoms of a hip pockets. A wallet will drop out pretty quickly if there's nothing to keep it from falling."

The conversation now turned to other methods of pickpocketing, burglary, and cheating tourists in Beijing. Each person there boasted about how much he could bring in one day. Inevitably, the stolen money brought us back to our most favored topic – good dishes in Beijing restaurants.

One day, Tian Chi from Squad Three wove a net with nylon thread. It was about thirty yards long and five yards wide. The threads were so fine that the net was almost invisible when he propped it up between two high stacks of bundled rice plants. Its purpose was to catch sparrows.

Sparrows rose and landed on one stack after another in large flocks, chirping noisily and merrily. Many knocked into Tian Chi's net and slipped down along the slippery threads to fall into small pockets in the net. The boys of Tian Chi's squad took the birds out of the trapping pockets and snapped each one's head between their thumbs and forefingers. With a small "plop," the birds would be dead.

The squad members would then dig a hole in the ground, and put the birds into it, covering it with a thin layer of earth. Then, they would pour boiling water over it. After a couple of minutes, they took the birds out and easily plucked off the feathers. The stewed sparrows were delicious.

If any officer happened to be present, they gave him a share. Other squads were jealous, since there were few other animals or insects around the threshing ground to pacify their protein-starved stomachs. There were mice, but the mice at Chadian were too small to be worth slaughtering and cooking.

Someone devised a way to husk the rice by grinding

the grains between two bricks. Clumsy as this technique was, it quickly spread among the inmates. At noon breaks or after supper, each squad could be found cooking rice in metal lunch boxes. Unfortunately Instructor Feng discovered this the following week, and gave strict orders that no one was to bring grain inside the Big Compound. Still some managed to smuggle in enough rice grains to cook a lunch box full on Sundays.

The Mid-Autumn Festival on September 19, and National Day on October 1st, were both occasions for family visits, which meant food packages and cigarettes. The atmosphere in the Big Compound became livelier as the dates approached. There was a feeling of anxiety, too.

My feelings were mixed. I longed to see Shalin but the meeting would be painful and awkward. The Mid-Autumn Festival, was a time for family reunions, but without privacy, the reunion would only be a torment.

Also I was concerned because Shalin had to travel by train to Chadian with our three-year-old son, changing trains at Tianjin. When they arrived at the Chadian station, the bus took them only to the general headquarters. It was four miles from there to Farm 583. She might hitch a ride on a cart, or someone might be willing to take our son with him on a bicycle, but she might not be so lucky. Then she would have to walk the whole distance, carrying our son on her back.

Pan Rong was perhaps the most eager for a family visit. His mother and sister would bring him two huge bags of food, part of which he would use to "bribe" Chang Fei, and two other thugs to provide him with protection from the other inmates. Chang Fei, the Terror of the West District, had become his patron after Pan Rong gave him half of a roasted chicken and some candies.

Pan Rong also wanted to show off his sister. She had caused quite a sensation during her last visit. Her laugh had a silvery sound and she had waved at the boys, who had cheered back at her. After that visit, Pan Rong found himself in favor for several weeks. Chang Fei frequently talked about his sister.

He was quite proud when others talked about his sister. "I would like to make you my brother-in-law," one of them said to Pan Rong. Instead of feeling offended, he replied, "Then you'd call me 'elder brother'."

To further increase his popularity, Pan Rong boasted that the famous film actor, Hsie Tien, was his uncle on his mother's side. He told the others how many children the actor had, how old each of them was, and where each of them worked.

"His third son and I went to the same middle school," he said in rebuking Tiger for doubting the truth of his claims. "If I am lying about it, I'll let you treat me like your son!" After that we all stopped questioning him on this matter. Many would have liked to have his sister as their wife, but no one wanted him as a son.

Several fame-awed boys wrote home to ask members of their families to check the famous actor's family tree. No answers ever came. This was probably because their relatives couldn't find anyone close to Hsie Tien, or because they thought it absurd for the boys to indulge in such matters while they were doing hard labor. The actor, himself, had written no autobiography, and no one else had written at length about his life yet. It was totally impossible for us to prove or disprove Pan Rong's relationship. He, in turn, grabbed every possible opportunity to remind us of his famous maternal uncle.

Pan Rong had been a shop assistant selling pork. He liked good clothes and to be seen in fancy restaurants. He would spend his whole month's salary of forty-five yuan on a dinner with his "buddies," who always looked him up on pay day. He had free meals at home and his mother never refused to give him pocket money.

After he learned that the family savings were dwindling fast, he devised a way to make easy money. He asked a friend of his sister, White Lotus, to cooperate in this scheme. The girl would come to his shop to buy half of a pig's head. He would stuff ten yuan in bills in the pig's ear before he gave it to her. Or, she would buy a pound of meat for five yuan. He would then give her change in ten yuan bills. In this way, they made a hundred yuan in one month. This thievery went on for two months until finally, to his great dismay, he was found out. The neighborhood police agreed with the shop manager that he should endure two years of hard labor to repay the damages.

He had no previous record with the police and no street skills to speak of. So the other inmates – the street thugs – bullied him and played all kinds of tricks on him. They made him do all the chores when they came back from the fields and they burnt his thighs at night with lit cigarettes. In the beginning, he was desperate to find a protector. Then his mother and sister came, bringing the resources he needed to make "friends."

Although we disliked Instructor Feng, we were at least grateful that he sent Master Chao with his cart and horses to the general headquarters to meet the visiting relatives. In fact, he did so for four days from September 19 to 22.

We were returning from the threshing ground, around half past eleven, when we saw the cart with the first batch of visitors. Master Chao slowed down and cracked his whip loudly as he passed us on his way to the Officers Compound. We screened the dozen people in the cart, each of us looking for our kinfolk, and at the young women relatives of others. I knew Shalin was not among them. She was coming on September 22, the last day of the festival. So I looked at the cart with less interest.

White Lotus, Pan Rong's sister, stood up on the cart to wave at us. Her mother pulled her down. Pan Rong waved back. Several boys waved toward the cart and gave her a hearty cheer. She was nineteen, had fair skin, and grew her hair long. Her fine features were enhanced by a pink blouse and a white cashmere sweater. A sky blue windbreaker draped over her shoulders. She was certainly pretty, but she didn't appeal to me. Her bearing seemed cheap, like that of a street walker.

Master Chao reined in his two horses at the gate of the Officers Compound. The relatives got off, stood there and looked back to seek their dear ones among us. Officer Niu herded us into the iron gate of the Big Compound. "There'll be time for you to meet your relatives," he said sternly.

That night I received some "tribute" from those whose relatives had arrived: a pack of cigarettes, some candy, three preserved eggs, and a piece of roast duck. Han Jen received his share of "tribute" too, a little more than I did. I gave him the packs of cigarettes, since he had no relatives to visit him, and anyway I didn't smoke.

While we met our relatives, the police presence was minimal, compared to the Liangxiang Detention Center. Only one officer was in the duty office supervising the dozen inmates with their relatives. The visitors felt much more lighthearted than they would have at Liangxiang. There were no tears, but smiles and occasionally laughter.

The Big Compound wall, though crowned with barbed wire, looked much less formidable and menacing against the high, broad sky and open fields than did the gray one at Liangxiang. Visitors could see the row houses through the open gate. The laundry hanging on the lines gave an atmosphere of family life. The doors and windows were not barred. The officers, in civilian clothes, looked and talked like nice country folk to the visitors from Beijing, who somehow felt superior to them.

Around two o'clock in the afternoon on September 22, a group of us were called to the duty office. Shalin was there. She had brought a bag of food as heavy as the boy, even though I had told her not to bring so much. We sat on benches in small clusters at the four desks. Most of us talked and stared at the desk tops.

Shalin told me that she and our son were in good health. The neighbors had become friendlier now that the initial shock of my detention was over. The children in our courtyard were even helpful to her. They helped with buying the grain and coal bricks.

She also told me who among my friends had been given formal prison sentences and who had not. "Li

Chuan was sentenced to death, and is on death row now," she said. "But we don't think they will carry out the sentence. None of them were tried in public."

Our son had grown much during the eight months since I left home. "You should have left him with a neighbor," I said, trying to smile at him. "And don't bring me so much food next time. You have to change trains at Tianjin. It's too troublesome."

"It's no problem," Shalin smiled self-consciously. "The boy insists on walking when we go out. He's learning to play chess with Danping."

"We'll play chess together when I come home," I said to him.

"When will you come home?" he asked.

"Not very long now," Shalin answered for me.

I looked away from the boy. Tiger and his mother were sitting in a corner diagonally from where I sat. Tiger was pouting, rolling his upper lip to block his nostrils. He was getting impatient with his mother, and his mother was shaking her head almost imperceptibly. Tiger winked and squeezed his eyes in persistence.

His mother cast a glance in the direction of Officer Guan, and then slipped her hand into her trousers pocket to withdraw a folded envelope that she passed into her son's hand. It contained cash, and the old lady had prepared it beforehand! Tiger had gotten into trouble because his mother had spoiled him. Now she gave him cash against the farm regulations. Keeping cash was considered an incentive for escape.

The forty minutes of meeting time seemed to go on eternally. Then, all of a sudden, we were told the time was over. Shalin and I both realized we had not said much to each other, and now we felt we needed time to talk. We looked at each other. I stood up and took the food package that had been opened and examined by Officer Guan before we came in.

Shalin and the other relatives were escorted to the Officers Compound, where they would stay in guest rooms for the night. Early next morning they would go to the railway station to catch the 8 o'clock train. We inmates returned to the row house. Another batch of visitors were brought into the duty office, and another batch of inmates were called over to meet them.

After supper Officer Niu sent for me to come to the duty office. "You may talk to your wife one more time if you wish," he said.

Gratitude brought tears to my eyes. "Thank you," I said.

Officer Niu took me to a small, empty guest room, went out and returned with Shalin. "You two have a chat," Officer Niu said. "I'm going over to see if the boys are behaving themselves." He had left us completely alone.

Actually there was not much to talk about. She told me not to take things too seriously and to take good care of myself, and I told her to take care of herself and not to worry too much about how little savings were left in our bank account. After half an hour, both of us became anxious. We hoped Officer Niu would return and take me back to the Big Compound. It was a risk for Officer Niu to let us have this second meeting, especially without supervision.

Officer Niu came back with a thermos bottle. "Shalin, you can wash the boy with the hot water in here," he said.

The next morning before we went out to the threshing ground, we heard Master Chao's whip echoing sharply outside the high wall of the Big Compound. Our loved ones were apparently on their way back to the general headquarters.

Pan Rong had received the most packages. His mother was only fifty-three and in good health, and his sister was young. Between the two of them they could have brought their dearest son and brother triple the amount if they had not been warned by Officer Niu that no more than ten pounds of food were allowed. They brought twenty pounds, ten pounds each in accordance with the regulations.

"It's a pity, really. I only have the Qianmen brand

this time," Pan Rong said as he was distributing a pack of cigarettes with an air of generosity. "Officer Niu wouldn't allow them to bring the Zhonghua brand for me."

"Your mother must have a lot of money," Black Head said as he took a cigarette from Pan Rong, stuck it behind his ear and then took another one and put it in his mouth. "Every time she comes she brings a mountain of good stuff for you to eat. Where does she get all the money? Does she work nights with your sister?"

Pan Rong looked at the extra cigarette on Black Head's ear ruefully and said with a rough edge, "My father left us money. We have a lot in the bank, more than you will ever see in your whole life. The interest is enough to keep us going, we don't have to work nights on the streets with your relatives."

No one made any comment. They were all smoking Pan Rong's cigarettes, puffing rings into the air.

"How could your father make so much," Black Head asked, not wanting to have his humor ruined, "wasn't he a lowly middle school teacher?"

"My grandfather left it to him," Pan Rong said proudly. "My grandfather was a minister of the Qing court. My father donated two thousand taels of silver to the government in 1951, to aid the fight against the US imperialists during the Korean War. We still had a box full of gold bars when the Cultural Revolution began. My mother wanted to give them to the government, but she was afraid that if the Red Guards found out we had them we would be in serious trouble. My father said we had a written government permit to keep the gold and silver, and he refused. After he died, my mother gave the gold to the government and threw all the pearls, gems, and silver ingots into a sewage hole. There were a lot of them. I helped take them out of trunks at night."

His words attracted attention. "You should have buried them under the floor, or in a wall," Pet Tong said regretfully.

"Why bother?" Pan Rong replied. "We can't spend

them anyway. No shop will accept them. If you go to the bank, they will confiscate them."

"But times will change," Pet Tong said. "Paper money may become useless after the regime falls, but gold, silver, precious stones and pearls will always be worth more and more. These things have been valuable for several thousand years and they will remain so, no matter what kind of a government there is."

Pet Tong was outspoken in political matters and got one year on the labor farm for it. An assistant lecturer at Beijing Foreign Economics Institute, he liked to argue with his colleagues that capitalism had its good points, and that China could learn from it. He was a member of Team Four, and often came to my squad to talk politics.

He considered me an equal – a fellow political prisoner. He reminded me somewhat of Liang Yu at the Liangxiang Detention Center. But Liang Yu was ten years younger than I was, and came from a big official family. Pet Tong, on the other hand, came from an office clerk's family and was thirty-seven. He was old enough to have learned the danger of talking against government policies.

"It was stupid to throw them away," Pet Tong continued to shake his head. "You can smuggle them to Hong Kong, and live like a millionaire there." Others joined the conversation, in agreement with Pet Tong.

"You're bragging, Pan Rong, aren't you?," I said. "You have never looked like someone from a rich family. If your father had so much gold, your family wouldn't have lived near the west city wall for twenty years."

"That's right," Black Head said, happy that Pan Rong was being exposed. "Pan Rong, you're bragging. My father never saw any gold in his life, but we didn't live anywhere close to the city wall."

Pan Rong's face flushed. At that point Tan Ching crawled over from the other end of the platform bed. "Hey, check this out," Tan Ching said. He smoothed out on the bed a page from the *China Pictorial* magazine. It showed a colored picture of Imelda Marcos, the First Lady of the

Philippines, kissing the aging Chairman Mao Zedong on the cheek. Her off-the-shoulder white silk dress revealed the upper part of her creamy breasts thrusting forward tantalizingly.

"I would die satisfied if I could lay her for one night," Tan Ching announced.

Tan Ching had been given two years for forging train tickets. A reticent man in his mid-thirties, he always finished his work load, and ate his meals quietly. After supper he would take a book, or old newspaper to read in a corner of the courtyard, or on the platform bed away from others. When younger men ordered him to do chores, he did them without complaint. We all believed he must have some mental ailment.

It was ridiculous for him to make such a statement all of a sudden. But I was glad he turned the talk to women and got the conversation away from the subject of hiding wealth from the authorities – an area that could be politically dangerous.

I wrapped some of the sugar and cooked the pork Shalin brought to me in two packages and gave one to Han Jen, and the other to Teacher Sun. I also gave Teacher Sun some fried soybean paste with pork pieces in it. Han Jen didn't lack things to eat, since many boys paid him tribute. But no street boy cared whether or not Teacher Sun received any gifts. His wife hadn't come this time.

"No, you keep them," Teacher Sun said. "I'm all right without."

"No letter from her?" I asked.

His wife had not answered his letters since she visited him on May 1. He was worried. "No," he said weakly.

"Perhaps she's waiting for National Day. It is only one week away."

Teacher Sun said nothing.

"Many families didn't come this time," I comforted him. "There will be more visitors on National Day. For many, that's more important than the Mid-Autumn Festival."

Even I felt that my voice was unconvincing. Teacher Sun had been away from his wife for nearly a year, long enough to alienate an attractive wife from a disloyal husband. Some other man had probably gotten her attention by now.

"You should write her more often," I suggested. "One letter every two weeks is not enough. The farm regulations allow us to send a letter home every week."

"I'm not worth her suffering," Teacher Sun said, tilting the small stool backward, so that he could lean his back against the wall.

The autumn sun was warm in the west, casting a soft light through willow tree branches onto his rugged face. The willow had begun shedding leaves. In Beijing, willow trees would still be golden green now.

"I've suggested in my last letters that she find another partner," Teacher Sun said as he looked through the willow tree at the setting sun.

"You shouldn't have done that," I said. "You're not a bad guy. Ask her to forgive you and promise to make it up to her when you get home. You'll live together happily."

"No. There won't be happiness for me any more. I'll be burdened with guilt for the rest of my life. One wrong move and the whole game is blown, as chess players say. Sometimes I think that because I have made this one wrong move, I should not go on with the game. It would be much easier for me to quit right here. Why are men's feelings strange? Why do we drag on until the end, even when we have lost all hope?"

"Things will change," I comforted him, aware that I was making empty talk.

"Change? Ha!" Teacher Sun laughed bitterly. "For me? Not in this life. My predicament is different from yours. Yours is political. There may be a chance for you to be exonerated. But for me? I have to carry it to my death. There are people who are sympathetic to your plight, but there won't be any people sympathetic to mine. A bad egg with rotten morals, that's what I am."

"Everybody makes mistakes, or as you say, makes a wrong move, or two in a lifetime. That doesn't mean the end of a person. Even if things turn out for the worst, say your wife leaves you, you'll be back in Beijing in another year. People will judge you according to how you behave from then on."

"I'm forty-two. There are not many years ahead." Teacher Sun said quite dejectedly. "Why bother?" he suddenly laughed. "When I was young I read some Buddhist tracts that said everything happens without consequence, and that as long as your mind was at peace, your life would be peaceful. In later years, I came to worry about too many things. Perhaps I should start believing in Buddhism again. Would you go out with me for a stroll in the fields?"

"My pleasure," I said jokingly, affected by his sudden turn of mood. "Indeed, why should we worry so much?"

16

Another Year at Chadian

Pan Rong's mother came for another visit on October 1, China's National Day. It didn't surprise anyone that she came to see her son for the second time in less than two weeks. But it was a great disappointment to the boys that she came without White Lotus. Therefore, when Pan Rong was called to meet his mother, none of the usual crowd gathered under the two back windows of the duty office to eavesdrop.

White Lotus had "made off" with one of Pan Rong's buddies, an inmate who was released two months earlier. Among the street boys, the term "make off" might mean many things: going out together as casual friends, joining a consorting with the opposite sex in public or sleeping together. Most often a girl like White Lotus – a chick with a pretty face – would do all of these things in order to impress the boys as to how worldly she was.

"What kind of friends have you made here?" Pan Rong's mother yelled at her son. "They eat your gifts, and when they get out, they come to cheat your mother and sister! The first time I came, I knew immediately there are no good people inside this damn place. What did I do in my previous life to deserve a useless son like you!"

The other visitors in the room looked at her in utter disbelief. The other inmates snickered and made faces at Pan Rong.

"This is no place for decent people," Pan Rong's

mother scolded her son savagely. "You'd better watch out so you don't become one of them."

Pan Rong tugged at his mother's jacket, and pleaded with his eyes for her to calm down.

"Oh, my lord in heaven! I give up. I've lost my poor, stupid son. But my beloved daughter! Oh!" Pan Rong's mother wailed, swore, and delivered a genuine swat to Pan Rong's face. She then hit the desk so hard and often that the other relatives in the room could hardly be heard.

All of them stopped talking and watched the mother and son. Officer Niu, on duty that afternoon, stood up and walked over to Pan Rong's mother. He said coldly, "Do you realize how idiotic you look, behaving like this in front of your son and other visitors? You can either stop yelling, or you can leave!"

Pan Rong's mother looked up at the officer, bewildered. She suddenly realized where she was and put a buttered-up smile on her puffy face. "Yes, I'm sorry," she said. "My good-for-nothing son made me lose my head. He has never given me a day of peace since he was born. He always makes bad decisions, and he never listens to me. It's God's retribution that he's suffering here. He deserves it. I must thank you officers here for helping him make a change."

"That's our duty. No thanks needed," Officer Niu replied.

Officer Niu didn't extend the meeting as he usually did, and called it off in exactly forty minutes. The other relatives glared at Pan Rong's mother ruefully, as they filed out of the duty office.

Pan Rong's mother lingered behind for a minute and tried to push a bulky bag over Officer Niu's blocking hand to her son.

"No, you can leave only half of the things for Pan Rong," Officer Niu told the mother firmly.

"But last time I brought more than this," she complained "and that officer on duty let me leave all of it."

"*I am on duty today,*" Officer Niu raised his voice. "And another, it is less than two weeks since your last visit. Pan Rong has not eaten one third of the food you brought last time. All you're doing is making it easier for him to be one of them."

Before his mother could plead again, Pan Rong scooped up the part of the package Officer Niu had brushed toward him, and left the room. His mother stretched her hand to grab him and missed.

"You useless son," she shouted after him. "Don't share the food with anyone. Eat it yourself!"

So once more, Pan Rong became the topic of conversation in the Big Compound. The boys speculated wildly as to what relationship Fu Dan had developed with White Lotus.

I remembered Fu Dan well because he came almost every evening to see Pan Rong during the first week after Pan Rong's mother visited. They would sit in a quiet corner near the latrine to share Pan Rong's delicacies. The two soon became sworn brothers. Fu Dan had been at Chadian for two and half years, and had made a name for himself among the thugs. Tall and handsome, he won admiration from Pan Rong, who was softer, rounder, and more feminine in his looks – definitely, not the type to attract girls.

Fu Dan looked White Lotus up and down on her visits, and she returned his looks with sweet smiles. If he was capable of "settling down" with her in a normal life, they would seem a compatible pair – as far as their looks and interests were concerned. But Mother Pan wouldn't like it. Her ambition was to marry her daughter to an office worker with a university education, or better still, a department chief. She thought highly of her daughter's beauty. To have Fu Dan, an ex-labor reform farm inmate as son-in-law, would have killed her.

"Fu Dan was lucky to get out earlier than me," Chang Ping said. "She should have been mine. Fu Dan doesn't know the first thing about women. How could he possibly take proper care of a nice girl like White Lotus?"

"Quit daydreaming, and get in line," Black Head said. "There are at least a dozen candidates ahead of you. By the time your turn comes around, that piece of flesh will have become one big callus. You would break your dick in it. Only person she'll be fit for is Mill Stone. His dick is as hard as an iron rod." Black Head guffawed at his own humor.

I could see that Pan Rong's right hand was becoming white with tension as he clasped onto the handle of his sickle. I told Black Head to shut up and get back to work.

We were cutting grass in the orchards. The rice threshing was almost done, and didn't need so many hands. Tractors were plowing the fields for winter wheat sowing. The drainage ditch water was still too high to do any repairing or dredging, so the officers gave us a long period to relax. The daily work quota became quite flexible.

For three days Team One, under Officer Niu, was assigned to cut grass in the orchards. In each plot, we found two or three baskets of pears and apples that had been hidden in the waist-high grass by the farm workers. They were apparently waiting for the weather to become cold so that few people would be moving around in the orchards. Then the workers would take these baskets home. They didn't realize that we would be sent out to cut grass there. The fruits of the orchards were forbidden to inmates.

Working in the orchards was a privileged job for us inmates. Normally, only the officers' wives, children and relatives were allowed to do it. When the fruit was ripening, the orchards were guarded. Through the entire summer, we were only allowed to buy grapes from the orchard once, and then just the loose ones, the ones that couldn't be shipped out. At the same time, they allowed us to buy some pears and apples with bruises on them.

Although we found a dozen hidden baskets, we couldn't take any of the fruit back to our row houses for later consumption because we had no way to hide them. And we could eat only two or three pears or apples at a time. I tried eating some of them, but they felt sour around the base of my teeth and tart on my tongue.

As a way of retaliating against the farm workers, the inmates searched the whole orchard to find as many baskets as they could, dragged each one out of its hiding place, kicked it open to spill out the fruit, and then either crushed it into pulp with their heels or shoveled feces into the baskets to spoil the fruit. "To make the fruit tastier," Tiger would say cheerfully. Then they covered the baskets again with grass.

One day Han Jen was sitting against a tree smoking. I went over and sat down next to him. He had become even more reticent recently. Two family visits at the Mid-Autumn Festival and National Day must have affected his mood.

"A cigarette?" he offered. I took one from his pack. I could now handle a cigarette from time to time, though still no Big Cannons. He lit it for me. The grass was high. Everyone was resting somewhere waiting for the whistle to blow. It was nearly lunch time, judging by the soft sun in the southern sky.

"I got a letter," Han Jen said and extracted one from his shirt pocket. "Officer Guan asked me who sent it. I said my sister."

Like all our mail packages, our letters were opened and examined by the officers before they gave them to us. When a woman's name appeared, the officer would make sure it was not from some former girlfriend among the gang members.

"You don't have a sister, do you?" I said, spreading out the neatly folded letter to read it.

"Of course not. She's a fellow worker in our factory. I didn't want to waste my time trying to explain that to Officer Guan. He's a bonehead. If it was Officer Niu, he would understand and ask no further questions."

"I can see by the letter that she's very concerned about you," I said.

"Concerned, indeed," Han Jen grunted.

The letter said Han Jen's factory had a new director, who had passed the word around that his predecessor had made serious political mistakes in management, and that he was going to redress these mistakes. Han Jen's fellow workers had appealed to the new director on his behalf. The new director had concluded that Han Jen had struck a bad person in order to help a good person. The director said that to take the law in one's own hands was not right, but a punishment of two years on a labor reform farm was excessive.

"So you see, no one will discriminate against you because of your record," the letter went on. "The director said he would go to the police to get you out right away. But the procedure may take several months. You have less than three months left to your sentence. Please be patient. We are looking forward to your coming back." The girl signed her name Shui Ying.

"They needed only one week to go through all the procedures when they sent me here," Han Jen said. "They signed only one paper, and then they packed me off in a factory jeep."

"The letter says the factory will send a jeep to pick you up. How grand that will be!" I said.

"To hell with the jeep! I've spent two years in this pig's asshole already! They give you a good beating, then say to you, 'I'm sorry, I made a mistake.' So you forgive them and start licking their boots again. No way, not me. Old director or new director, all crows under the sky are black. They proclaim things to be right or wrong according to their own interests, just like the bigwigs at the very top. Fuck that. To hell with them all. I wouldn't give a damn if they sent a delegation with a Red Flag limousine to meet me."

"You're right," I agreed, remembering what Shalin had written in a letter I received the day before. The leadership at the Beijing Foreign Trade Bureau had also changed recently because the political atmosphere had changed. They were talking of giving a death sentence to my friend Li Chuan only two weeks ago, and now the new leadership was asking the prison to move him from death row to a regular cell.

"We are mere pawns, manipulated by those with the

power to do so," I continued. "My time here has taught me a great deal about life. You may believe that your life is important, but if others think you're nothing, especially those in power, then you are nothing, and you go nowhere. That is why we ended up here in the middle of nowhere."

"No way, I'm not a nothing," Han Jen retorted. "To myself, I'll always be important."

I felt I had offended Han Jen, and quickly changed the subject. "Who's this girl?" I asked. "You've never mentioned her to me before."

"A fellow worker," Han Jen said. His expression told me he was recalling her image. "A group leader of the Communist Youth League. Very active in politics, and orthodox in her attitude toward political matters – I mean she always believes in authority. When I think about it, I feel ridiculous that I, someone who was never interested in political matters and born recalcitrant, got along so well with her. If I hadn't hit that drunkard, we might have been going steady by now."

"You can make up for it now," I said.

"Make up with that girl?" he laughed in his throat. "No, never. She's all right, I guess. She doesn't have evil intentions. But she's too flexible. She rides the political tide, always changing her opinions to suit the incoming leadership. I wouldn't call her an opportunist because she honestly believes in what she is doing."

"There are many people of her type, people who change sides automatically," I said. "They claim it is unwavering faith in the leadership of the Communist Party. To them, the Party is always correct, glorious and great, no matter how fast or radically it changes its policies. They believe that it's only a few bad guys in the Communist Party who make mistakes. So the Party has to stage campaigns from time to time in order to purge those bad guys. It's like it is in the West: God is always right. Only a few unfaithfuls make mistakes. The girl sounds like she's unsophisticated and just plain ignorant about politics."

"Well, whatever she is politically speaking, the girl

is all right as a person," Han Jen said. "But I don't think she's my cup of tea."

"Right. It's better to keep away from such people. My wife told me that because the political situation has shifted, my colleagues have begun to talk to her, and say that I shouldn't have been sent to a reform farm. But just a few months ago, many of them were shouting denunciations at me during their weekly political meetings. To hell with those bastards!"

Han Jen looked at me. "You've learned to swear since you came here," he commented.

My face must have flushed. Han Jen shifted his eyes away and said, "Shui Ying is a nice girl, like I said. She's too honest to be dishonest, but she's not my cup of tea. This is the only letter she has written me since I arrived here. Perhaps she is just writing from the angle of a Communist Youth League leader so that I will not lose hope in the Communist cause. Well, let's forget her. I won't write back.

"You said you wanted to learn some qigong routines. I will teach you a simple way of doing it. Put one of your hands in front of you, bend the elbow so that the hand is one foot away and aligned at your eye level. Then imagine that the big tree over there is about to fall. There is a thread attached to your hand and to the tree, and you hold the thread with a force that prevents the tree from falling. Try it, and see how you feel."

I did.

"Do you feel any tiny shocks of electricity emitting from your fingers?"

I felt a swelling in my fingers, but there were no electric shocks coming out of them.

Han Jen said this was because I didn't totally concentrate my mind in doing the exercise.

Actually my mind was wandering to Shui Ying. She must have been pretty, otherwise Han Jen wouldn't have set his eye on her. I didn't blame her for "riding the political tides." She was probably not a person who won favors from the authorities by saying what the authorities wanted to hear. She was just politically naive. I knew many people like Shui Ying. They changed their attitudes toward a political issue overnight. When the authorities condemned a person as a counter-revolutionary, they walked up to the platform of the public meeting to denounce him. When the authorities exonerated the same person later, they immediately walked up to him to extend congratulations.

"You can also do it this way," Han Jen said. "Put both hands in front of you at waist level, as if you are holding a big ball and the ball is buoyant. Now imagine the ball is rising and you are holding it down. You get the same effect as you do by holding the tree up, though it may take a couple of minutes. In qigong, this kind of exercises is called 'seeking action in inaction.' Taiji boxing is 'seeking inaction in action.' The highest form of qigong is seeking action in inaction."

"My mind is too active for qigong," I said.

"Then start with Taiji. It's easier."

"Tell me how you can throw a person down in one push," I asked, remembering the time Han Jen pushed Pan Rong into the drainage ditch. "You don't look very strong."

"A person's strength is much greater than what they actually use," Han Jen explained. "It's just that people don't know how to exert their strength to full capacity. For most people when they strike someone, they use the power of only one arm, or one leg – only a small part of the power in their whole bodies. A good qigong practitioner can exert all the power within himself, and 'borrow strength from his rival' when he strikes. This is called exploding force. Of course, it takes many years of practice to be able to do this. Some people have too active a mind to be able to do it, like you, and some people indulge themselves in drinking and women. They can never do qigong well."

He stood up, spread his feet as wide apart as his shoulders, bent his knees to assume a horse stand, raised his arms straight in front of him, and placed his palms on a pear tree. "See, in my mind I'm bringing the strength from the earth through my feet, up my legs, through my spine, and into my shoulders and my hands."

He breathed deeply and evenly and then yelled: "Hi!" The tree shivered, shaking off a shower of leaves.

I stood there, trying to imagine what it would be like to bring strength into my legs from the earth. I only felt the tendons of my ankles were going to cramp.

Han Jen sat down. "Don't bother learning this kind of stuff," he said quietly. "I can teach you Taiji for building up your health, but fighting routines are no good. They only cause trouble. After you've learned them, it's difficult to keep from using them when you meet a thug in the street."

I genuinely wished I had the martial-arts skills that Han Jen had. I could put them to good use. But I realized I couldn't accomplish much by practicing qigong. As Han Jen said, I had too active a mind. And I doubted if I could learn Taiji either.

The job in the orchard lasted only three days. We guessed the orchard workers had found out that we were destroying the fruit they had stolen, and complained about our working there. Next, we were sent to trim the willow trees along the edges of the fields, and along the drainage and irrigation ditches.

Although the rich coal mines around the city of Tangshan were only fifty miles northeast of Chadian, the general headquarters set a meager supply of coal for consumption by the inmates, an hour's worth of burning every two days. Officer Niu told me to have my squad collect as many tree branches as possible to supplement the coal supply.

"You'd better ask Master Chao to check the stove for heating the bed," he said. "You'll need it. The coal won't last long. Besides, a warm bed is more comfortable than warm air in the room."

The bed we slept on was a platform bed, called a *kang* by local people. It was like the beds on which most peasants living north of the Yellow River slept. This type of bed was built with adobe bricks, and took up about one-third of the room space lengthwise. It was composed of a number of elongated bricks, erected on the floor in such a pattern that heat and smoke can circulate underneath the bed. The smoke then vented through a chimney at the far corner of the room. Large square bricks were placed flat on top of the standing bricks, and a layer of mud mixed with chopped wheat stalks was spread across the surface so that the bed was not too hard to sleep on. In the country villages, the peasants would rebuild these beds every two to three years. They would use the ash and pulverized adobe bricks for making compost.

The platform beds at Chadian were built with baked bricks, and thus lasted a long time. Those on Farm 583 must have been built half a decade ago. The surface was uneven, and there were spots that threatened to cave in.

The coal stove in each squad room was a Chadian invention of ingenuity. It was actually a fireplace, built for heating the room rather than for cooking, connected to a fire tunnel that zigzagged under the bed through three hairpin bends, one on top of another. A layer of bricks sat on top of the fire tunnel. The fire was not allowed to get high, so one filling of coal could last for many hours. Most of the heat was absorbed and radiated before it went into the chimney. If there was enough coal, the stove could heat the whole room, despite the many cracks in the walls and windows.

Before I noticed the change in color, the willow and locust trees had all shed their leaves, and the grass and reeds had turned dry. In another two weeks, a thin layer of ice appeared over the drainage ditch. A squad of inmates from Team Four worked for a week, transporting coal from the railway station to the officers' homes and offices. Each squad of inmates received two buckets full of coal for the first week of December. As Officer Niu suggested, I asked Master Chao to check the platform bed stove in our squad room. I helped him dismantle the stove and clear out the soot and ash in the fire tunnel leading under the bed.

"You'd better send someone up on the roof to see if the chimney is blocked. Sometimes rats and birds will make nests in it."

Several members of my team vied for this mission.

"There won't be any birds' eggs at this time of the year," Master Chao told them. "So don't fight for the job. You may fall down and break your legs. Then you won't be able to enjoy the corn-flour buns, and salted turnips from the kitchen."

We put the stove back together, replacing the bricks and cementing them with mud. Each room was issued a cast iron cauldron, which we placed on top of the stove. We sealed the crevice between it and the bricks with more mud. Pan Rong brought in a bundle of corn stalks, poured some water in the pot, and lit the stove. He blew hard to get the fire going. The room was soon filled with smoke, which came from the stove and some cracks in the platform bed.

We moved the reed mat away, and patched the cracks. Some spots were caving in and Master Chao said if we didn't want trouble after winter set in, we'd better repair the bed right then. So we scraped away the top layer of dried mud, removed the bricks under it, changed some of the broken and tilting bricks that supported those placed on top, and patched the spots with a mixture of mud and chopped wheat stalks. The job took most of Sunday. I doubted if the stove would work properly through the winter, or give us enough heat.

I wrote Shalin not to come during the New Year Festival. It had been only little more than two months since the Mid-Autumn Festival and the Spring Festival was coming in little more than one month. She came, nevertheless, bringing with her our son and a bag full of food. "Aunt Yin offered to look after our son," she said. "But I thought you might want to see how much he has grown."

He had really grown a great deal, now almost reaching his mother's armpit, but he was thinner. His large eyes had became more conspicuous. Shalin must have taught him how to behave. He held my hands while I asked him how many songs he had learned, and with whom he played.

Shalin brought some cheerful news: the bureau authorities had been arguing about the counter-revolutionary charges against my friends. "Families of those in prison are encouraged to intensify their efforts in appealing to higher authorities for wrong charges," she said. "Someone in power has promised to re-investigate the cases. So you see, you may not have to stay here for three years after all."

I wanted to tell her to stay away from the wives of other counter-revolutionaries. During the ten months at Chadian I had worked out a strategy for dealing with the constant changes in the government policy. I would no longer get myself involved in any political issue. Nevertheless I didn't tell Shalin about this. She was too straightforward and honest to restrain herself from speaking out her mind at political meetings. She always believed that every wrong thing that was done was the action of individual Party leaders, and that the wrongs would eventually be redressed by other, wiser Party leaders.

The news was, of course, good. But Shalin sounded overly optimistic. I probably would stay at Chadian the full term of three years. If things were as simple as Shalin seemed to think, Han Jen's new factory director would have gotten him out three months ago.

Pan Rong's mother came again, and brought him another huge bag of food. Officer Niu was quite annoyed, and ordered her to take most of it back. This time the old lady didn't make a strong protest. Master Chao and his cart and horses were not sent to fetch the visiting relatives this time. All of them had to walk for nearly an hour to get to Farm 583.

When Pan Rong's mother and other relatives set off for the general headquarters the next morning, Officer Niu stopped her, saying, "The bag is too heavy for you to carry on this long road. Since you have already brought it here, you may leave it for your son." Pan Rong's mother, looking much older and more dejected than she did on the last visit, thanked the officer profusely.

It was reported that White Lotus had an abortion, bringing enormous shame on the Pan family. After this visit no one in the Big Compound showed any more interest in Pan Rong's sister, now that she had become a "tattered shoe", which translated to "a loose woman." Pan Rong was very quiet after his mother's visit.

"I have a lot to learn about life," he said to me. "I don't know how to make friends. The friends I have made here all want to take advantage of me. There are no good people in this damn place! Oh, I'm sorry. I didn't mean to include you. You're a good guy. From now on, I'll listen to you."

"You really need to learn something," I said. Pan Rong was not a man I wanted to be close to. He was weak minded, and easily intimidated or flattered into attempting things far beyond his abilities. He would probably betray a friend when his own interests were threatened. "But don't listen to me," I continued. "You should listen to the officers, and try your best to turn over a new leaf."

Pan Rong lowered his head and said, "You don't trust me, do you? I don't blame you. I'm too cheap to be trusted by real guys like you and Han Jen. I reported on you several times. But believe me, from now on I won't say a single word against you. I need your help in this place."

"That's all right," I said. "I'll do what I can."

I didn't want to solicit antagonism from any inmate. Why not let him believe I would help? As the saying goes, "Better to make a hundred enemies among gentlemen than to make one enemy among the riffraff." Pan Rong was merely a weakling who fawned over those stronger than him. What he said was true, though. A weak person like him needed protection from others. His problem was that he had sought protection from the wrong people.

Pan Rong was laughed at and teased by even the most timid boys in the Big Compound. As soon as they heard that his sister had taken up with Fu Dan, they crowded him. "Did you give your sister to Fu Dan before he left?" one of them asked. "Did you tell Fu Dan which part on your sister's body is the most sensitive in arousing her?" another asked loudly. I had to disperse the crowd by threatening to call for Officer Niu, which I wouldn't have liked to do.

Shortly after New Year's Day, a jeep drove into the Officers Compound. Officer Niu accompanied a middle-aged man and a young woman over to the Big Compound. Han Jen was called to the duty office room. When he returned to his squad room, he began to put his things into a net bag. He was leaving. He gave his mattress, quilt, and most of his toilet articles and clothes away. I went over to say good-bye.

"Those bastards," Han Jen swore. "If they were sincere in correcting their mistakes, as they told me they are, they would at least have come before the festival. I think the guards would have let me out several days earlier if they had insisted. But they waited until my full time was up – to the very hour, to the very day."

"What's the difference of several days?" I said. "The real thing that matters is you're now out. After you get back to work, don't make a fuss over the two years here. Try to forget it and enjoy your life. What did you say about fucking?"

"Hold on as long as you can, enjoy every second of it," he recited, as he laughed. "Ah, Huang Longsen, you are learning at this 'school of thugs.' I hope you won't become too tainted by the education."

"I won't," I said light-heartedly. "I have begun studying English in earnest. I am not expecting to learn much, but at least I won't forget too much of what I learned before. I feel the time will be less unbearable now than it used to be."

"The hardest time for an inmate here is the first six months," Han Jen observed. "The second year is comparably easier. The last six months are hard too, but in a different way from the first six months. You are anxious to get out. Now that you've begun your second year and you have Officer Niu on your side, things will be easy."

"You'd better watch your temper when you get back

to Beijing," I said, wanting to end the talk. Officer Niu and the people from Han Jen's factory were waiting.

"Don't worry," Han Jen smiled bitterly. "From now on, I'm going to turn the other cheek whenever I am slapped on the face. I'll pretend not to notice if someone is being killed. The officials talk nicely and urge us to do good things for society, but the only thing they really take seriously is protecting themselves. They are 'prostitutes who want to build themselves a memorial arch to virtue' – they want both money and a good name."

"You'd better go. They're waiting for you," I said.

"If you trust me, Huang Longsen," Han Jen said, "tell your wife to let me know if she needs help. I have many friends in many places."

I said thanks and then forgot to ask him if the young, pretty woman waiting for him in the duty office was the one who had written him the letter.

Their jeep sped up the short climb to the Chaobai River dike, kicking up a swirl of dust in its wake, and disappeared to the south. I felt a heavy loneliness, as I did every time someone was released. It reminded me once again how many days I had left to count before my turn came. But I was glad Han Jen left before what, for me, was one of the hardest times at Chadian.

Now the ground was solidly frozen. Every day each of us was assigned three cubic yards of earthwork to deepen the irrigation ditches. The first strike of our picks only made a white dent in the ground. It was frozen solid. As I dug the drainage ditch during the spring, I worked out a way to make the job easier to do, and quicker to finish. After I dug below the frozen layer, I continued to dig deeper and to enlarge the cavity in the unfrozen earth below the top layer as far as I could reach with my pick. Then I struck the frozen layer from above, which broke easily. I removed the broken pieces by hand, shoving them up over the banks. I taught my squad to dig in the same way. We could finish our quotas an hour earlier than the other squads.

The Spring Festival was coming. Shalin agreed not to

visit me during that time. My excuse was that Chadian was too cold, and the guest rooms were not heated properly. She and our son might easily become sick. Life would be even more miserable for both of us if she were ill. Without the anxiety of anticipating her visit, I felt better.

The snow at Chadian came early and was heavy. I had not seen such thick snow in Beijing for many years. The whole universe seemed to be wrapped in white. Trees were literally bursting with ice blossoms.

The Spring Festival meant more to country folk than to city folk. As the last month of the lunar year came to an end, the officers became more friendly toward the inmates and less demanding. When there were ten days left before the Festival, we stopped working altogether. Then, we were ordered to clean our rooms, wash our clothes, and cut our hair, and we were taken to the general headquarters for a bath.

The political commissar at the general headquarters called a grand meeting in the auditorium. Twenty five inmates from the nine sub-farms were awarded by having their terms cut for conscientiously reforming themselves. Five were punished with additional time for disobedience and fighting. On this occasion, we were allowed to buy cakes, each for two yuan, and each squad was given the privilege of making *jiaozi* dumplings. Extra coal was issued for our stoves. They also slaughtered three pigs for the occasion.

Tiger brought a chunk of fat from the pigsty, heated it in the cast iron pot over the bed stove, and fried our corn-flour buns in the melted fat. "Did you steal it?" I asked him. "Steal?" he laughed. "After a whole year of hard labor reform? No. I'm not that stupid. I have only one year left, and I want to go home on time. The cooks threw it away, and I picked it up."

"What part of the pig is this?" I looked at the sizzling piece of fat with suspicion. It was of an indistinct color and gave off a foul smell.

"Don't ask," Tiger said, annoyed. "It's meat. Why do you care which part of the pig it came from? What's the difference whether it's the pig's ass or cock? I tell you a pig's anus and penis are delicacies in many of Beijing's best restaurants. So enjoy your fried corn flour buns."

The fried buns did taste delicious, although my stomach felt queasy during the night.

On the last day of the old lunar year, the kitchen issued each squad some wheat flour, chopped cabbage, ground pork, soy sauce, spice powder, and other ingredients for making the" jiaozi" dumplings. We scrubbed our washbasins thoroughly, and mixed the ingredients in them. We also cut spade handles into sections to use for rolling out the dough.

Tiger's mother came on the fourth day of the Spring Festival. She brought a food package from Chi Fei.

"Remember him?" Tiger said to me. "He was the squad leader at the Liangxiang Detention Center. You slept next to him in Room Number Three. He's out on probation due to illness."

I remembered him well. He was the first street boy I met at Liangxiang who had given me any help. Black Head and Tiger worshipped him and talked of him constantly.

Tiger distributed the food between Black Head, himself, and me. "I knew he would be able to get himself out in less than a year," Tiger said happily. "He's a very smart devil. He knows how to make the guards like him. With his record, he would have been given three years on a labor farm or two years in prison. But the guards at the neighborhood station put in a good word for him. He only got two years.

"Remember Officer Wang at Liangxiang? He was the guard who checked you in. Chi Fei managed to worm himself into Officer Wang's trust. Two months ago Officer Wang obtained probation for Chi Fei because of an illness. Now he's out enjoying himself."

We ate a half of a Beijing-style roast duck. "Chi Fei said the chocolate drops are for you," Tiger said, pointing at a small package with his greasy finger. I was grateful that Chi Fei still remembered me.

"Where did he get the money to buy these expensive things?" I asked.

"He has a lot of it," Black Head answered. "He's a big player, not like us spending all we can lay our hands on. He puts some money aside, either in the bank or at his girlfriend's place. When the situation becomes hot, he sits tight, eating from the funds he's accumulated. He got to behave himself now, calling members of the neighborhood committee uncles and aunts, and helping with the street sweeping. He won't steal under these circumstances. Soon the neighborhood committee will report to the guards that Chi Fei has become a nice boy and will ask them to terminate his remaining labor-reform time. Then he's free. He has twice as many smarts as we have."

Shalin's letters kept me informed about the developments in the political situation in Beijing. It seemed that the national capital had arrived at a state of indecision. The people in high places seemed to be hesitating on what step to take next in the Cultural Revolution. The economy was on the brink of collapse; too many people had been made the enemies of the Communist Party; the central leadership was splitting. While freezing in bed, I tried to think about these matters, but the complexity of political affairs exhausted me quickly. I would rather let my mind wander elsewhere.

Winter was over, then spring. My squad was once again assigned the job of tending the rice fields. Half of the members of the squad were new. Black Head and Tiger had little difficulty in convincing them to follow my orders. Political Instructor Feng was promoted to the general headquarters. Officer Niu then had a freer hand at Farm 583, though he complained more often that it was unfair for the authorities to appoint a new political instructor from outside, while leaving him at the bottom of the ladder at Chadian.

I was happy to see Political Instructor Feng go. His departure immediately removed an immense obstacle to my early release. Officer Niu argued ardently on my behalf. I appreciated the fact that he did this despite the fact that my case was of a grave political nature. Finally, after weeks of argument, he succeeded in obtaining a six months' cut in my term.

17

Home at Last

I waited in the squad room on the evening of July 16, 1975, for Officer Niu. I was to be released the next morning. Either he or Officer Guan would come and give me my release papers. I figured it would be Officer Niu in my case. Inmates with whom I was on friendly terms had already said good-bye to me, and I had distributed my odds and ends among my squad members.

Thanks to Officer Niu's persistent recommendations to the Communist Party committee at Farm 583, the general headquarters had approved a cut in my three years sentence to two and half years. Six months meant a great deal to any inmate. I had been calculating the remaining weeks and days for the last two months, and I had written to my wife about the day I would arrive in Beijing. She would meet me at the Yongdingmen railway station.

It was already 9:45, a quarter of an hour till bedtime, which meant all lights off. My anxiety was mounting to an unbearable point. I didn't think I had made a miscalculation in my release date, but I checked the pencil slashes I had made on a calendar card over and over again. There was no mistake. The others had already gone to bed. I laid down too, dressed properly, pricking up my ears for the familiar steps of Officer Niu.

Customarily, release papers would be given on the second to last day at the farm. Officer Niu should know how I felt, and have given it to me earlier. At that moment, I began to resent his inconsiderateness. "A man who has never starved doesn't know how a starving man feels," as the saying goes.

Finally, I heard him coming down the hall. I got off the platform bed, and walked out the open door. Officer Niu was there. "I'll give you the paper tomorrow morning," he said tersely, as he approached. "Get your things together after you get up. Master Chao will take you to the railway station around eight o'clock."

I wanted to say something to thank him, but said nothing. Officer Niu was not the kind of person who received flattering words graciously.

"You may go to bed now," he said, and walked away.

I don't remember if I slept that night or not. When my eyes got tired and dry from staring at the ceiling, I closed them for a rest. I tried to shut off my brain, too. Stubbornly, my thoughts refused to stop coming. In the quiet of night, frogs croaked in the rice paddies and ditches, and insects and mosquitoes dashed and bashed against the bare bulb and mosquito nets. I felt removed from everything, my surroundings and the other inmates. I was going home.

I was thinking about how I should act on the train back to Beijing, how I should greet the neighbors in our courtyard, and how I should deal with my colleagues at the office. What would they do with me? Would they give me a decent job, or assign me to clean the corridor and toilets on the fourth floor of the office building?

I would have to re-register my residence at the neighborhood police station. Police there would deliberately ignore me, and let me wait while they chatted. I would have to be humble, as one released from a police establishment should be. I would also have to endure many more embarrassments.

I had dreamed night and day of ways to avenge the wrongs I had suffered: of changing myself into a dragon so I could cleanse the world in a deluge; of inventing a powerful laser gun with which to kill all of my enemies;

of becoming invisible so I could walk into my persecutors' homes, and rip their eyes from their sockets.

But now, suddenly, all the hatred I had harbored so long and so deeply was gone. I was returning home. This was the only thing that mattered. To hell with the bureau officials, the police, and my colleagues who might despise me. I would ignore them from now on. I had my life to live, and I was determined to live it to its fullest potential.

I shifted my mind to my wife and son. I would do everything to make my home comfortable, compatible and happy. I would bring my son up to appreciate the good things and despise political maneuvers. I would make my wife realize that all politicians were liars and should not be trusted, no matter how nicely they talked, or how much they promised. I had been cheated by them, and I wouldn't let my loved ones be cheated again.

Dawn broke as the whistle blew. People poured out of the squad rooms to rush to the latrine at the northern end of the compound and to the single tap near the entrance at the south. Unhurriedly, I spread my old blanket on the platform bed and bundled up my clothes, quilt and bed sheets. I couldn't afford to give all my things away, as many younger men did – more for a show of gallantry than because of real generosity. Furthermore, the clothes and bed things my wife sent me were the best of our family. I would need them in the future.

None of the men released before me ate their last breakfast at Chadian. They smashed their bowls and broke their chopsticks to "cut the link with Chadian." At the age of thirty-four, I didn't need to demonstrate such sentiment. I went to the kitchen and received my share of two corn-flour buns, a bowl of corn porridge, and a pinch full of salted leeks – the seasonal vegetable. The kitchen at Chadian was the only place that I have ever had salted leeks.

After the others had gone to the fields, I borrowed a wheelbarrow from the kitchen and put my things on it. Both Officer Niu and Officer Guan came to say good-bye and to wish me well. I had thought of leaving my home address for Officer Niu, but changed my mind. He was a good man, yet still a policeman. How should I, a counter-revolutionary with a record of forced labor reform, expect to keep in contact on equal terms with a policeman? That he had been nice to me, and gotten me out six months earlier didn't mean that he considered me as a friend. He may have had his own reasons for treating me well. After all, I had kept eleven inmates from making trouble for him.

I had served the role of a buffer, and an intermediary between the rival factions in the Big Compound. In my particular position, I had done what an officer wouldn't be able to do. So I deserved to be rewarded with six months reduction from my term.

Officer Niu, in his more than twenty years' service at Chadian, had dealt with many inmates like me. That was why he was so cool in seeing me off. He may have already forgotten me as he turned his back. The saying goes that "As a guest leaves, the cup of tea gets cold in no time." Why should I be so sentimental?

As I read the two lines of characters in bold type on my release paper, and examined the red seal at the bottom superimposing the date, tears came up in my eyes, the same kind of tears of shame and anger I had exactly twenty-eight months earlier at the Liangxiang Detention Center when I was ordered to sign the registration forms. I wanted to tear the release paper up. But I would need it to buy my train ticket and to get my resident card back at the neighborhood police station in Beijing. I put it in my shirt pocket and pulled the wheelbarrow over to the Small Compound, where Master Chao had already hitched the cart, his two horses neighing proudly.

"You've survived," Master Chao congratulated me. "You have a nice wife, and a smart son. You'll live happily."

"Happily?" I said. "With the brand of a counter-revolutionary on my forehead for the rest of my life?" I wanted him to understand that my future wouldn't be much better than his, so he shouldn't be too sad to see that another person had got out of the grip of Chadian.

"Still you're out of here," he said. "This is no place for decent people. Even the officers hate it. I don't know if I will ever have a chance to go back to Beijing."

I was about to remind him that he once said he didn't want to go back to Beijing, but preferred to live at Chadian because life here was much simpler. Yet I shut my mouth in time to look at his face – a dark shadow making him seem ten years older.

Master Chao stopped his cart at the open lot below the railway station, and helped me up the slope to the waiting room with my luggage. "I'll buy the ticket for you. I know people here," he offered.

I was grateful for his thoughtfulness in saving me from having to encounter the contemptuous scrutiny of the station workers. Master Chao waited on the short platform till the train puffed away. I watched him lumbering down the slope to his horses.

My wife, my youngest brother, and my five-year-old son met me at the Yongdingmen station. My wife and brother averted their eyes, not wanting to appear to be staring at me. My son, however, stood aside looking at me strangely. I had not seen him for six months, not since my wife brought him to Chadian during the New Year festival.

I must have been quite a sight then, with an emaciated face, skin like that of a mummy, and dressed in rumpled clothes. Many years later, my wife told me that I had looked like a ghost from the Beijing opera stage when I walked out of the train station lounge. No one at the station would have doubted where I had come from.

To avoid embarrassment on the public bus, we hired a three-wheeled taxi to take us home. The light car sped and swung dangerously through the crowded Beijing streets for about fifty minutes, until it arrived at our tiny, dark and dilapidated room, which we called home. It faced a large courtyard under the Greater White Pagoda in the northwestern part of the city. I felt a great relief at being home at last.

The courtyard was quiet at the time. Since it was

around noon, only kindhearted Granny Yen was at home. She brought a bottle of boiled water over to our room for me to wash my face, and make a cup of tea.

People returned from work at about five in the afternoon. They greeted me with an awkward warmth, "Glad to see you back."

I smiled and answered, "Thank you."

The three of us slept on the double bed to which a length of wooden board was attached. Our twelve-by-twelve-foot single room had no space for another bed. The close quarters, however, brought our family even closer. The room seemed dark to my eyes, which had become customized to the lit bulb in the squad room at Chadian.

"You haven't gone to sleep," my wife said as she was awakened again and again by my turning and twitching. "Is there anything wrong?"

"I have slept with light on for too long," I said. "I need time to adjust."

She got up, drew back the curtain, and went out of the room to turn on the light in the courtyard. "Better?" she asked when she returned.

"Our neighbors won't like to pay more for the electric bill," I said. "Besides, I can't sleep with the light on for the rest of my life."

I got out of bed, walked outside, and turned the light off. "You go back to sleep. I'll stay outside for a while," I told her.

The sky in the city was not as clear as it had been at Chadian. The stars were blurred by the perennial shroud of dust and smoke over Beijing.

The next day, I went to report to the office. A small desk had been placed for me in a corner of a big office room. Throughout the day, I typed clean copies for others, and was left alone most of the time. When the kitchen needed a hand to transport grain or coal, or the compound behind the office building had to be swept, I was obliged to help.

The office library was richly stocked with novels in English. I indulged in reading them, one book a month at first and then one book every week, from Shakespeare through Dickens to Hemingway.

I was exonerated in 1979, shortly after the downfall of Jiang Qing, the widow of the late Chairman Mao Zedong. Jiang Qing had played a vital role during the Cultural Revolution, and was blamed for all the bad things that took place during that period. In 1980, I successfully passed an examination to become a member of the first group of Chinese scholars to be sent by the government to study in the United States.

Everything I have done since I left Chadian has been relatively successful. I have published two books in English and several books in Chinese. My wife has gained a middle-age gracefulness, and our son is now in college. But I am still often awakened from a dream in which Officer Niu has forgotten to give me my release permit. In the dream, I am afraid of asking him for it and wait sometimes for two weeks, sometimes for two months, before he remembers and sends me home. The horrible dream of fighting airplanes also occurs from time to time. But during the day, I have been too busy to think about those twenty-eight months of imprisonment.

I didn't keep up contact with any of my fellow inmates. Although, during the two and half years I was at Chadian, I made quite a few friends among them, and some were quite devoted to me. They would fight for me, share with me the precious food their relatives sent them, and do more work when I was put in charge in the fields. I credit part of the fact that I got my six-month early release to them. However, they were not my type of friends. They were what might be called "contingent" friends, persons with whom I would have little to do in normal times.

One sunny June day in 1985, as I was asking directions to a painter's home on busy Gulou Street, a man stood up from beside a motorcycle he was examining, and came over. "Aren't you Huang Longsen?" he exclaimed happily.

I looked at the familiar face. "Aren't you Han Jen?" I replied.

Han Jen began to stretch out his hand, looked at it, and then withdrew it. It was smeared with black grease. I grabbed it in my hand.

"How have you been all these years?" he asked.

"Fine, very fine," I said. "I was cleared in 1979, and now I'm a reporter for a magazine published in English. How about you?"

"I'm fine," he said with a proper amount of enthusiasm. "How much time do you have? I mean can you have lunch with me?"

I hesitated. I only had a ten yuan note and some change in my pocket. It would have been enough for two five years ago, but now a decent lunch required four times as much.

"On me," Han Jen seemed to be reading my mind. "How about Indian food? There's a nice Indian restaurant at the crossroads." So saying, he propped up my bicycle on the sidewalk, and called to a young man in the repair shop, "I'll be back in an hour."

"You work here?" I asked.

"It's mine," he said, smiling. "Let's talk while we eat."

The five waitresses in the restaurant seemed to recognize Han Jen, and smiled at him as we entered the establishment. The restaurant was fancier than I would ordinarily go to for a casual dinner.

"You sit here while I go wash my hands," Han Jen said and departed through a curtain that separated the customer section from the kitchen. A middle-aged waitress came to the table to pick up the used bowls, plates and chopsticks, while a younger waitress wiped the table clean. The middle-aged waitress returned with two sets of plates, spoons, chopsticks, and glasses.

"Want a beer, or something?" she asked courteously.

I said I wanted to wait a minute until my friend returned. She smiled understandingly. The earlier customers looked in my direction with hostility. I was being given preferential treatment – being served before they were. I lowered my head to look over the menu. I had come in with Han Jen, who apparently was a special customer here.

"How much can you handle?" Han Jen said as he returned.

"A bottle at the most," I answered.

"I mean hard stuff, not beer. You must be accustomed to banquets since you're a reporter."

"Yes, but I still can't handle much. Two ounces, tops."

The middle-aged waitress came again. "A bottle of Maotai," Han Jen said to her in a whisper.

"No!" I stood up to protest. "That's too expensive."

"Don't worry. I can afford it. You're my old friend. There should be something special for this rare meeting."

The price of Maotai had escalated rapidly in five years from a dozen yuan to over a hundred yuan a bottle. Most of it was consumed by government officials, who paid in office checks. The price had gone beyond the reach of ordinary people, even for family reunion dinners on major holidays.

"Almost all the motorcycles belong to the children of big officials, or private business owners," Han Jen explained. "A motorcycle is worth over five thousand yuan on the black market. If an owner can afford that much, he doesn't mind paying me a hundred extra for repairs. As a matter of fact, some of them offer more so I will take better care of their precious machines. You can put your conscience at ease and enjoy this dinner. They are paying the check."

"When did you start this business?" I asked.

"Right after the government started allowing people to set up private businesses. In 1980, I borrowed some money and tore down a wall of my father's house, the wall facing the street. The house was confiscated during the Cultural Revolution, and returned to me in 1979. The location is excellent. First I repaired bicycles. When motorcycles became the fashion, I added some tools. The bike owners swindle money out of the government, and I take a tiny part of it from them. Ah, try the roast mutton, a favorite of mine in this restaurant."

The dinner bill was 185 yuan. Han Jen stuffed 200 in the hand of the middle-aged waitress, who smiled and nodded her thanks.

I gained the courage to re-acquaint myself with others who shared any experience at Chadian. I first contacted Officer Niu who informed me that the three workers of the Small Compound had been redressed in 1980, and all had been reassigned to jobs in Beijing. Master Chao now worked for the Encyclopedia Press, not far from my office. I found him on the fourth floor of their new building, next to the Fuchengmen overpass, and promptly took him to lunch. During our forty minute conversation, several men and women came in to ask Master Chao to sign various papers.

"To be a section chief is too much of a burden," he complained, showing his pride in holding such a responsible position. He was still stocky, and moved his short legs and arms like pistons.

"Lao Huan and Lao Fang are retired, taking care of grandchildren." I noticed Master Chao had dropped the prefix "Master" before their surnames and, instead, now used "Lao," which means "old" or "senior." This is a respectful way of addressing older white-collar workers. "Master" is more often used among factory workers.

"Still single?" I asked.

"Yes, still single. As I said at Chadian, 'after filling my stomach, I don't care anymore if the world goes on starving.' My job keeps me busy and free from thinking of other things."

I heard that Black Head was running a small restaurant of his own with his wife. Like all up-and-coming private entrepreneurs, he had become a "ten-thousand-yuan man," which in the eyes of most Chinese was like being a millionaire.

Tiger had "stumbled" into police hands again when he broke into an apartment and badly hurt a deaf old lady who happened to be inside. This time, he was serving in a real prison cell.

18

Return to Chadian, This Time with Honor

On April 26, 1988, I took the 6:50 a.m. train to the Chadian Labor Reform Farm near the Bohai Sea. I planned to stay there for two or three days to interview police officers and inmates, if possible, and to look at the places where I had experienced the extreme heat of summer and the freezing cold of winter for two and half years because I was considered a "counter-revolutionary."

I was going to write a book about the hard-labor experience, and I needed to see the police officers, the farm fields, and the houses once more to recall the many obscured memories.

The train traveled slowly, stopping at every small station. The otherwise monotonous journey of nearly five hours was made pleasant by Li Sia, a young policewoman assigned by the Beijing Public Security Bureau to accompany me.

Li Sia was attractive and eager to make an impression on me when she learned I was going to write a book in English. Soon she was inquiring if it was possible for her to go to the United States to study. I asked her how much English she knew.

"I'm following an English class on radio," she said, cheerfully. I asked her what she wanted to study at her age of over thirty. "Anything," she said. "As long as I can get to the United States. Many of my friends have left for Japan, Australia, Canada, and the States. They didn't have a definite idea of what they planned to do."

"How about your family?" I asked. "Does your husband mind your going?" She had told me her husband was an army officer, and that they had a seven-year-old daughter.

"That's one of the reasons I want to go abroad. My husband and I have not been on very good terms for several years. I don't think we can work things out. It will be an emancipation for both of us if I can go abroad. You must have a lot of friends in the States. Can you help me?" She looked up at me. Her eyes were bright and large, nose slender and straight, and her mouth sensitive, showing neat ivory teeth. She wore a civilian blouse of light material with the two top buttons undone. I detected the white strip of her brassiere.

I felt a bit uneasy in the face of her frankness, but wished I could promise her that I would help. "It's not easy to live in a strange place like the States," I told her, trying somewhat to ease myself of the obligation. "I've been there several times, the first time for two years. My homesickness was terrible." I quickly shut my mouth when I saw her expression of disappointment in me.

Today many young people in China are trying to get to the West by hook or crook. They don't believe there is any future for them in China. Every morning in front of the visa office of the US embassy, in the eastern suburbs of Beijing, there is a crowd of two or three hundred people lined up to get into the office, some having arrived many hours before the office opened at 8:30 a.m.

Young Chinese with university education are shoveling garbage and carrying waste down staircases in the high-rises in Japan, or washing dishes for ten hours a day in Chinatown restaurants in the United States. The jobs are poorly paid and of the most menial kind. Still, those who have managed to go abroad are the envy of those left behind, because they can make much more money than they could in China.

The United States has tightened up its policies on issuing visas to Chinese. Ten years ago they accused the Chinese government of restraining Chinese from going to their country. Now that the Chinese government has relaxed its restrictions, the Americans have become afraid that too many Chinese are going to their country and they have tightened their own restrictions accordingly.

"Well, if you could find a financial sponsor, I might be of some help," I added hurriedly. "I do have some good friends in the States. But none of them is rich enough to provide a financial guarantee for a Chinese citizen. Several of my younger colleagues have gone to the States after three or four years' persistence. You keep trying, and keep up your English study. You'll make it some day."

The train was full when it pulled out of the Yongdingmen station on the southern edge of Beijing. People who got on the train at Tianjin had to stand in the aisles or in the area between two cars. The Chinese have recently taken to vacationing away from home, and the government now allows peasants to be vendors, moving from place to place to seek higher prices for their goods. Also young men from rural areas, with their bedrolls, are traveling back and forth between the cities where they work on the booming construction projects and their native villages.

North China had suffered from droughts for over a decade. Rivers were now showing their bottoms. Wheat grew limply, and the alkaline soil north of Tianjin that used to grow an excellent strain of rice when there was plenty of water now produced little. Many of the paddy fields were overgrown with reeds that spread over to other fields and choked the abandoned irrigation ditches.

As the train approached Chadian I saw huge flat-bottomed, rectangular pits. Several bulldozers were digging them. Li Sia told me the local people had found a new way to make quick money – breeding shrimp by letting sea water flow into the pits.

"That's an excellent idea," I commented. "The sea water is plentiful, and shrimp sell for more money than rice."

Our train jerked roughly, and stopped. People using this out-of-the-way Chadian station were few. Thirteen years ago it was no more than a shed of red brick and tiles, surrounded by a wooden-strip fence. Now, It had been renovated and enlarged to hold at least fifty people. The tracks were guarded by cast iron railings on both sides that stretched for over 500 meters. The platform had been extended to accommodate a passenger train with twenty cars.

Li Sia led me down the embankment to an open lot where two buses were waiting for the train passengers. They would take us to the general headquarters of the Chadian Farm, and its nine sub-farms and workshops. In short order, the buses were packed with police officers, their family members, farm workers, and relatives visiting inmates. Li Sia told me regulations were now much more lenient for family visits.

There were multi-story apartment buildings clustered around the general headquarters. An open-air market with vegetable sellers from nearby villages was doing brisk business. People were going in and out of three of the Farm's new restaurants. Horse drawn carts, trucks, and occasional jeeps and cars sped on the highway that skirted the complex. I wondered if I was actually within the boundary of the notorious Chadian Labor Reform Farm, at which tens of thousands of counter-revolutionaries, gangsters, cutthroats, thieves, hooligans, and various other types of criminals had been confined to serve terms of forced labor since 1951.

Director Ren of the general headquarters office, a pompous policeman in a thick woolen uniform, gave me and my companion a welcome dinner. "All these are our own products," he said as he swept his chopsticks over the half dozen dishes on the table, "including the shrimp." He picked up a big shrimp and placed it in my rice bowl. "I was the discipline officer at Farm 583 when you were there. I recognized you immediately when you stepped into the office. You may not remember me, though. See, we are old acquaintances. So don't stand on ceremony. Have another shrimp." He picked up another one, and placed it in my bowl.

I smiled, feeling awkward. After so many years I still felt uncomfortable in the presence of police.

Later, I took a stroll by myself around the old dilapidated auditorium where I had attended two annual reward and punishment meetings. At the second, my name was read out. My term had been cut by six months for my good behavior, hard work, and conscientiousness in "reforming my counter-revolutionary ideas." I went out of the front gate to the stream that passed by the general headquarters. It was now cleared of rubbish. Flowers had been planted and a low wall built. Obviously an effort had been made to give superiors from Beijing, who stayed at the guest house, a good impression.

The police officers and civilians looked at me, admiring my Western suit and the camera I was carrying. As a journalist for a magazine published in English, I had long ago learned how to dress on different occasions. This time, I dressed to make the Chadian people believe I was a person of importance from Beijing. I felt an aching desire to be avenged.

I walked back to the spacious room Director Ren gave me free of charge at the guest house, took a shower in the private washroom, tried the color TV set, which failed to provide a clear image, and lay down on the soft bed to think about how unpredictable one's fate could be.

Thirteen years ago I was doing hard labor here, and sleeping on a platform-like brick bed with eleven others, packed in like canned sardines. I had not dared to curl up my body when it was freezing on winter nights because my allocated strip on the bed didn't allow me to do so. If I did, I would intrude into the space of the next person. Then I dared not look into the eyes of police officers, but kept them riveted on the tips of my shoes. Now I was being received by the Chadian authorities with honor, and I was sleeping in one of their best furnished rooms.

Outside, the night was quiet and peaceful. The stars were much brighter here than they were in the smoky Beijing sky. I knew, within a perimeter of fifty miles around Chadian, four thousand inmates were sleeping on platform beds, and dreaming of their release day.

The next morning Director Ren came with a young police officer. "He will look after your welfare during your stay here," the Director said pleasantly. He also assigned a jeep to my disposal.

First we drove to Farm 583. The jeep ran smoothly on the asphalt road stretching toward the West. The wooden bridge was still there, and I recognized a huge rock at the base of one of the bridge piles. The road from there onward used to be dirt. Chadian's dirt had high alkaline content. When it was wet, it was as sticky as glue; when it was dry, the ruts became hard as iron.

My wife had traversed back and forth on the dirt road many times to visit me during the time of my incarceration at Chadian. The bus would stop at the general headquarters then. After that, she would have to walk the four miles to Farm 583, often dragging along our three-year-old son and a bag laden with jars, cans, and packages to supplement my poor diet from the inmate kitchen. The walk would take her two hours. If she was lucky, she could hitch a ride on the back rack of a cyclist or on top of sacks in a horse-drawn cart that happened to come this way.

"There are no more inmates of your type at Chadian," the young officer offered. From the way he talked and his manner, I assumed he must be the son of a Chadian veteran officer. He had probably failed to make it to a Beijing college, and had enlisted in the local police.

"My type?" I was brought back from my reverie.

"Labor reform elements," the young officer said. "Now the farm only takes real criminals. You know what I mean."

"Yeah," I said.

Squads of inmates were working in the vegetable plots. Though the officers guarding them still wore civilian clothes, the inmates wore black prison uniforms with white shirts made of a coarse material. When I was an inmate, we had to wear whatever clothes we brought from our homes.

There was a new, high wall surrounding the site of the Farm 583 Big Compound. It was mounted with barbered wire, and red electric bulbs which shone dimly on top. Guards in military police uniform, a sector of the regular army, and a policeman stood at the iron gate, their bayonets shining brightly. I peeped through a hole cut in the gate. The courtyard where we used to drill on the three basketball courts was now filled up with red brick row houses. The whole complex was deadly quiet.

"Want to go in and have a look?" The young police officer invited. I said no. He told me that the row houses I had lived in collapsed during the 1976 Tangshan earthquake. "But the whole thing is not much different," he said. "Except the walls are more solid, and each window has iron bars."

The row houses of the Officers Compound, and those in the Small Compound, where three farm workers and cows and horses had lived, still stood there and were in use.

I walked over to the station that once pumped water from the Chaobai River. The water no longer flowed there and the dry riverbed was planted with wheat. Where there was no wheat, tall weeds grew. Apparently the river was so low, no more water could be led into to the channel under the pumping station. I was told that the pumping station had not operated for at least two years. The canal to the paddy fields was dry. So were the fields where I had looked after rice crops for two seasons.

Niu Denghai and Li Fang, two police officers in their late fifties, were happy to see me. Their hair had turned totally gray. Before they reached fifty, most of their faces had wrinkled, their skin had become cracked and their hair had turned dry and gray. The two officers looked much older than anyone of the same age in Beijing.

I particularly wanted to see them because they had treated me with more dignity and integrity as a human being while I was an inmate of Chadian, than they were supposed to as police officers. Now my exoneration and new social status verified their judgment of me thirteen years ago.

After sharing a cup of liquor which I had brought them from Beijing, they began to complain about the skyrocketing prices at the market and their continued low pay after having served on the farm for over three decades. They said that they hoped that by being friends with me, now an influential person with many connections in Beijing, I could do something about their situation. If only I could. I would have to find another way to show my gratitude for their kindness during the hardest years in my life. But, for now, all I could only give them was empty, comforting words!

In two days I visited three sub-farms and two factories. Then I returned to Beijing to start writing this book.